PENGUIN BOOKS

I'LL DRINK TO THAT

Betty Halbreich is the director of Solutions at Bergdorf Goodman. The author of *Secrets of a Fashion Therapist*, Halbreich regularly dispenses her unique brand of wit and style in a wide range of media outlets from the *Today* show to the *Wall Street Journal* to *Refinery29*. The legendary personal shopper—who has been impeccably dressing her clients for forty years and herself for eighty-six—was featured in the *New Yorker* and the 2013 documentary *Scatter My Ashes at Bergdorf's*. She is also the inspiration for a forthcoming HBO television series written by Lena Dunham.

Rebecca Paley is the *New York Times* bestselling coauthor of several memoirs and has written for numerous publications ranging from *People* to *Mother Jones*. She lives in Brooklyn with her husband and two children.

Praise for Betty Halbreich's *I'll Drink to That*

"Lena Dunham, creator of HBO's *Girls*, is now developing a series inspired by Ms. Halbreich's life. The impatient, however, can satisfy their curiosity more immediately with *I'll Drink to That*, the long-anticipated memoir in which Ms. Halbreich chronicles her life in the dressing room and beyond." —*The Wall Street Journal*

"Sartorial style becomes a philosophy of life in this spirited memoir. . . . Halbreich comes across as sage and gracious as she narrates a life full of incident, taking us inside the fashion industry and one of its great institutions." —*Publishers Weekly*

"Every woman has a piece of clothing that she can't live without, because in it, she feels most like herself. Betty's memoir has that effect on a reader. Authentic style is a form of self-knowledge. And in that respect, *I'll Drink to That* is like Betty's famous three-way mirror.

She sizes up her own life fearlessly, and in the process, not only helps you to diagnose your own flaws, but to embrace your own beauty."

—Judith Thurman, author of National Book Award–winning *Isak Dinesen: The Life of a Storyteller* and *The Los Angeles Times* Book Award–winning *Secrets of the Flesh: A Life of Colette*

Praise for Betty Halbreich

"Betty was born to sail through people's lives telling them what to wear (and even what to do). The other day I overheard her chatting with a client, 'Oh, she's been my friend for thirty-five years, and she's only thirty.' Lines like that are good enough for George Cukor. The whole scanrio is. Maybe she's known that all these years. Fashion is not only about necessity but also a form of entertainment—and that is what Betty sells."
—Isaac Mizrahi, fashion designer

"I would trust this woman with my life—closet!"
—Joan Rivers, television personality

"She's the go-to celebrity. She's also the most fun."
—Patricia Field, costume designer for *Sex & the City*

"There's a pragmatic principle behind the way Betty dresses people. It's very inclusive. There's room for everyone in her process. [Betty] is able to be in the fashion world, but also take it down a peg at the same time."
—Lena Dunham, writer and actress

"The fashion doctor is in. . . . Even as designers and editors seem to be conspiring to lure women into their latest whims, Betty Halbreich is a scrupulously practical truth-teller. She considers it her job to protect women from clothes that are wrong for them. She takes pride in pushing the least expensive items she can find, when it's appropriate. . . . A brassy Chicago native with a manner that's part Angela Lansbury and part Lucille Ball, Halbreich believes in taking chances with color and accessorizing lavishly."
—Bob Morris, *New York Magazine*

I'll Drink to That

A LIFE IN STYLE, WITH A TWIST

Betty Halbreich

with Rebecca Paley

Penguin Books

PENGUIN BOOKS
An imprint of Penguin Random House LLC
375 Hudson Street
New York, New York 10014
penguin.com

First published in the United States of America by The Penguin Press,
an imprint of Penguin Random House LLC, 2014
Published in Penguin Books 2015

THE LIBRARY OF CONGRESS HAS CATALOGED THE HARDCOVER EDITION AS FOLLOWS:
Halbreich, Betty, 1927–
I'll drink to that : a life in style, with a twist / Betty Halbreich.
pages cm
ISBN 978-1-59420-570-5 (hc.)
ISBN 978-0-14-312770-3 (pbk.)
1. Halbreich, Betty, 1927–   2. Image consultants—United States—Biography.
3. Clothing and dress.   4. Fashion.   5. Beauty, personal.   I. Title.
TT505.H24A2 2014
746.9'2092—dc23
[B] 2014009695

Printed in the United States of America
5   7   9   10   8   6   4

Designed by Gretchen Achilles
Illustration on pg. 273 by Meighan Cavanaugh

Some of the characters described in this book are composites, drawn from
the author's many years of experience. The names of some of the author's
customers have been changed out of respect for their privacy.

Penguin is committed to publishing works of quality and integrity.
In that spirit, we are proud to offer this book to our readers; however,
the story, the experiences, and the words are the author's alone.

To Kathy and John, my grown-up children,
and the wonderful accomplished grandchildren
they have blessed me with:
Gillian, Hannah, and Henry

When you are Real you don't mind being hurt. . . .

Once you are Real you can't become unreal again.

It lasts for always.

—The Velveteen Rabbit

ACKNOWLEDGMENTS

It would take many chapters to mention all those in my life* who play such momentous roles.** They know who they are, and there are many heartfelt thank-yous for keeping my dance card filled!

*E.B. and R.A.

**To Emily's expert transcribing skills and being an ear to the world; and Rebecca, the writer-listener par excellence, who really got it.

The pieces I pulled the day before were lined up in my dressing room with military precision, in the order I planned to present them to my client—a very tailored woman who typically wore extremely expensive clothing—were a cashmere double-breasted jacket, various tops in crisp white percale, cropped khaki pants, and dresses categorized into ones for day and others for night. They weren't separates unified simply by taste but rather possessed a continuity that I saw in my head and would introduce to the client on her body. The cashmere jacket was to be paired with the cropped pants for a weekend afternoon or matched with the charcoal gray skirt for a business lunch—and white percale goes with practically anything. Together the disparate items I gathered made a series of outfits. A story, if you like. To have a closet fully packed and presented to you is a gift. That is not to say that the women I work with adore all the items I choose, but the experience of walking into my dressing room for an appointment makes for something individual and special. The clothes I work with as a personal shopper (a title I have never particularly favored) are an extravagance unto themselves—the price tags on many are often too rich for my midwestern sensibilities. Yet the true luxury of what I do is the knowledge my client has as I slip a sweater over her shoulders or zip a dress up the back that I was thinking only of her when I selected the garment.

Many women are nervous when they first step into my office. I am the antidote to the intimidation of shopping, but it is difficult here at Bergdorf Goodman, probably the most beautiful store there is because of the years on it. Even the location of its elegant, mansard-style building on the site of the former Vanderbilt mansion is venerable. One walks into the store and gasps: It is truly opulent. Light twinkles from crystal chandeliers at the center of magnificent white rotundas. Even updated, the French moldings and paneled walls display old-fashioned charm that simply cannot be built into new stores.

It's beautiful, but the store itself is not all that my clients are seeking. Often their need runs deeper. A great many of them require mothering, which I provide in various ways. The simplest is the advice I dispense from the list of purveyors I have amassed over the years in a leather-bound book I keep handily on my desk. My clients don't just ask me about what to wear; they also want to know the best nursery schools to send their children to, a hand laundry that does linens, or the best chocolates I have ever eaten. And I oblige—with dentists, party planners, bakeries, whatever they require. I am the ultimate trusted source, because when a person enters my dressing room and takes off her clothes, I must instill confidence. I also become a listening post and hear things my clients won't tell their husbands, best friends, or real mothers. I don't mind. It's much easier to take care of other people than it is yourself. I put a lot of myself into the heads and bodies of my clients, whom I want to dress as well as I would myself. Having grown up around and lived with beautiful clothes and fabrics all my life, I sometimes find it difficult to see the new and appreciate it—even here at Bergdorf Goodman, a store many consider to be the ultimate in fashion and my place of work for the last thirty-eight years. But I romance the clothes in my mind. Instinctively I feel the fabric, see the allure.

When I'm gathering, I can have only one woman in mind. This approach takes longer, but I've never been much of a multitasker. It also has the blessed benefit of making the seven floors of the Fifth Avenue store new every time I travel them for a different client. By the end of a season, the clothes are like old relatives that one knows all too well. But in the game I play with myself, looking closely at the same departments and clothes as if I have never seen them before, I always find something new.

In the dressing room, I straightened a persimmon sheath dress and considered the woman arriving in several hours for an appointment to answer two different needs: a new dress for a benefit luncheon hosted by her daughter and a few pieces that were more casual than she was used to for a trip to Aspen with an old college friend who was not nearly as dressy as she. Calling them *"needs"* was something of a misnomer. In truth, we need very little. Certainly nobody needs all these clothes. Want, however, is something else. Whether they buy them at H&M or Bergdorf, women love clothes. You can get someone at the lowest point of her day and make her feel good (at least for a moment) with a new shirt or, even better, a dress. It doesn't matter how erudite or worldly someone is—doctors, bankers, artists—they all want a fix. The client in question, a lawyer who worked at a top Manhattan firm, was no exception. Her large frame, however, made fitting her a challenge. Over the years I had gently nudged her away from her comfort zone of jackets and matching suits to a softer, more feminine look.

The mere fact that she was big didn't mean she wasn't a woman. As with most of my clients, I had known her a long time. Her mother-in-law had been one of my first friends when I moved to New York and has been dead twenty-seven years. I don't believe in disposable fashion or people.

The phone rang in my adjacent office. Back at my desk to answer the call, I looked out at the stunning view from my office window that unfurls past the Plaza and the Pulitzer Fountain, to Central Park, and up Fifth Avenue. Although it was raining when I got into a cab to come to work, I could see the sun breaking through over the Upper East Side.

On the end of the telephone line was another long-standing client calling to say she needed new pants.

"What do you need new pants for?" I asked. I'm the only salesperson on earth to dissuade customers from buying; I'm known for it. Here was a woman whose husband of forty years was dying of pancreatic cancer and she was contemplating pants?

"I know exactly what you have, because I sold them to you," I said.

"They are not very exciting. Exciting pants I've never seen. Unless we are talking about what's inside pants."

The woman on the phone didn't need pants; she needed a visit. She had fallen out of my life for a long time but reappeared six months earlier, after her husband's diagnosis. Ever since then she had come for a lot of retail therapy. I kept the appointments frequent but the bills low.

I made a mental note to find out where one could buy those special tabs to affix to zippers for women who have to get into dresses by themselves—another client of mine, whose husband had had a stroke, showed me the clever invention last time she was in the store. This client, too, would need them to zip her own dresses when her husband would eventually lose his battle to cancer.

"We will get you something," I told her, taking out my well-worn leather-bound datebook. "When do you want to come in?"

Just as I finished writing the word "pants" under her appointment entry in my book, in walked my first client of the morning, a new person I had only previously talked to on the phone.

Through all the years of being "at the same station" and seeing the many hundreds of personalities who've come through the door during that time, as soon as someone enters my office, I pretty well know what I'll be dealing with. The unsmiling woman before me, clad in all black, birdlike in stature and movement, clutching a small purse as if it were a life preserver, was a reluctant patient. No doubt about it.

Now standing on my threshold, Mrs. P, the silver-haired society wife of an industrialist, had been adamant when we talked on the phone prior to her appointment about why, after nearly fifty years of dressing herself, she'd decided to come to me.

"I have to dress appropriately," she'd said. "None of my beautiful clothes are appropriate for me anymore." She named every French, American, Italian couture designer in her closet!

"You're making it too important," I had replied. In our subsequent conversation, the frustration in her voice lessened as we talked about her desire for a change to suit her age. In other words, she needed an updating.

Yet as I now made eye contact with this woman, who lived in

an apartment with a prominent address, full of art and beautiful clothes, I could see she was absolutely petrified. It's a peculiar phenomenon, but generally when women first come to me, they are very apprehensive. I don't know why: Maybe it's the store that people have adorned with so many absurd titles, like "Mecca of Style" or "Fifth Avenue's Finest." Maybe it's me. Maybe it's my white hair!

Sensing this apprehension in Mrs. P, I immediately sat her on the soft love seat beside my desk to make light chatter. After all, I'm here to serve. My bedside manner settled her down while we retraced ground on her needs and desires.

"I would like to look like *you*," Mrs. P said.

As she gave my ensemble of twenty-year-old black pants, a chartreuse collarless jacket, and gold star pin that had been my mother's the old up-and-down, I thought if she only she knew how little clothes meant to me. I have often toyed with the idea of wearing a vendeuse smock like the kind they used to wear in the ateliers in Paris, but I must keep a semblance of my personal fashion sense in my line of work.

"And *I* would like to live in *your* building!" I replied.

The one-liner made her laugh and eased any tension. We weren't in competition. "Come on," I said, "let's look. I will lead the way, because it is very bewildering. We'll go slow, and you don't have to feel compelled to buy anything."

We set out from my cozy office, blessedly hidden away at the end of a long corridor of dressing rooms in a nondescript corner of the third floor. Walking the floor—which I do alone every morning before the store opens, irrespective of weather, tragedy, or sickness—is not something I like to do with clients. Unlike the singular and luxurious experience of having a whole wardrobe brought to you, doing the large, crowded floor is confusing, overwhelming, and not in any way one-on-one.

But I always walk through the store with a new client. The first meeting with anyone is something of a test run. I can get the feel of a new client's body just by looking at the person, but to understand her personality, lifestyle, sense of color, fantasies for herself? For that I find I'm not successful unless I eyeball her in action. Our going through the floors of the store together is a lot of wasted walking time (I can do them so much faster myself, for I know all seven like the back of my hand). There is much touching and feeling of material—and talking, not just about clothes but also about what the women do for a living, how they act with their children and husbands, the depth and breadth of their social lives. I closely watch their reactions as I show them things they would never put on themselves. That is what I'm here for—to open them up to new worlds. Why else would they come to me? While I was escorting Mrs. P onto the elevator, a woman exited with a stroller that held an infant who couldn't have been more than a few weeks old. When we got off the elevator, in rolled an elderly woman in a wheelchair pushed by an attendant. A large mix of people walk through the store, every nationality and every age, even if it is just to look. I don't care where the person who walks in hails from—Saudi princesses or tourists from the South—they are awed. Many don't stay. They walk in one door and directly out the next. Sometimes it worries me that the place feels too out of reach. I don't care for that kind of snobbishness.

Mrs. P and I arrived at the second floor, which houses the luxury brands that can be found in malls stretching from Beijing to Birmingham. In general I don't do much there. I prefer individuality to ubiquity. Strolling past a dress in glove leather by a popular Italian design house, I couldn't help but peek at the price tag, only to roll my eyes in disgust; one drop of red pasta sauce and the wearer would be out three thousand dollars. Mrs. P, looking as lost as a little girl in a deep forest, asked, "How do you deal with these clothes?" I pulled her away from a dress splattered with paint à la Jackson Pollock and beckoned her into the fur department, where one of the designers who had started as a furrier had become a grand dressmaker as well.

"He makes lovely clothes," I said about the designer. "A lot of people don't make nice clothes anymore. They use what once was lining material and call it a dress. This designer uses extravagant, beautiful fabrics, but his prices are absolutely obscene. One pays for quality."

She held up a jacket made of white sheepskin and black leather, with monkey-fur epaulets, a misstep in an otherwise perfectly beautiful collection, as if to prove me wrong. She reminded me of a petulant child who finds the one exception to every rule.

"Let's go up to saner clothes," I said.

"I believe in you."

"Don't believe in me."

On the fourth floor, I showed her a dress by a young American designer with a pattern of colorful bunches of flowers against a royal blue background. "It has a nice fit for your body," I said.

"It's awful."

Instead Mrs. P turned to a sleeveless shell dress with matching three-quarter-length coat in elephant gray. "This I like," she said.

"And you probably already have it in your closet. Every New York woman does. Let's move on."

It was becoming clear that Mrs. P wasn't going to let go of her hang-ups without a fight. Tough cookies, however, are my specialty.

I kept moving. At a black wool cape with a dramatic, positively clerical, white collar that tied, I commented, "Isn't this beautiful?"

"But it isn't fun."

Oh, I did not like this game. Not one little bit. Mrs. P veered off into a boutique I don't frequent very often, a society designer too mundane for my taste in his overuse of sparkles, feather, and tulle.

"My mother loved feathers," I reminisced out loud at the sight of a dress trimmed with white feathers around the neckline. "Wherever she went, she left a trail of them. Feathers are not my favorite. I like birds, but not feathers."

Mrs. P took a sparkly black blouse off the rack and said, "This is like a white horse—you could take it anywhere."

It was gracious and feminine in its round neck and it had sleeves. A miracle!

"It's actually very pretty," I said, putting the garment over my arm to bring back to my dressing room. "Now let's leave this department."

Mrs. P protested, to which I said, "Well then, you don't need me. You can just shop at the store."

Stomping her foot, she said, "I don't want to spend the time. I want you to do it for me!"

While I kid by calling myself a "clerk," I am pleased to be of help whether it's to hunt for a wedding dress or just to provide a diversion for an hour. At times, however, when I deal with difficult women—those who let me *know* they're spending money, for instance—I put my foot down. If not I'll get run over and killed. I am most definite about how I work. Mrs. P and I needed to gather a few items to whet her appetite and then return to the dressing room. Otherwise we were headed for a tantrum.

I pulled a sumptuous cashmere turtleneck with an interesting block print by a brand that, having begun as a manufacturer of fabric in Italy's Lake Como, still took pride in craftsmanship. Its extravagant materials are what fabrics were like when I entered this business. "Just feel it," I said. "It has a European flair."

"I want to be very simple. I don't want to be cluttered."

"Try it on so we don't have to go through this next time," I said, and laid the sweater on top of the sparkly shirt.

My next find, a cherry red wool dress with puffed bracelet sleeves, went over a little better. It seemed that Mrs. P, like so many others, needed a firm hand.

"That's not bad," she said.

"The color is nice."

"This is an education."

"This is a dream."

We moved quickly through peplum skirts and swirling prints, sheaths and leather, to add a cropped tuxedo jacket, a round-necked jacket with a ruffle front, and a charcoal knit top to our collection. It was a small pull, but Rome wasn't built in a day, and neither should a wardrobe be.

On our way to the elevator, we cut through the shoe department, a very confusing department with each pair of shoes more unattractive than the next. A platform bootie in red water snake under a spotlight looked like an artifact on display from an ancient culture that took perverse pleasure in deforming people's feet. A leopard-print stiletto with a heel topping out at six inches, on a platform as well, would have made a drag queen blush. Whenever I walked behind women wearing these shoes, which was unfortunately quite often, I was struck by the strange, Frankenstein-like gait they produce. Legs in these shoes simply can't support the height and weight.

"Hello, ladies," I said to a line of salesgirls buried in their phones. "You look like you're waiting for the bus."

Even though they weren't the type to respond, they were scared to death *not* to. My age has earned me that deference at least. After they squeaked out a few hellos, they quickly returned to their light world.

Back on the third floor, I ran smack into a pair of palazzo pants, swingy and patterned with large tropical flowers made bolder by a black background. Where had those been hiding? It was sort of a wild idea. Not for Mrs. P (the tiny woman would have drowned in them), but for my tailored client coming later in the day. They were unlike anything she had ever looked at, but I just had a feeling about them. They reminded me of the luaus, the balmy romance, and the feminine dressing I'd seen on my Hawaiian honeymoon a hundred years ago. I draped them over my free arm.

Back in my quiet corner of the store, I took a moment to tuck the palazzo pants into the lineup, placing them at the end—risks always come last. Then I went to the next-door dressing room to deal with Mrs. P.

First I slipped the tuxedo jacket on her—jackets are the easiest place to start, not least of all because one doesn't need to get undressed to try them on.

"That's pretty," I said.

"I don't like the way it fits in the back of the neck," she said, tugging at her collar like someone being pulled offstage. Sometimes it's a wonder I don't drink at work.

"I guess you're used to couture clothes," I said, removing the jacket and placing it outside the dressing room.

I approached her with the turtleneck, but she lost her nerve.

"I can't wear turtlenecks. I get way too hot."

I knew it was the mirror. She trained the same harsh judgment she used to quickly dispense with clothing on herself. Mrs. P was starting to panic—I had seen it a million times before—and in a complete reversal of her previously negative pose wanted to buy the red dress and the sparkly top still on their hangers, without trying either of them.

"Oh, no, I don't sell clothes like that," I said.

"They'll be perfect."

"How do you know until you put them on your body?"

I got the dress over her head. After thirty-eight years of doing this, nobody zips or buttons faster.

"How does it feel here?" I asked, patting her on the hips, knowing full well how it felt.

"Not good. It's awful. My rear end is sticking out."

I took the dress off and put on the sparkly shirt, which was very becoming. The silver sequins complemented her bob.

"It's not exactly me," Mrs. P said.

"You don't always want to look like you. . . . It's beautiful with your hair."

"What about this?" she said, pointing to her neck, angry at the signs of its age. "I think the scoop neck is too much with *this*. My legs are the only part left that's any good."

Mrs. P looked at herself again and then turned to my reflection to ask, "What do you think?"

What do you think? I'm asked this question constantly. Even the new clients who arrive with very assured thoughts about their likes and dislikes wind up deferring to me in the end.

Mrs. P, so tough and critical on the outside and so desperate on the inside, came to me because she said she was sick of holding on to the past. Confronting her long-gone youth through a closetful of couture clothes that were making her unhappy—and yet, inside my dressing room, she couldn't let go. Of her youth, her couture clothes, her mother. I made up my mind that I wouldn't sell her anything, not this time. We still had more work to do—at a later date.

"What I think is the next time I'm the boss," I said, putting an arm around her tiny frame. "Everything will be compiled and ready for you, whether you like it or not."

I escorted Mrs. P back to the elevator (I spend so much time in the elevator I should wear a red carnation in my lapel) and down to the basement for some makeup. It's a must with me to make each woman I deal with, regardless of what shape or look she is, leave my clutches feeling different from when she entered, even if it is only through a new shade of lipstick.

Having dispatched Mrs. P, I had no sooner returned to my office when my tailored client plopped her sizable purse on my love seat. After a quick catch-up about her husband (long-suffering), the dog (ditto), and the apartment (like the store, forever under renovation), we set to work.

I slipped a double-breasted blue cashmere jacket on first to warm her up.

"Quite gorgeoso," she said.

I put it to one side and followed it up with something more challenging: a white dress with polka dots and a black plant pattern that emanated from the bottom as if it were growing up from the hem.

"It's the year of the print," I said. "You just have to close your eyes and pray."

Before she had a chance to zip the zipper all the way, I was pulling it down. With as many changes of clothes as I've seen, I know these things immediately.

"No, take it off."

"I liked it on the hanger," she protested.

"It's too broadening. All you need is a frame and you'll look like a botanical picture."

A draped woven-crepe dress in black was just as bad.

"Oh, God, please, you look like you're in a shroud," I said. "Off!"

"Well, you're certainly not out to sell anything," she replied.

I brought forth a pink suit whose deep, saturated color I could tell intrigued but also unsettled her.

"Whose is it?" she asked.

"It looks like an old Saint Laurent jacket," I said, then told her the name on the label.

"What size is this?" she asked while pulling up the skirt.

"It doesn't matter."

She twirled in front of the mirror. "This looks like me but more festive, me but in a wilder color!" she said.

You but happier, I thought.

"It's good for the luncheon regardless of weather. It could be cold, or we could have a heat wave," I offered.

"Could I wear black pearls?" she asked.

"Beautiful," I replied.

Success emboldened my client. She truly was starting to feel good and relaxed, which is not easy in this city or this life.

"You know that flowered dress you sold me last year?" she said. "Everybody loves me in that dress. You can throw it in a shopping bag, and out it comes crisp and ready to wear. I get so many compliments whenever I put it on."

Hearing that always makes me feel good. Now, with the luncheon dress a reality, it was on to the vacation problems, but first I added a few structured shirts I thought were to her taste, including an oxford-cloth point-collar shirt with long sleeves.

"I'm wavering," she said, looking at herself in it.

"Don't. You have to like it instantly. Nothing gets better the more times you look in the mirror. I agree—it looks like your husband's pajama top. Off!"

The next was a paisley-and-geometric-pattern silk blouse.

"This I love."

"You are now in a different ballpark. That's *très élégante.*"

The designer I had pulled the blouse from was very popular this season. Still, I didn't like the entire collection. I never do; I glean individual pieces from many collections.

"The paisley pattern is vintage," I said.

"How do you know?"

"I know because I'm old. I remember the original."

"What would you wear with it?"

"Black pants."

"Tucked in or out?"

"Both."

I placed the silk blouse beside the suit, which was separate from the blue cashmere jacket that I would most likely talk her out of in the end. The definite noes that I hung outside the fitting room had already been spirited away by Emily, my assistant.

We disagreed over a blue-and-white cotton trapeze shirt.

"You have to take this off," I begged.

"But I think it's cute."

"No, no. Children will talk behind their hands about you."

"Does it come smaller?"

I threw my hands up in the air. "It probably does," I said, turning to Helen, the fitter who had just arrived with her pins and scissors in a clear plastic Birkin-style bag. "Please take up the cuff on the blouse while I look for this terrible blouse."

I zipped to the department where I had found the blouse in the first place, and wouldn't you know my luck? In a store with very few sizes, of course they had it in a size smaller.

"Here's your favorite blouse," I said when I returned.

"I know I'll wear it."

"Well, it's cotton at least. This is the easy part for you. We haven't gotten into the nitty-gritty part of the fitting."

That meant pants. After my client squirmed through a pair of ill-fitting capris and stretch pants that made her feel like her "granddaughter," she started asking for her security blanket. "Any Chanel jackets floating around?" she asked demurely. It might have been an exorbitantly priced blanket, but a blanket it was nonetheless. A cloak behind which to disappear. She has so many of them she could have filled a warehouse.

"You have enough Chanel jackets," I said.

"It's been a couple of seasons. I'm going through withdrawal."

Is the customer always right? Not in this case, but still I went back down to the second floor and gagged as I pulled a Chanel bouclé jacket in red, white, and blue with silver buttons.

"It fits me perfectly," she said.

"Do you *really* want to look like this?" She was not going to make such an insecure and costly purchase on my watch.

"I guess not."

I rushed the jacket out of the fitting room before she could reverse herself again and used the moment of confrontation to push her boundaries all the way, revealing the palazzo pants. She paled and shook her head no.

"Just for the fun of it, try them. It's an experiment."

After years of our working together, she knew I wasn't going to take no for answer. She slowly picked up the black silk pants as if they were slimy. But as she buttoned them and found the courage to raise her head to the mirror, I saw the light go on.

"These are adorable! And comfortable!"

She loved herself in them. It was as plain as day. But she wanted to know what to wear with them. While all they needed was a casual white shirt (Brooks Brothers makes the best non-iron in cotton—the collars stay crisp), I couldn't send her home without a complete outfit. If I didn't find the missing piece of the puzzle, she would never have the courage to put them on after they entered her closet. The door of my office is where I draw the line. I'm not part of the package—I don't go home with the pants.

I left her swishing around happily in her palazzo pants and went through the third floor yet again. Perhaps I had missed something. I passed a fashion victim in a short black minidress with pink polka dots and a ruffled skirt, carrying a big tote emblazoned with a designer logo. Too many people wear a label rather than what is becoming. I grabbed a slouchy sweater out of desperation.

Back in the dressing room, the neck of the sweater was too high and made my client's bosom look matronly, which turned her divine pants into clown pants. I got the sweater off before she had a chance to get a complex from looking in the mirror and was off again, but not before Emily stopped me: A young designer was on the phone.

"I need vodka," said the brilliant designer of true one-of-a-kind clothing, who was in the middle of a trunk show for the store. I recently put one of my clients into an exquisite three-quarter-length coat of his with crystals he affixed to the front but not the back. Why? Who knows? The inconsistency is what I love.

I had to let him down—no vodka in my office, although I do understand how this business can drive you to drink.

Into the elevator and up to five, I revisited a collection that I like because of its chic, clean lines and the fact that it's made in America, which is extremely important to me (I try to sell it every chance I can). But the fit is not easy; all the clothes run very small. That would not do for the woman patiently waiting.

I went up and down the escalators and in and out of the fitting room until I could not contemplate those palazzo pants for another minute (I, too, have my limits). I had to send my forlorn client home without the pants but told her not to worry: I, who do not know the meaning of the word "satisfaction," never give up. I would hold on to them and, rest assured, find something that would suit her perfectly. Another day, another time, I would try again and see things differently. I find that once I have cleared my head, I'm game for a new beginning. I am like the doctor: You confide in him, he diagnoses you, and then, when your time is up, he's on to the next case! Over the years I have learned how to turn away from the patient and move on. There is a cutoff period to my involvement, but with me at least one gets an hour or two.

CHAPTER

One

In the 1930s, the South Side of Chicago was filled with good things: a dubonnet dress trimmed in white piqué; snowballs made from the inside of angel food cake hand-scooped out and rolled in homemade marshmallow and fresh coconut; the dining-room table set by Mother with china, silverware, starched linens, and an abundance of fruit and flowers; shopping at Kiddy Kicks, where an X-ray machine was used to fit shoes and make sure you were getting your money's worth; the vegetable peddler's heavily accented song floating up from his horse-drawn wagon to the third floor and through the window of my bedroom, where, awake but still, I dared not move until my nursemaid let me know it was time to rise.

Morning was easy, particularly because I always laid my clothes out the night before. They were a cheery greeting. My Best & Co. blouse hanging from the wardrobe was ironed using a special small board for the puff sleeves alone, so that they wouldn't get creases. Its Peter Pan collar, which came on and off with fasteners for easy washing, was a snowy white. The topstitched knife pleats of a brown gingham skirt I chose as a well-suited companion had been pressed to razor sharpness. My patent-leather Mary Janes, the ones that required a buttonhook to fasten, had been treated with Vaseline, then buffed to a high shine with a cloth.

And how good everything smelled! Our laundress, Isabelle, came every Friday to boil our clothes in a huge tin vat in the basement, where I intently watched her cook starch on a burner and stir the water with a wooden spoon. From the deep creases in her black skin, I figured her to be about a hundred years old. After she was done with the washing, all the laundry went into the backyard, adjacent to the alley, where it hung on the clothesline even in a light rain. Once the linens were washed, the sheets were put through a machine called a mangle, and the rest ironed by hand. Then she folded and tied them together with moire ribbons before they were returned to the linen closet. When I climbed into bed on a cool evening, my sheets gave off a heavenly aroma of starch, sun, and lavender sachets.

My perfectly pressed and polished outfit helped with the "school stomachs" I suffered. A new teacher, a hard assignment, or any change in my daily activities threw me into delirium and often made breakfast intolerable. The dreaded cream of wheat, toast, and orange juice that awaited me had to be consumed on pain of a tap from the switch of my nurse, Nora. Very strict and very Irish, she believed that children cleaned their plates. To that end she plucked a twig off a tree in the park, removed the bark to reveal its supple green inside, and made it whistle if any food lingered.

There wasn't any reason to worry; I never had problems at school. The teachers liked me. In fact, I was often referred to as the teacher's pet by the other children. But while I was a diligent student, I suspect that the label had more to do with how well dressed I was sent to school. My mother, Carol, had excellent taste. Whether it was a Lanz dirndl with a ruffled white blouse, a royal blue bodice, and a sweetly contrasting apron or a Tyrolean sweater with silver buttons, she made sure all my clothes were nice. My father, Harry

Stoll—who worked for his uncle running a chain of fur departments before becoming president of the Chicago department store Mandel Brothers—had had a gray squirrel coat with big round buttons and a Peter Pan collar custom-made for me when I was five.

It was the Great Depression, and yet I never remember wanting for anything. I guessed I was the most privileged child in elementary school, because not only did I have beautiful clothes but I also brought the best lunches in my pail: yummy sandwiches, homemade cookies, and fresh fruit. But I had no idea how privileged I was, since my parents and their friends, all part of the well-to-do Hyde Park Jewish community, didn't talk about money. Mostly of German heritage and entirely irreligious, this insular community didn't call the clergy at its high Reform temple "Rabbi" but rather "Doctor." Services at Congregation Sinai were a once-a-year affair on the High Holy Days for my family, and I had never heard of a bar mitzvah. Ours was a proud cultural and intellectual tradition that wholeheartedly embraced the lushness of Christmas.

Mother might have had to be dragged to temple, but she went all out for Christmas, preparations for which began in September with a trip to the gift show to buy her wrapping paper. The sunroom became the most exciting room in the house from October through December, as she filled it with enough Christmas materials to rival Santa's workshop. My mother turned wrapping each and every present (and there were a lot of them) into a grand art. She even went so far as to dip the tips of plastic straws in gold sealing wax and tie them in the middle so that they popped open to look like a huge, magnificent chrysanthemum. That was only one element of the production. There was also the cookie baking that started in November. Mother sent to Dallas, Texas, for the elaborate forms for our sugar cookies, which, along with fruitcakes, handmade popcorn trees, and lebkuchen—German gingerbread snowy with confectioners' sugar—were gifted to friends.

Mother never cooked—she was too busy smoking—but we always had the most marvelous food. Like all her friends who were married to doctors, lawyers, retailers, and business owners, she didn't work but ran a household maintained by competent persons. In our apartment on the top floor of 1218 Madison Park, we had a cook and a second girl, who for seven dollars a week lived in, sharing the large maid's room outfitted with two Murphy beds. (On Thursday nights, the cook's day off, we delighted in a Chinese-food feast pedaled over from a small local shop.)

My mother wasn't a terrific eater. She was basically an eater of sweets, through she wouldn't admit to it. Our cook, Martha, who had a terrible drinking problem but was a divine baker, filled Mother's afternoon coffee klatches with schnecken, German sticky buns, and fragrant cinnamon toast that complemented the warm and civilized low part of the day. As sure as four o'clock came every afternoon, so did the rolling tray.

Daddy, on the other hand, loved food so much that he couldn't walk into a grocery store without practically buying out the place. He never met a double lamb chop he didn't adore. Although he was diabetic and supposed to restrict his diet, how many courses we consumed at home! Every night the candelabra illuminated a blue-and-white china relish tray whose compartments were filled with bread, chutney, cottage cheese, celery, carrot sticks, olives, and our own bread-and-butter pickles. We did a lot of pickling in the fall, and the big crocks of brine and marinating Kirby cucumbers sat in the pantry throughout the year. Once we sat down, out came soup, hot bouillon or cream of mushroom garnished with a dollop of whipped cream, and egg timbales. Sometimes herring, in sour cream or German style with beets.

A natural lefty, I found it awkward when the main course of meat, vegetable, and potatoes was served from a large silver tray on my left by the maid. Although my teachers at school allowed me to write with my left hand, at home I was taught how to serve myself and eat with my right. I struggled through many meals until I mastered using a fork in my left hand and knife in the right. Etiquette demanded nothing less.

There was always bread on the table, homemade yeast rolls accompanied by butter balls rolled to the right consistency with wooden paddles and topped grandly with a piece of parsley.

To round it off, dessert. Profiteroles with custard, rhubarb-and-strawberry pies, baked apples with sour cream, homemade cookies—linzer cookies, sandies, butter cookies—really anything as long as it wasn't store-bought. Heaven forbid. Even though my father's diabetes prevented him from truly indulging in candy or sweets (though he was known to ruin a perfectly good box of chocolates or a beautiful cake by plunging his hand into it for just a fingerful), he wouldn't tolerate anything less than homemade.

Once at a dinner party at a friend's home, Father took a dig at the quality of the dessert served. "In our home we don't serve cake from Askow's," he teased the hostess, referring to a popular Hyde Park bakery and embarrassing all.

No one would ever have accused my father of being easy. His

photographic memory and obsessive newspaper-reading habit resulted in encyclopedic knowledge and confidence that provided a lot of ammunition for arguments. He spoke his mind whenever and however it directed him. Indeed, my father was *the* only Republican of all their friends. In the 1936 presidential election, Franklin D. Roosevelt received more than 95 percent of the vote in the Jewish 24th Ward, leading the president to call it "the best ward in the whole country." Father, so devoted a Republican that when he died my mother received a letter from President Nixon, truly loathed President Roosevelt.

Mother—my brilliant father's intellectual peer, who was loved by many and feared by even more for her caustic tongue—saved the mortified hostess who'd made the awful mistake of serving bakery cake by giving it right back to him.

"Well, Harry, at least they don't wear short sleeves to dinner," she said, rolling her big blue eyes and breaking the tension.

Mother was referring to his peccadillo regarding long sleeves, which he hated so much he had them removed. Mother bought him beautiful shirts from A. Sulka & Company, only to discover when he lifted his arms at a dinner party to cut his prime rib that his cuffs had disappeared. No matter that the shirts came from the preeminent haberdashery, whose loyal customers included the likes of the Duke of Windsor, Clark Cable, Gary Cooper, and countless Rockefellers. He had all their sleeves lopped off.

Clothes were never a big part of Father's agenda. My mother was forever coaxing him into buying a new suit, but the extent to which my father shopped involved sneaking into Abercrombie & Fitch to buy the same coat with raglan sleeves he'd owned in another tweed and Brooks Brothers for light blue button-down shirts (of course with the sleeves off) that he felt were perfectly fine for all occasions—even fancy dinners and business meetings.

While he wasn't crazy about clothes, he did love his heavy, dark brown British cordovans, which he kept at a high shine. Whatever train station, airport, club, or man on the street he happened upon, he stopped to have his shoes shined. Many a shoeshine boy was tipped very highly. He also owned one of the very first automatic shoe polishers, in which an electrically powered soft red ball rotated and buffed the shoes. He simply adored a perfect shine. I think it made him feel tall, thin, and very well dressed.

His love of shoes over clothes might have stemmed from his weight problem (after all, no matter how heavy you get, a new pair of shoes will always fit). He refused to take insulin, opting to control his diabetes by dieting. Daddy's weight went up and down like a yo-yo. Periodically he restricted himself to consommé and coffee, proudly demonstrating how much he'd lost by the newly freed holes in his belt. Then he went back to gorging on triple-cut lamb chops. Even his cordovans couldn't trump a good meal. He managed to get through all of World War II in only two pairs, because my mother traded our shoe rations to Mr. Kline, the butcher, so we could get Father his lamb chops and maybe a nice roast beef.

Whether because of my father's appetite or my mother's good hiring, our house always smelled as if we were expecting the door-bell to ring. And more often than not, it did. My very social mother and father had a lot of parties where there was lots of good food, lots of drinking, lots of screaming.

Dressed for bed, I silently watched the raucous cocktail hours where plenty of highballs, martinis, and even the occasional man-hattan were consumed. People say Jewish people don't drink. Well, these did. I marveled at the glamour of my mother and her friends having a merry old time in their strapless dresses with brooches pinned to the cleavage. (Nowadays everybody under fifty wants to be nude and everyone over fifty covered up like a nun. Whenever I put a strapless evening dress on an older client and hear, "Oh, no, no, no. I have to have sleeves," I remember all the bosoms and arms of those voluptuous women of my childhood.)

After cocktails the party moved to the dining room, where the table was covered in one of my mother's beautiful linens. Mother adored table linens, which she purchased from a man who came to the city once a year with stock specially ordered from Europe. They were embroidered often with flowers, sometimes fruits, in many colors. The theme was carried out in two Steuben horn vases at each end of the table and a large boat-size vessel in the middle filled with flowers or fruit or both, which my mother arranged herself. Every night we ate on linen place mats with matching napkins, but or-gandy cloths were for big parties.

While the guests started on egg timbales topped with caviar, I snuck into the butler's pantry to sip the dregs of the leftover cock-tails collected by the maids. Naughty girl. With the pleasant warm feeling spreading from my chest to my head, I returned to my usual industrious self, darting in between the kitchen and cold pantry to help the cook and the second girl get the huge filet of beef with fresh mushrooms; asparagus with hollandaise sauce; and salad of persimmon, watercress, and homemade French dressing out to the table. I, in pajamas and robe, dutifully shadowed the second girl, in her black uniform and organdy apron, until the last of the strawberries Romanoff or swan-shaped meringues that held ice cream and butterscotch sauce (another favorite) had been cleared.

Although the members of the dinner party cooed at the cuteness of my playing maid, for me this was no game. The kinship I felt to the people who worked in our house went far above what I felt for many of my parents' friends. My upbringing, strict and sheltered, demanded that I be seen and not heard, always correct. A life of quiet discipline. As an only child in an often-empty house, I took shelter in the cook and the second girl's gossip about boyfriends or groused over the guests my father invited to dinner without notice. As cakes baked and sauces thickened, I, a small girl who looked like an angel in precious outfits, listened silently without giving any trouble whatsoever. Little pitchers have big ears.

The warmth and camaraderie meant I spent most of my youth in the kitchen, but there was another place with an opposite form of protection that had the same strong pull. I found a wholly different companionship in closets, which offered up their private comfort for an endless game of dress-up.

I began in the closet of my dear, chain-smoking nana, whom we visited every Sunday afternoon. It was the highlight of my week: Auntie Mill, Auntie Emmy, and other ladies gathered over strong coffee and delicious coffee cake to dish on their grown children and husbands, reverting to their native German when the conversation became unsuitable for little-girl ears.

My mother's mother provided the spiciest content herself. While her sister, my great-aunt Corrine, who wore her waist-length hair in a regal coronet braid twisted around her head and had the most incredible collection of glass paperweights, was the beauty, my square and nearsighted nana did very well with the men (particularly her type—married doctors).

She was spunky, and loved men back, though it was hard to imagine her ever having loved my grandfather, who had divorced her and married his Christian Scientist secretary, Lenore, just like in the movies. You took your good manners to see my maternal grandfather, Sigmund Freshman, a stern man who in the mid-1920s had produced with his brother Charles a radio called the Freshman Masterpiece. For many American families, it was their first radio, because it cost only $60—also available as a kit for only $17.50! While competing radios went for $75 to $150, the Freshman's low price was attributed to the tough, if not ruthless, methods the brothers used to drive costs down. (In our home we had much grander radios, lovely consoles that were nearly pieces of furniture, and we listened constantly to *Your Hit Parade*, *Fibber McGee and Molly*, Hans von Kaltenborn reading the news, and, best of all, soap operas like *The Guiding Light*.)

My visits consisted of my grandfather's chauffeur, Otis, a southern black gentleman in a peaked cap, leather gauntlets, and a gray uniform that matched the gray car, delivering me to the restaurant in the apartment-hotel where my grandfather lived with Lenore, where I sat very straight and quiet for the duration of the meal, because Papa did *not* like girls who wiggled.

Nana, a cigarette forever hanging out of her mouth, was worlds away. She wasn't like any other grandmothers I knew. She was fun and expansive—she didn't go out and about a lot but liked to travel to Europe and Hot Springs, Arkansas (mostly on her alimony)—and she was far from perfect. Her hair, which she kept blond, was the bane of her existence, so she changed styles from week to week, which I found terribly exciting. But what she never changed were the peignoirs she wore on her 1890s figure at all hours of the day and night.

During the Sunday coffee klatches, I faded into the background of disapproving clucks, clinking cups, and the rich smell of coffee. Then I happily disappeared into her closet.

Secluded in my own world, the ladies' clacking reduced to a comforting murmur, I opened the doors of an armoire to reveal Nana's impressive collection of negligees (my mother bought new ones for her wherever she went shopping). My chest thrilled at the image of all those slinky, silky things. Pearly cream, moody silver, petal pink, they hung in perfect array like impractical soldiers. After running my hand over the delicious materials, I pulled one out by instinct: a white silk negligee that zipped up to an accordion-pleat top.

In my game of dress-up, there was never any plan or story line. My nana's negligees recalled the seductive screen sirens of the day, but I wasn't pretending to be Carole Lombard, Joan Crawford, or Norma Shearer. Mine was the methodical enjoyment of an only child. I didn't even bother too much with the mirror—in fact, I really dislike mirrors of all kinds and am known for leaving the house with my buttons askew and my clothes inside out. The pleasure was simply getting into the garment and seeing what happened. The game was wearing this and that, sensing how the silhouette slimmed with a twisted rope belt or the hem seemed to lengthen with Nana's satin boudoir mules. The game was putting it all on.

The game was also private. I never would have thought to parade out before my nana and my aunties, and although they knew what I was up to, I would have been mortified to be caught in the act. Similarly, as soon as my mother went out for the evening, I went straight into *her* closet.

Inside my parents' bedroom, she had two enormous walk-in closets where everything was tidy, tucked away, and inviting. There was soft carpeting underfoot and the smell of lily of the valley in the air, my mother's scent. The dresses hung on one side and blouses and skirts on the other, divided by a marble-topped dresser with delicate perfume bottles and atomizers gathered on a mirrored tray. Inside its fabric-lined drawers, all manner of treasures nestled: stockings, underwear, and scarves. I inhaled lily of the valley and Joy from empty bottles she kept deep in her drawers after using up all the perfume.

A staggering number of kid gloves lay immaculate in a "glove drawer," as though my mother had just bought them and not worn them to drive, have lunch at the Drake Hotel, or go shopping at Marshall Field's. Even the white kid dinner gloves looked new, thanks to their rigorous cleaning regimen in which they were gently rubbed with a washrag doused with cleaning fluid to remove spots, blown into, periodically turned on a Turkish towel to dry, then smoothed down.

My mother's robes took up quite a bit of space. She loved them as much as Nana did her negligees. The minute Mother was in the door, off came her clothes and on went a dressing gown. The lovely ones were worn to dinner. The wraps were for lying down or after the bath.

I trod lightly when I came to her handkerchief boxes for hankies made by nuns living just outside Chicago. Ribbons kept the intricately embroidered quilted satins, taffetas, and linens pressed together nice and flat—and who was I to destroy all of Isabelle's precious handiwork? Separately, large grosgrain ribbon similarly kept packets of six folded nightgowns. The firm order of so many delicate things made an enormous impression on me.

The one area I ignored was hats—although it wasn't easy, since there were so many. My mother and her hats. She adored and wore all manner of them, from fedoras with great big feathers to doll hats with small veils of nylon netting. Many were made by Bes-Ben, run by the fanciful milliner Benjamin B. Green-Field, otherwise known as "Chicago's Mad Hatter." One would never have suspected that a man so uninhibited in his use of lobsters, clocks, firecrackers, skyscrapers, doll furniture, and even cigarette packages to decorate his hats was the son of an ironworker. From such humble beginnings, he created a business with his sister Bessie that catered to celebrities such as Lucille Ball and Marlene Dietrich, as well as all of Chicago society. His strange and quirky little hats were perfect for Mother. Changing with the seasons, she wore a cloche covered in cherries with her mink in December and a confection of silk flowers that looked like a wedding centerpiece on her head for spring. My father, crazy for Mother in chapeaus, encouraged her purchases, even though the hats at Mr. Green-Field's shop on posh North Michigan Avenue started at a pricey $37.75 and went all the way up to an insane $1,000. (Mr. Green-Field was no snob, however. Every summer he held a midnight sale where hat lovers could buy his creations for as little as $5 until 2:00 A.M., when he began simply tossing them out the front door to committed bargain hunters.)

My mother became known for her hats, but I was never tempted by the hatboxes piled to the ceiling. I hated wearing them, more than anything else in the whole wide world. I loathed anything on my head. Felt, wool, even the silk of the babushkas that all the girls my age wore made me feel claustrophobic. As a small child, I tried to ease off the dreaded heavy knit hat that my nurse, Nora, outfitted me in for winter walks to school. But she pulled it down hard over my ears to make sure it stayed. (When everyone was wearing fur hats in the 1950s, I had a sable one made and wore it a few times. The exorbitantly luxurious fur didn't change anything, and the old hate came back. The poor thing still sits captive and unworn in a see-through hatbox on the highest shelf in my closet.)

I tried on everything else of Mother's and walked around, imitating her as best I could. I loved how my mother looked. Her taste was superb, even when times weren't great. In addition to her unique hats, she wore scarves when others didn't. And the way she threw a fur boa over the masculine suits that were stylish at the time put her own imprint on a popular look. With her expressive blue eyes, red lipstick, lean figure, and personal flair, I thought my mother always dressed the best.

I loved to watch her put it all together. With the logs crackling in the wood-burning fireplace in their bedroom, she got ready for an evening out while I sat at attention on one of the two huge blue-and-white sofas and Daddy stretched out on his bed with the newspaper. He had plenty of time to relax, since he didn't need very long to pull on short sleeves and a suit.

Playing dress-up in my mother's closet was not as much about being in her clothes as it was being with her. I was gifted so many good and beautiful things. Still, what I wanted above all else was to be with my mother. But she and my father weren't home a lot.

Daddy, a workaholic, traveled all the time for business. He always seemed to be taking the Broadway Limited back and forth between New York and Chicago or catching a ride on a mail plane to even farther-flung places. When he was at home, my mother picked him up most every night, because that's the only way we got him home. When she bundled me (in my pajamas, after my bath) into the car to drive downtown with her, it was the biggest thrill of my life. I'd been released from jail, if only for a night.

That excitement, however, paled in comparison to the times when Mother picked me up at school to run errands! She at the wheel and I by her side, we careened past the shops of Fifty-third Street, Hyde Park's shopping district several blocks north of the University of Chicago campus, stopping first at the butcher, where chickens (later to be our dinner) kept in a pit outside the store squawked at our arrival. The unevenness of the sawdust that dusted the white tile floor felt good underfoot. Mr. Kline, frenching the bones of a slab of pork ribs for a crown roast, put down his slender silver boning knife when he saw us walk through the door. All weapons were useless against Mother.

After deciding that what truly looked the best were the tournedos of beef, although she'd been hoping for five-inch sirloin steaks, and reluctantly accepting a pound of unctuous sweetbreads as a gift from Mr. Kline, we were off to my most favorite store—the Italian grocery, where my love of everything green began. Tony, an awfully kind man who adored my mother and me, showered us with hidden delights. He held out a basket filled with the bright pods of fresh lima beans for my mother and a tissue-wrapped bunch of Concord grapes as pretty as any bridal bouquet for me. Pride swept across his face as he saw my mother's reaction of joy at the sight of his persimmons. (I do think he was in love with her.)

The butcher, the grocer, the baker, and the florist—shopping was not one-stop. It took forever, pinching and poking everything, politely answering questions, and accepting little gifts of a macaroon or an apple. I was in no rush, though; the attenuation of every minor transaction meant a longer reprieve from the rigidity of home.

While I would happily have shopped with my mother for cream of wheat, true heaven was a trip to Marshall Field's. It was impossible not to feel fancy as soon as you arrived in the Loop and glimpsed the department store that took up all of its State Street block (at the time it was the second-largest store in the world after Macy's at Herald Square). That was just the start of the grandeur. Inside, the Tiffany mosaic ceiling, an iridescent trinity of blue ovals surrounded by swirling hues of gold, capped a six-floor atrium in the jaw-dropping manner of a Byzantine church.

The mosaic of hundreds of thousands of handmade pieces of glass wasn't at all an outsize gesture. At least not in my book. Marshall Field's was no ordinary store, but a wonder of the world, a civic institution, a temple of quality! Once surrounded by the ground floor's dark-stained wood, marble floors, and white Corinthian columns that were grand enough for Cinderella's ball, you could find anything. Replacement bags for a Hoover vacuum or a Mikimoto cultured-pearl necklace. *Anything.*

Any day I got a whiff of the cocoa, Oregon peppermint, and butter wafting down from the large melting pots on the thirteenth floor that produced Frango mint meltaway chocolates was a good day. But if I were really lucky, Mother would take me for lunch and a fashion show in the Walnut Room, where the Great Tree dripped with lights over diners during Christmas. It was oh so glamorous in the massive wood-paneled dining room where Austrian chandeliers glittered overhead.

At our table for two, I took boundless delight in my usual order, the Field's Special Sandwich, a wonder in itself with a piece of buttered rye topped with Swiss cheese, turkey, iceberg lettuce wedges, more turkey, enough Thousand Island dressing to puddle around the plate, bacon, tomato, egg, parsley sprigs, and, lastly, a stuffed green olive. Mother, though, hardly broke the crust of her chicken potpie, preferring instead thoughtful drags on her cigarette. We made some small talk, what I imagined to be the regular gab of ladies who lunch, but mostly I watched her large blue eyes take in the fashions on the runway as the models paraded around our table.

I saw how other people looked at and talked about Mother, who was the opposite of staid or housewifey. She always ran a good house, because she had good help, but she never did housework. Instead she was front captain among her circle of friends and beyond. There was no doubt about it. Mother did all sorts of pacifying when her friends were fighting among one another. She took them to buy clothes and to have abortions. How many and how often, I had no idea. My mother was very secretive about things she didn't want made known. My entire family was quite Germanic in that way. Lots of "Shhh, the baby is in the room." Still, I heard enough to know that Mother, strong-willed and take-charge, was the leader of the group in every sense.

I completely adored her, but I didn't have that much of her. I was the child left dusting and rearranging my room. That's why those grocery-shopping or Marshall Field's expeditions were very important to me. I never knew when our next excursion would be, because I didn't dare ask her. I was as frightened of her as I was in love with her. The last thing I wanted was to do anything wrong.

My mother's comings and goings weren't the only mysteries I wasn't supposed to know anything about. The other, much larger mystery was the man she was once married to, the one who was my real father. I had understood that the man I called Daddy wasn't my biological father from as early as I could remember. My real father would resurface unexpectedly out of the shadows from time to time. Other than the fact that he *was* my father, I knew very little else about him, because Mother kept the details of his identity in her pantheon of secrets and Daddy hated him enough that any mention of his presence was barred from our home.

Occasionally, out of the blue, he would be waiting across the street from my elementary school to pick me up, a stranger in an ordinary dark suit. I felt like I was doing something wrong. Perhaps he had told my mother he was picking me up, since I was never unattended as a child, but I was not privy to that information. Instead ours felt like a sneaky affair. When he took me out for ice cream, I felt the burden of living with a lie and a deeply shaming embarrassment. Nobody else had two fathers.

Despite my otherwise very good memory, I remember little of the visits and not much more of my father, as if my memories, too, obeyed my parents' wish to obliterate this man's existence. Tall and slim, he had overly kind brown eyes that always seemed to be filled with tears when he saw me. He had attended the University of Chicago. And both my mother and father called him "weak."

Just as no information about my real father was permitted, neither were any physical traces of him. I never had a single picture of him, and if he brought me presents during our secret meetings, I had to get rid of the evidence. The maids were my accomplices, helping me to hide the Mickey Mouse watch or the charm bracelet I came home with when I returned from one of my sneak visits.

I imagined that Mother or Daddy would be furious if either found out I'd been seeing my biological father—and had accepted a cheap gift from him! Both had epic tempers for which they were unapologetic. (After smashing an ashtray against the wall in anger, my father simply said, "We can afford another." When my mother left hairbrush marks on my arm because I didn't want to go to school, it was Nellie, my nursemaid after Nora, who cried in my room with me.)

The fear when my real father rang the bell of our apartment one night, however, was new. Paralyzed in my bed, I could hear every single sound of the altercation on the outside landing as if it were one of my programs playing on the radio. I wished I hadn't heard Daddy yelling at the man, hitting him, and the man falling down the stairs, but I was always listening. After that there were no more sneak visits or presents, as he, too, agreed to disappear.

The chronic nightmares began soon after. Everything was taken care of for me, and yet I had no control over anything, even when the adults in my life came and went. One Christmas, Mother and Daddy went on holiday to Florida without me. But they left a very lonely child, who on Christmas morning, terrified of the big, empty rooms of the apartment that were typically bustling (and of waking Martha, who would certainly have a raging hangover), crept toward the living room. After soundlessly opening the doors, I found there under and around the tree, spilling out like a department-store display, many, many presents that were all for me. I methodically undid my mother's lavish wrapping, trying my best not to rip the stunning paper or crush her straw chrysanthemums. She'd bought me the wonderful doll I wanted, but more—a high-chair and a complete layette, too. Without any siblings I was secure in the knowledge that I wouldn't have to share any of it. That was *all* I was sure of.

Nana picked me up after a tense breakfast with Martha, and I took my new doll, dressed for the cold weather, with me. On the ride to her house, a block from Lake Michigan, you could hardly tell the water from the sky. The bleak gray of winter was very beautiful as well as forbidding. Dolls and dollhouses made up for a lot, but they couldn't make up for what I believed others had. Later, sequestered in Nana's closet, I had all but forgotten about the doll. A gorgeous clementine-colored peignoir that tied at the hip bone in a great floppy bow was taking up all my attention. In this secret world of clothes, a world that I controlled, there was no need for the company of playmates, because the clothes were my playmates.

CHAPTER

Two

Outside my great-aunt and great-uncle's cabana in Miami Beach, I took in the rays, absorbing them internally like a medicine I desperately needed after the last six devastating months. Although I had always loved the sun—it's terrible for your skin but wonderful for your being—I had never before experienced anything like the therapeutic heat of Florida.

Mother and I had flown to Miami to join my father's uncle and aunt for a couple weeks of their season wintering at the Atlantis Hotel. The express purpose of the trip was to get me away from the boy next door with whom I had had an unpleasant breakup. While I found the sea and salt water extremely soothing, I was already beginning to bore of spending every night with my family. Uncle Sam, a dour man, had seemed old to me even when he was young, and his long-suffering, second wife, Aunt Etta, was always complaining of how her son, whom they had to take care of, never did anything right.

As if someone were reading my mind, a shadow and a polite voice broke the sun's intense hold on me.

"Excuse me, miss. Sorry to bother you."

I opened my eyes to a cabana boy standing over me.

"There's someone who would like to meet you," he said. "And his father owns the hotel."

What a direct request! A blush appeared under Aunt Etta's snow-white hair and across her proper bosom. I pictured some ninety-seven-pound weakling with his swim trunks up to his chest sidling over. No, thank you: I wasn't *that* bored. But my mother just rolled her big blue eyes.

As soon as the cabana boy was out of earshot, Aunt Etta, Uncle Sam, and Mother started to confer.

"Otto Halbreich is quite something," Aunt Etta said.

"He's in the dress business," Uncle Sam added.

"And you should see his wife, Florence," Etta added, "and her jewelry."

"Mother," I protested, unsure about some hotelier's son.

"My, Betty, have a little fun," she said.

I sighed in resignation and smoothed down my light blue Mabs of Hollywood bathing suit out of nerves rather than necessity. Wrinkles were simply not possible, since it was made out of Lastex—a corset material that dancer Mabs Barnes had first used to create clinging swimwear in the 1930s and that later set off a revolution when Marlene Dietrich walked into a department store and ordered twelve suits, one in every color. The last thing I wanted to do was spend the rest of my holiday trying to dodge the hotel owner's son.

But the cabana boy's request was immediately followed by the most handsome human being I'd ever seen. The man's six-foot-tall frame was athletic and suntanned. His coal-black hair was cropped short, and his eyes, a chocolate brown, had a slightly Asiatic slant to them. There was a small beauty mark under the right one to give his obvious good looks a signature. It was love at first sight. But that was hardly unusual for me.

There weren't enough boys in the world for me. When one of my best friends back home said that boys were obsessed with me, I explained that, well, they might or might not have been obsessed with me, but I was definitely obsessed with them. From the age of twelve, when I started going with Danny, a long-lashed lonely child like myself whose father had passed away and whom *my* father called a "lounge lizard" because of how much time he spent at our house, I had averaged a new boyfriend every month.

Through high school I liked dancing with boys, hayrides in the country with boys, double features with boys—basically anything that involved lots of kissing and believing that one was in love. There were many first kisses, because one came with each new fellow. And that was the best part, because after the chase and capture I often tired of them as quickly as I'd fallen for them. The game of catch and release got a little hairier when, at sixteen, I arrived on the campus of Colorado College as a freshman.

When it came time to attend college, I wanted to get as far away from home (and my father's strict rules) as possible. I wanted to go to the University of Southern California, but Mother and Daddy said that was *too* far. So when my best friend, Annette, applied to school in Colorado, I did, too.

As World War II wound down, I found college filled up with girl-hungry veterans of overseas combat and occupations earning their degrees on the GI Bill. These were not boys, but men who had seen war in Europe and the Pacific.

Sprung from the strictures of Chicago, I dove into a heady social life. Preppy and young in Shetland sweaters, blouses with Peter Pan collars, pleated skirts, and one of the first pairs of penny loafers (with the penny stuck in, naturally), I went to lots of "beer busts" where dinner was 3.2 beer (that tasted like dishwater) and hard-boiled eggs. In cocktail dresses I danced at the ballroom of the Broadmoor Hotel. And everywhere I went, there were men: members of the air force, sailors, army officers. (I even went out with a captain in the ski troops just back from a tour in the Italian Alps.) They were years older than I, decorated to the hilt, and sexually sophisticated. Not that I did anything with them, although they sure wanted to do something with me.

I was smitten with being on my own and let my attentions guide themselves, which they did everywhere but academics. In no time at all, I went from being a very good high-school student to an undergraduate who flunked modern dance, no less! I only got more distracted sharing a room with Annette from home.

When Annette and I boarded the Rocky Mountain Rocket with the same trunks we'd taken to all our years at camp together, I couldn't imagine a better person to start the rest of my life with. I met Annette because her grandparents, who doted on her after her very beautiful mother became a widow and took to her bed, lived in the same building as my grandmother. Although we grew up eating and sleeping at each other's house, we lasted only one semester in the same dorm room. Annette did not partake in the new social experience the way I did. When I took to wearing mascara, Annette exclaimed, "What would your mother say if she saw what you have on your eyes!" I was deeply saddened by the rift, one that grew so big we put bookcases in between our beds to separate us until we got our own rooms.

And a little mascara was the least of it. If Mother were scandalized over my makeup, how would she react to my latest beau,

George? A hockey player from Saskatchewan, he was one of a group of Canadians brought down to play for the college while American boys were fighting in the war. A WASP from the northern prairies who supplemented his living by selling homemade sandwiches to coeds in the dorms was not exactly what my parents had in mind as a suitable partner. On campus, however, George was a star athlete and different from any man I'd ever met. I don't know if it was the rum and Cokes or mountains made gorgeous with wild lilacs, but by the time I headed home, I thought maybe I would marry him.

Except that when I returned the next semester, things weren't going right. He changed and grew distant. Not really a talker, George didn't offer much by way of a reason. But the why hardly mattered. His coldness turned into a physical hurt, a punch to the stomach or a kick to the kneecaps. Desperate and crying constantly, I couldn't go to class. I couldn't do anything. For the first time in my life, I found it difficult to get up in the morning.

George's abandonment brought up an old sensation. With a real father who was a stranger waiting outside school for me, I felt the trauma of desertion run through my core.

I stopped eating and didn't get out of bed for days. My inability to function bewildered and terrified me. And I didn't even have Annette to turn to. In my single room, a housing decision made while high on love and adoration, there was nowhere to go. Who was going to come? I had to get help for myself.

Although I'd never had therapy before, in my great distress I sought out the school psychologist. I talked through the whole situation, but if she offered insight, I didn't hear it. While I plaintively asked why George was doing this to me, why he had changed, I had the distinct impression that this was nothing more to her than a dumb love affair.

I stuck out the semester, but when I returned to Chicago, my family, alerted to my visits to the therapist's office, decided I wasn't going back. At home for good, I would apply to college in the city. Somehow, though, I never got around to it. I blamed the heat for my lethargy, but the truth is, I hardly noticed the choking humidity, because I didn't feel anything at all. A thousand miles and worlds away from my experiment with independence, I still smarted from my breakup with George.

I had no appetite but still took refuge in the kitchen, where Martha had been replaced by Margaret, a wonderful cook with a quick smile and a heavy Irish brogue. In a saucepan she whisked yolks, water, melted butter, and lemon juice together into an immaculate hollandaise (everything Margaret did was immaculate, including changing her uniform and apron twice a day). It was an attempt, I knew from my corner perch, to get me to eat. I normally adored eggs Benedict, but in this moment the frothy, pale yellow mixture Margaret set carefully over heat made me gag.

"You've done enough furrowing of your brow, my child," she said, whisking in a measured speed all the while. "God'll take care of all of this, he will."

While envious of Margaret's deep religious belief as a devout Catholic, I could not share in her faith for the future. She gently coddled a pair of eggs, placed an English muffin into the oven, and detected my wordless skepticism.

"You think a broken heart can't mend any better than a broken leg?"

She lifted the eggs out of the water and retrieved the perfectly browned muffin.

"The heart's much stronger still."

After assembling the egg and muffin, she poured the rich sauce over them and placed the plate on a white linen napkin, used as a makeshift place mat over the butcher block in front of me. There was no use. I just couldn't. And the quickly congealing hollandaise only added to my guilt. I adored Margaret—her mile-high popovers, the way she left looking like the "lady of the house" on her day off, and how she was known for her old-fashioneds (it was something in the muddling). Wasting her food was a sin.

"Och, come now. If God can't convince you, then maybe the tea leaves can."

Margaret took the teacup that was her constant companion, swirled the dregs three times, dumped the excess liquid out into a saucer, and turned her cup back over. Then she set about discerning my fortune by concentrating on the clumps of tea leaves and droplets of liquid.

"Look here!" She pointed to a squiggle halfway down the cup's side. "This section represents the future of no more than a fortnight, and there, as clear as day, is a fish. Why, that's wonderful news!"

"What does it mean?" I asked.

"As my dear old mother used to say, 'There are more fish in the sea than anyone ever pulled out of it.'"

Sweet Margaret and her tea leaves proved prescient, because

soon thereafter I started dating the boy next door. Just as the sadness with George had come upon me like a wave, practically drowning me, so like a wave again it ebbed and I was over it.

Buddy was literally the boy next door; I could look into his apartment from ours. He was a sad soul, sweet but a bit light. This was the summer of 1945, and all the availables were at war. Buddy, who suffered from a sort of asthma, was definitely a 4-F'er, but he had a brand-new Hudson, a car that impressed me greatly. Not for long, though. I soon tired of him, as I had done with so many before.

Despite my own experience with rejection, I was just as terrible at terminating a relationship as ever—and I was the girl who once made a date for New Year's so far in advance that by the time the date arrived, I no longer liked the boy. However, I was too honest to pretend I was having a good time and too guilty to hurt him by calling it off. So I hid in my room and refused to come out—even after my date arrived! My poor mother had to make up some excuse, anything short of my being dead. I didn't have a clue how to untangle myself, except to beg my mother to do it for me.

So instead of my saying to Buddy, who clung to me like a particularly smothering leech, "This is over, even though from my window I can see your mother and father, who drive me around on gas rationing," my mother packed me up and whisked me to Miami Beach for a vacation with my aunt Etta and uncle Sam—which is where I met the handsome hotel owner's son, Sonny.

Less than a week after arriving in the place I'd come to get away from a boy, I'd fallen in love with another. Sonny came over to our cabana, and the next thing I knew, I was in his convertible. Not only was he handsome, but his car, a brand-new blue Lincoln Continental with red leather seats, was one of the first luxury cars off the assembly line after the war. It was his father's expensive welcome-home gift to him.

Everything about Sonny was spectacular. While we drove around exciting Miami Beach with the top down to enjoy weather my mother described as "balmy," he told me about how after two years at the University of Virginia he'd enlisted in the army. After officer's school, I learned, he spent his war years leaning against the bar at the Copacabana in tailor-made uniforms. Alluding to a secret division of the army, he played it up as very important and hush-hush. Spies in nightclubs? All I knew was how marvelous he was to look at. Indeed, after his discharge from the army, Sonny went to the Racquet Club—a favorite of Hollywood celebrities and birth-place of the Bloody Mary—where he was spotted around the pool of the Palm Springs resort by the comedic troupe of the Ritz Brothers, who set him up with a screen test for a biopic of Rudolph Valentino.

I was gone. Here was this twenty-seven-year-old eastern sophis-ticate in linen trousers and a button-down, spread-collar blue shirt who introduced me to stone crab. I couldn't believe that someone like Sonny wanted to be with someone like me, a nineteen-year-old whose favorite piece of clothing was a Liberty of London print cot-ton skirt that you wound around and bound to a broomstick handle when wet and out it came a pleated skirt. What did he see in me?

He saw something, because things moved very quickly. We spent every day and evening together, and then he asked me to meet his parents and his sister, Mildred.

Walking hand in hand with Sonny down the rows of cabanas alongside the boardwalk, I wanted to run into the ocean and swim away. The closer we got to the big cabana in the corner, the more panicked I became, so that by the time we stood in front of it, the blood in my ears pounded louder than the surf.

"Mother, Dad, Millie," Sonny said. "This is Betty."

His mother sat under the shade of the cabana's thatched roof in a long cover-up, her skin brown without sunning. On one of her extremely well-cared-for hands, she had a huge star-sapphire ring. His father smoked a cigar near a big pitcher of iced tea and large bowls of fresh fruit. I could see where Sonny got his looks. Otto Halbreich, just starting to go gray, was handsome—not in a distinguished, older-man way but rather with the virility many men half his age would envy. A moment of silence felt like an eternity as I bore the weight of their stares, until Sonny's beautiful sister piped up.

"Oh, I didn't think you were going to be so pretty," Mildred said.

At her own joke, her small, delicate features broke out in a hearty laugh that I wouldn't have thought them capable of producing. Her laugh prompted the rest, and they all started laughing big, open-mouthed, loud laughs that defused the tension. I was glad to have the attention shifted away from me but could not bring myself to laugh. I'm not a laugher.

Still, they invited me to go to the Colonial that evening, and I agreed. If, after the war, gangsters and former bootleggers opened enough horse-betting parlors and carpet joints in Florida to make it the gambling capital of the nation, then the Colonial Inn was its high temple. When I walked into the first of many lavish rooms filled with tourists playing roulette, craps, blackjack, and every other kind of betting game, I was surprised by how the women really dressed. Everywhere I looked, there were cocktail dresses with big skirts and cinched waists in satins and taffetas, gloves that went to elbows, and enough jewelry to make you tear up. It was very posh and, to me, unexpected.

On our trip to the casino, both Sonny's mother and sister wore custom-made cocktail dresses from Kreinick's, high heels, gloves, and loads of diamonds. In a Kelly green dress from an unknown label, I might as well have been Cinderella before her fairy godmother appears. Not that I didn't look right. I wasn't as glitzy as the women around me, but I didn't worry about competing. Appearing in the wrong clothes was never my problem.

Otto, not to be outdone by the ladies, imitated his idol, George Raft, the dancer-turned-actor, who was so good at playing mobsters in movies like *Scarface* that many wondered if he was a gangster in real life. He certainly set the style for them in jackets with wide lapels, dark shirts with long collars, white ties, high trousers with sharp creases, and spats. Otto, dressed just like him down to a light gray fedora pulled over one eye, headed straight for the chemin de fer table.

There were plenty of other things to do at the Colonial, such as enjoy a luxurious dinner of crab and steak or take in a floor show starring Carmen Miranda. We spent a moment, however, watching Otto play.

Sonny, who stood by my side, had been explaining everything to me since I'd arrived in Miami, and tonight was no different. The Colonial was partly owned by the infamous gangster Meyer Lansky (whom Sonny's father knew); the boisterous groups of players sat at what were called gaming tables; and his father's game, chemin de fer, was a version of baccarat. I appreciated the lesson but didn't want Sonny to suffer on my account.

"You can play, too," I said to him.

"I never gamble," he said. "That's my father's game."

A showgirl in a green sequined playsuit (no doubt about it, the playsuit was in) stopped when she walked by us and squealed, "Sonny!" After she planted a kiss on his cheek that lingered a little too long for my taste and told him to give her a call sometime, he turned to me and winked. "Copacabana." I did *not* share the Halbreich sense of humor.

Concentrating on the game instead of Sonny as punishment for the showgirl, I watched Otto reveal a roll of cash the likes of which I had never seen. It was so thick that I couldn't figure out how on earth it had fit in the man's pant pocket, no matter how forgiving the pleats. He peeled off ten hundred-dollar bills and handed them to the dealer. A thousand dollars? What for? My parents didn't allow me to go to the casinos in French Lick, Indiana, and here I was in the ultimate den of vice. My dismay must have announced itself on my face, because Sonny leaned in. "That's just the buy-in, the amount to get started in the game. These guys can play for hundreds of thousands. They're high rollers."

I had never seen a hundred-dollar bill before in my life, but I didn't reply to Sonny's remark. Where I came from, you didn't talk about money or those who had it. We were comfortable, and that's all I needed to know. Money wasn't nice, according to *my* family.

It was back to reality when Mother and I returned to Chicago—

and the reality I faced was breaking the news about Sonny's existence to my father.

My mother, a terrible romantic, had encouraged the relationship while we were in Florida. I never had to keep any secrets from my mother about men. She, like my grandmother, felt just as strongly about them as I did. Mother thought Sonny walked on water, most probably because of his looks. If my father had been with us on vacation, things would have been very different. He was the person we kept secrets from.

From the time I was a young teenager, he'd wait up for me on the stoop of our apartment in his pajamas until I was home from a date. He didn't care about what others thought. I was expected home when he dictated the time. A rule was a rule. No exceptions. He was so strict that it prompted my friends to coin the expression "Don't be a Harry Stoll!"

We would probably have kept Sonny a secret from Daddy forever, but we didn't have that luxury. Sonny planned to fly to Chicago the first weekend we were back, and he wouldn't take no for an answer.

Daddy threw a living fit. Although he was a native New Yorker, he had a very large dislike of New York. "Why is he better than anyone here?" he yelled at me. My poor mother, however, took most of the blame. Why hadn't she watched the "baby," he demanded to know?

The irony of my father's anger is the great love that developed between the two that year as Sonny dutifully and extravagantly flew from New York to Chicago every weekend. I was surprised at how they became as close as brothers, since my father was nothing like Sonny. But whenever he arrived, off they went for lunch at the Standard Club, a private club that after its start in the late nineteenth century by German-Jewish businessmen catered to Chicago's elite. Only fifteen years apart in age, my father and Sonny talked easily about business or family or food.

Daddy's camaraderie with Sonny quieted the little doubts that popped up now and then: How come Sonny didn't know what "apoplectic" meant? Why did he have to call his mother every evening while in Chicago? Did his eye really linger on any pretty lady who passed by, or was it my imagination? Chicago's unabashed approval of Sonny didn't hurt either. Everyone was completely entranced with the man. (Even my dear nana, who gave him the third degree, got on board after Sonny answered all her questions, including how many rooms his family lived in. In her way and with cigarette ashes falling all down her front, she was a wonderful, delusional snob.) They truly couldn't get enough of the handsome New Yorker with the infectious laugh.

Everyone was still enamored with our liaison when Sonny and I were engaged in the winter of 1946.

My father, my mother, and I traveled together to New York, where we stayed at the Hampshire House. As a nineteen-year-old who wore very little makeup and washed her hair every day like a good girl, it was my first time in the big city, and my one wish was to have a black dress—another first. My mother and father didn't think I should wear black. No one my age wore black, they said, except to funerals.

Now that I was getting married, however, I could have one, and

I was taken to "Uncle Al's" office. Uncle Al was Al Neiman, the ex-husband of Carrie Marcus, who after getting her start in retail as a blouse buyer and saleswoman at the A. Harris and Co. department store became one of the highest-paid women in Dallas by the time she was twenty-one. Al, an orphan who somehow landed in Texas, married Carrie and together with her brother they created Neiman-Marcus. After their divorce he sold his interest in the specialty store and moved to Chicago, where he impressed my father as a tough merchant and eventually came to think of me as a daughter, since he never had any children of his own. Eventually he moved to New York to open a buying office.

I was very fond of him, and he spoiled me by taking me directly to the manufacturers to find the perfect black dress, which I did. It was a Nettie Rosenstein sheath with a light French lace off-the-shoulder top and a delicate little belt. It hadn't been put in the stores yet, but that didn't matter. All that mattered was that it was a very glamorous dress, or so I thought.

I wore it with high-heeled black suede shoes, a string of cultured pearls, and small clip-on pearl earrings to the celebratory gathering Sonny's mother and father held in their home at 25 Central Park West. Only a few short blocks from our hotel (the beautiful Hampshire House), their building, grandly called the Century, rose up to the sky in two ominous art deco towers that dwarfed all the other beaux-arts buildings around. Inside, their apartment was no less impressive. A gracious foyer gave way to a step-down living room with a view of Central Park from the fifth floor that just grazed the tops of the trees. A very expensive decorator had thrown around a lot of Persian rugs and ivory pieces to create an air of rococo opulence. The place was fancier than any other I'd ever seen. The only giveaway of Florence's hardscrabble beginnings and inbred thrift was the clear plastic that covered the upholstered furniture in the rooms not designated for our little party.

After Mother and I smiled our way through a tour of the apartment, Otto summoned everyone to the foyer for a champagne toast.

"Come in, everybody," he said, and then all of a sudden, without explanation, he grabbed my hand and he put a five-carat, emerald-cut diamond on my ring finger.

As a young girl, I had lusted after jewelry but wasn't allowed to wear much of it. I'd had an Add-a-Pearl on a gold chain and watches—I particularly loved one with the Orphan Annie logo—but broke them all (I've always felt there is something in my metabolism that stops the workings). How many times had I prayed for a ring? But I didn't want it this way. In my future father-in-law's grip, I went blank and looked to Sonny for rescuing. But he accepted this as a natural happening. If it hadn't been for the size of the ring, I would have run right out.

From that moment, through all the wedding preparations, and right up until the day of the big event, no one could talk reason into Otto. Toward the end we didn't know what he was doing. My mother, getting paler by the minute, had two hundred invitations out for the wedding at the Standard Club. Still, he kept inviting people by phone, in person, or by carrier pigeon up until the three cars he commanded on the Broadway Limited pulled out of Penn Station. New York was coming to a *party*.

As the date of June 7 neared enough to reality amid the crushing rounds of trousseau shopping, teas, and thank-you-note writing, I took refuge at the flower shop in the Drake Hotel, where the florist and I went over every petal and leaf. We were going to bank the club walls with tall spruce trees so it would look like a forest when one entered the candlelit room. The table arrangements were lily of the valley, lilacs, and peonies. My bouquet was lily of the valley and gardenia. The smell and sight of those delicious flowers were the only thing that seemed to bring me happiness.

I began to have a suspicion that this was not how a bride-to-be is supposed to feel two weeks before the event, and I became downright panicked. Sonny, in town early for the endless number of dinners and demands, and I were having lunch in a quiet corner of the Standard Club when all of a sudden I was overcome by the strongest urge to run out of the dining room and keep going until I was far, far away. I couldn't move to New York. I just couldn't do it. I didn't like it there. How had I let things get this far? In a strict upbringing such as mine, children don't say no. Now I felt I would stop breathing if I didn't speak up.

"I don't think I can do this," I blurted out.

Sonny pretended he didn't know what I was talking about, but the look he gave me said otherwise. He worked his jaw, and I saw anger in his eyes.

"I can't go with you to New York," I said. "I'm frightened and not ready."

He leveled a furious and threatening gaze at me.

"Yes, you can," he said in tone so flat it was scary, "and you will."

There was great strength and determination in that anger. I had never seen Sonny this way. I went silent, thinking that perhaps this was the assurance I needed to get me down the aisle.

As I walked the long, long road in the big, proper, satin-and-lace, off-the-shoulder wedding dress from Saks and a French tulle veil made in Paris with an apple-blossom crown, while all the guests oohed and aahed, my insides were still insecure. My chin always seems to get higher the more nervous I am. I did love the man, and despite whatever fears I had, I knew he would care for me.

Sonny and all his groomsmen wore white dinner jackets while my many, many bridesmaids were in long, soft pink dresses— except for my beautiful sister-in-law, who went rogue in a shocking, hot pink, jewel-encrusted dress that made her look like she was the member of an altogether different kind of wedding. My mother, in her simple soft blue taffeta dress by Pattullo, turned ashen.

The strain of the wedding on my mother—its myriad expensive details, inane for one evening—was staggering. If she looked like she needed a long winter's rest, though, my father, standing by her side, was even worse. He looked as if he'd just been shot out of a cannon (he had a kidney attack two weeks later). He wasn't my biological father. Still, I was his daughter, the only one he ever wanted. To him I was perfect. Once, while showing me off (something he did all the time) at the Standard Club, he asked a man he knew well, who was having a drink at the bar, "Did you ever see anything more beautiful?"

The man gave me a once-over and replied, "Yes, I've seen better."

My father never spoke to him again.

For my whole life, Daddy's concern over "watching the baby" bordered on obsession. To relinquish that control in one short ceremony, even to someone he liked as much as Sonny, was disorienting. After the reception, seeing me in my traveling outfit—a Suzanne

Augustine dress of gray silk and alpaca with white collar and cuffs, white gloves, handbag, and a hat to go ten minutes from the Standard Club to the Ambassador East hotel—he looked so sad.

Hawaii, where we honeymooned, was the antidote to so much reality. Not that the trip wasn't some kind of production in its own way. The enormous beige cowhide Hartmann steamer trunk I traveled with contained enough clothes for an unlimited stay.

The contents of the trunk were part of my trousseau, which included a complete wardrobe from morning to gala evenings. For my honeymoon wardrobe, there was a knowledgeable salesperson at a Chicago department store who knew every climate and resort. It was all effortless but took a great deal of time. I didn't even have to pack my own trunk. A woman, who came to the house, crumpled tissue and worked it up the arm of a garment until it looked as if an arm were actually wearing it. Then she used another piece of tissue, folded in three sections, to envelop the whole garment so that each item was individually wrapped (including stockings!). This was to ensure there wasn't a crease or a wrinkle in a single dress, blouse, or pair of underwear. For good measure she inserted a piece of flat tissue to divide different sections. When I unpacked, I was awash in tissue.

We were to be gone for a month at the posh Royal Hawaiian, recently reopened after the war (submariners had used it for R&R) and redecorated by Frances Elkins in island-themed chintzes, so we required a lot of changes of clothing. I didn't mind at all. All my new clothes were exciting. And the salt and sun, leis of fragrant ginger blossom, and volcano explorations, once we arrived in Hawaii, only made them more so.

We were very busy dressing, sometimes three times in one day. For lunch at a private surf riders' club, which my darling husband somehow talked himself into, I knotted a brightly colored sarong on the side over a new Mabs suit. On a tour of Dole's pineapple plantations, where workers were still finding grenades from the war between the rows and rows of fruit, I paired a striped long-sleeved blue-and-white boatneck T-shirt with white shorts that zipped down the left side so they didn't bag but truly fit a feminine waist.

For formal dinners at the hotel, I wore Clare Potter, who practically invented modern American sportswear with her incredibly easy and becoming clothes. Like the rest of his family, Sonny was such a good dancer that the only thing keeping me on my feet were her great floor-length silk skirts and matching long-sleeved blouses with a lapel in Asian-motif prints of soft yellows, navy, and red. At least a few nights out of the week, we went to raucous pig roasts with hula girls, where my ever-charming Sonny made more friends in one evening than most people do in a lifetime. There I opted for either a dirndl skirt and an off-the-shoulder peasant blouse or a Claire McCardell dress. McCardell, a considerable innovator during that fabulous period of American fashion, married quintessentially domestic fabrics such as cotton, denim, and wool with flattering shapes to give every woman what she wanted: simple, useful, interesting, and affordable clothes. My cotton dress had a halter bodice that crossed at the front—a typical McCardell touch—and opened up to a very revealing back.

My trousseau also contained the most delicate and lovely lingerie. Most of it was hand-monogrammed with my new initials and all of it also stuffed with tissue. There were full slips, half slips, nightgowns, pretty lacy bras, stockings, and garter belts. For my wedding night, I had the most extraordinary blue chiffon gown and robe. The first night together for newlyweds in 1947 was a novelty enhanced by exquisite silk and lace. (Bergdorf Goodman's once-legendary lingerie department became inconsequential when people started living together before marriage. Why spend a lot of money where there's no surprise?) I met the fright and mess of true sexual experience in a gown imported from France, which draped my body light as air and was held up by two blue ribbons that tied with bows at my shoulders.

What I was even more scared to face than my wedding night was the new reality waiting for me in Manhattan. I much preferred the impossibly romantic evenings of dancing under the stars and having Sonny all to myself. But after extending our honeymoon to a ridiculous six weeks, it was finally time to go home.

CHAPTER

Three

L et's give a hand for all the beauties here today at Lido's pulchritude contest," the emcee said before announcing the winner to the crowd gathered on the beach.

"Mrs. Lido Beach 1947 is Mrs. Sonny Halbreich!"

I was going to be sick. Worse than standing in front of the assembled guests now clapping politely, which was bad enough, was the fact that the halter bathing suit I wore was jersey. I had never worn a jersey suit in my life! Without Lastex there was no hold. I felt completely naked.

Sonny's parents were in residence for the summer at the Lido Beach Hotel, and although Sonny and I were just recently married, we spent the season with them on Long Island. The three-hundred-room hotel right on the Atlantic Ocean, recently reopened after the navy had used it as a discharge center during the war, was the utmost party place. There was a lot of dressing—even to the beach. Among the very exclusive and fashionable guests, one carefully considered what bathing suit and cover-up to wear before heading out to the cabanas.

Every night at the enormous Moorish-style resort, dubbed the "Pink Lady" because of its color, was like hitting the town. Its restaurant, where women wore gowns, mink stoles, and jewelry, had a retractable domed roof to allow for dining under the stars. Headliners such as Sammy Davis Jr. and Milton Berle provided the entertainment at the circular nightclub before it was off to the ballroom for dancing and more dancing. It was very New York, and very scary. People were so different from what I was used to. All gay and laughing, they carried on day and night. Compared to my insular South Side world, New York society was strange and aggressive turf.

I came from gentrified but very low-key people, who discussed clothes, food, business, and politics—anything but money. It was a good thing to have, but not to talk about. At the Lido, money was everywhere, including the tip of the tongue. This was a high-living crowd for whom no stakes were too high in a card game, no dress too glittery, no piece of jewelry too large. I had trouble following the conversations; I couldn't comprehend their lingo or their accents. Although I did understand the oft-repeated phrase "You're from *Chicago*?" I found their incredulity curious. All the guests of the Lido did was talk about going to Europe, but they didn't have a clue as to the location of Nebraska.

My husband and my family fit right into this society. Watching the four of them dance every night, I was overwhelmed by the whole situation. The Halbreichs—Millie always her father's partner, Sonny his mother's—were such good dancers that I became increasingly self-conscious with every perfect rendition of the rumba, cha-cha-cha, waltz, or boogie-woogie. I grew so intimidated by their performance that I refused to join them or anyone else on the floor.

Daytime diversions included distance swimming and dance lessons (no thank you). The men played marathon card games, smoking large black cigars under the hot sun, while cabana boys catered to them for huge tips (they could make a hundred dollars easy). There were also pageants where guests of the hotel paraded around. I don't know who pushed me out there (I could be pushed into anything except under a bus, where I longed to be in that particular moment), but *someone* thrust me into this exercise in humiliation. I didn't know how I ended up in that bathing suit, let alone winning the contest.

I was not fun-loving, like all the people I was surrounded by. The transience I experienced living in a hotel was compounded by the fact that I didn't belong there. I called my father to say I was unhappy, I wanted to go home. "Stick it out," he said. "Everything will be okay."

My summer at Lido Beach was just the beginning of a whole new life that didn't settle very well with me. Even the pampered art of shopping took on a tough veneer.

A nondescript shop hidden away on the twelfth floor of a midtown Madison Avenue building was not only the origin of my first Traina-Norell, generously purchased by my mother-in-law, but also a lesson in the rough-and-tumble world of New York retail. Long before the shop's owner, Martha Phillips, opened her famous Fifty-seventh Street salon catering to the couture needs of the likes of Brooke Astor and Gloria Vanderbilt, she spun me around like a top, praising this and that about the gown. While I turned, I caught a glimpse of Florence, in the Hattie Carnegie suit that fit her well-preserved frame like a glove, arching an eyebrow skeptically from under her close-fitting Mr. John hat.

Other than the deep blue and green moire taffeta print, the dress didn't look at all like the one I'd tried on weeks earlier. The sleeves were shorter, the low neck rounder, and the waist on the big dirndl skirt higher. Instead of altered, the dress had been remade, because in its original state it had been way too large.

Martha—a tiny woman who gained a few inches with her im- peccably coiffed hair, which didn't move as she burst into fitting rooms to tell half-naked customers what they should buy—was a saleswoman true as God made little green apples. From the time she was eight years old, selling blouses to bemused women by stand- ing on a crate behind the counter in her father's Brooklyn shop, she knew how to get people to buy. She had originally tried to push the Norell on Millie when she, my mother-in-law, and I originally visited the store a few weeks earlier. "Oh, no, no," my stunning sister-in-law demurred. She had her eye on a much more seductive Galanos crepe gown embellished with enough faux diamonds and rubies to make a sultan blush. "But it would look positively wonder- ful on Betty. Don't you agree, Mother?"

My mother-in-law wasn't there to buy me clothes, but Millie cornered her into it. Martha, not one to miss a dynamic, quickly switched gears, and before I knew it, she was pulling in the back six inches while I looked at the front, then running around to the front to do the same magic while I looked at the back.

"This dress suits a beautiful girl like you." Martha clapped her hands together. "How well it fits!"

Martha's routine was just like that of the salesmen at the old Barney's Boys Town, who pulled you in front, pulled you in back, and then exclaimed, "The suit fits!" The dress no more fit me than it fit the man on the moon, but Martha's in-house seamstresses had spent the weeks since our last visit turning it into a dress that did.

"Now that I'm looking at it, something isn't quite right," my mother-in-law said.

"What do you mean 'not right'? It's perfect," said Martha, who had mastered the art of the hard sale. You didn't go back to see her unless you bought something the last time you were in her shop.

The two tough ladies were off, *hondeling* until my mother-in-law wrestled a discount from Martha. My mouth dropped in embarrassment and confusion. To agree to buy a dress, have it altered, and then renegotiate its price was the height of rudeness. Admittedly, I was no bargain hunter, but where I came from it would have been unimaginable. Martha was much less upset than I. Once the sale was rung up, the two ladies were like best friends.

Beautiful clothes surrounded me my entire life, not just since my arrival in New York, but my new home was an introduction to an aggressive pursuit of fashion I had never before known. Shopping in Chicago's specialty stores was a serious, quiet, no-nonsense affair. One of my favorites was Stanley Korshak on Michigan Avenue, where no clothes were visible when one entered—maybe a hat or a handbag, nothing memorable. You were quickly ushered to a private fitting room whose only luxury was its size and its deep carpet. Then a fitter, coffee, cookies, and of course clothes followed. Stanley (Old Stanley, as we knew him) and his nephew (Young Stanley, groomed to be Old Stanley's successor) saved for me the original couture pieces they bought in Paris to adapt line for line in the United States, because I was a size 6 and they liked to see me in their clothes.

In this way I came to own a two-piece Givenchy dress in a deep blue-gray animal-like print that buttoned down the front in a low neck, small-sleeved jacket and tight skirt. The construction of another piece, the most beautiful taupe and black silk Dior wrap, no-waist chemise dress that gathered in the front, was something to behold. Everything was lined in the best silks—and beneath it all a bustier made underwear unnecessary.

The only other place that rivaled Korshak's serene luxury was Millie B. Oppenheimer. Tucked away in a small group of rooms upstairs in the Ambassador East Hotel, there was nothing more than a credenza and fresh flowers to connote a store. Her clientele was as small as her shop. The epitome of low-key graciousness, Miss Oppenheimer in her small hat and black clothing had the most exquisite taste; taste I have never seen matched. Beyond that, though, was her understanding of the women she dressed. Miss Oppenheimer cared about everyone who shopped with her; she was a rarity in that she bought with great insight for each individual customer. (Some specialty stores still do this; that is the great thing about them. Unlike department stores that buy a popular dress in a range of sizes, owners of these small regional boutiques will take a model in a size with a regular customer in mind.)

It was through Miss Oppenheimer that I got my first Christian Dior dress. It had three bows, one at the breastbone, another in the middle of the torso, and a third at the waist, with transparent netting underneath to give the illusion of nudity in the front. The skirt, with an inverted front pleat, had four layers of crepe and moire. This dress, which Bobo Rockefeller later wore for her wedding, became the most copied dress of the season. (In the following season, fall of 1948, Christian Dior also dropped the hemline from the knee to the ankle, thus rendering my entire costly trousseau obsolete.)

Everyone always thought New York was *the* place for fashion, except for my father, who said, "Do you think that Hattie Carnegie just makes clothes for women in New York?" It wasn't the only place, but it was different from any other place. I had always marched to my own drummer when it came to dressing—turning my cardigan sweaters backward when I was a teenager because I didn't want to look like everyone else, or pairing brown shoes with a navy skirt in a combination that most people assumed was mismatched but looked well on. They way I dressed myself was not unlike the way I'd dressed my dolls as a child. The pressure-cooker style of fashion in New York was a shock to my midwestern sensibilities.

And yet when I first arrived in this bewildering place, I took solace in shopping. Oppressed by the concrete landscape and not knowing a soul other than my husband's family, I would take myself downtown and sit in Sonny's office until it was time to go home. Out of desperation I learned my way around Macy's antique furniture and china departments, choosing the famous store not for its clothes (I never looked at the clothes, which weren't very up-to-date) but because it was across the street from the office. I spent many hours collecting Early American blue-and-white china that was more fit for a cozy country kitchen than for our first apartment on a nonresidential stretch of Sixth Avenue.

After the war, apartments simply weren't to be had, but my father-in-law knew Ben Marden, who owned the Riviera, a famous nightclub across the river in New Jersey, where big names like Lena Horne used to appear. Marden also owned the building, on West Fifty-fifth Street, into which we moved. We were lucky to have it, but I didn't feel that way. The apartment was small, noisy, and cramped with not a sign of green grass near it.

Housing was the only deprivation, for us, in post–World War II

New York. It was as if someone had exhaled a lot of problems, and suddenly everything from cars to clothes were back in abundance. The city seemed to be awash in money. We went to restaurants and nightclubs every weekend, with dinner parties at home thrown in during the week. "We" were a large group of Sonny's acquaintances (that got larger every night out on the town) who all had families, careers, and intimidatingly full lives—and they were almost a decade older than me. There was Charlie, who had a marvelous time partying with Sonny during the war, and his then wife, Charlotte; Jerry Silverman, another wartime buddy and owner of one of the country's most successful dress-manufacturing businesses (which he described as the "meat and potatoes of the dress industry, not the frosting"), who threw fun, decadent parties with his partner in their lavish penthouse apartment at the Mayfair Hotel (the terrace was carpeted with a Persian rug), where people from every walk of life (even the clergy) attended; and Sidney, who knew my father from the fur business. Sidney and his wife, Beverly, introduced me to Claire and her husband, Ted. Claire, extremely intelligent like her husband, had a steel trap for a mind. We used to rent vacation places in Atlantic Beach together.

On Sonny's arm I was just along for the ride. (Although he never let anyone get too close, everyone just adored Sonny.) But what a ride! Evenings out started with food, heaps of it. Every meal was a fiesta. There was the wonderful Italian restaurant, Romeo Salta, where pasta was prepared right at the table so that it could be eaten hot and al dente. Brunch at the Colony, "the boardinghouse for the rich," might be eggs Colony (a piece of toast, freshly cooked crabmeat, a poached egg, and a few drops of sherry) and then back for a dinner of truffled salade à l'italienne and chicken Gismonda. Just around the corner, on Sixty-third Street between Madison and Park, Quo Vadis served marvelous sunset salad, poached oranges, and chicken Quo Vadis. Steak Row, the neighborhood in the East Forties with so many steak houses—the Palm, Joe & Rose's, Danny's Hideaway—had its beginnings back in the 1920s when a former plasterer from Italy named Christ Cella opened a small basement kitchen in an apartment house. His eponymous restaurant grew into an institution where Frank Costello and Frank Erickson had a great, large table outside the kitchen. Right next to these fine fellows, who ran huge gambling empires, one could find us on most Friday nights, eating huge chopped salads, overflowing platters of french fries and onions, and steaks on the bone.

However did we go on to late-night entertainment following such feasts? Afterward there were exciting evenings at the Plaza Hotel's Persian Room watching the Williams Brothers and Kay Thompson, who seemed eight feet tall, with the largest hands I had ever seen. At the Waldorf Astoria's Empire Room, Pearl Bailey sang her heart out and danced around the stage while the man who would become her husband, Louie Bellson, played the drums.

We practically lived at nightclubs like the Copacabana, El Morocco, the Stork Club, and the Latin Quarter (opened by Barbara Walters's father, Lou), where all types mixed and the legendary acts performed in the ultimate café society. At the Versailles we watched Edith Piaf, frizzy-haired and very unkempt in a black dress with cigarette ash down the front (not unlike Nana), sing plaintive songs that, although we didn't speak French, moved us. Ben Marden's Riviera across the river in New Jersey was large but gathered the best.

It was there that Lena Horne's beauty first astonished me. (Many years later I saw her in Bergdorf's wearing large glasses but underneath her age still an incredible beauty.)

No matter the cabaret or restaurant, we always had the best table. There was a lot of greasing of palms that went on. Hail-fellow-well-met, my husband knew every captain in town. That kind of access meant we secured a front table at the Copa by entering the Wellington Hotel next door and walking through the basement alongside showgirls on their way to work at the nightclub.

The fun didn't end after dancing and a show. Then we headed to after-hours clubs like Gatsby's and Billy Reed's Little Club, where until very, very late we would sit on banquettes, drink, eat yet again, and rub elbows with early TV personalities and film people. Sometimes we did more than rub elbows. Once, at the Little Club, a hand gripped my neck and a deep baritone voice said, "You are some cute girl." Sonny shot up, seized the owner of the hand by the shoulder, and was about to give him a wallop just as the captain and a few of the waiters pulled him back. The cheeky fellow whose idea of hitting on a girl was grabbing her by the scruff turned out to be David Susskind, the notorious womanizer and legendary talk-show host whose program, which aired for thirty years, featured everyone from Nikita Khrushchev to Truman Capote.

Many a night Sonny and I heard the clink of the milkman's bottle deliveries as we made our way home. I didn't have to rise early. I lolled in bed until 10:00 A.M., taking breakfast on a tray just like Mother and Nana. Using half of the breakfast set for two that I'd received for my wedding and the three-division pot for cream, coffee, and sugar, I sat on the end of the bed with the telephone and a cigarette. My only responsibility was to find enough outfits for all these evenings. The task, however, quickly became a full-time job, because we really and truly dressed up to go out: all manner of cocktail clothes, satins, *peau de soie*, lace, cinched waists, off-the-shoulder, lots of sleeveless, diamond buttons that you were always losing. And you didn't wear the same thing twice (at least not in a way anyone would notice).

In the hunt for beautiful clothes, nowhere was off-limits. A few blocks from home, I journeyed to Bonwit Teller, a traditional store that had just about the same clothing as every other place of its ilk, but I returned again and again because of a funny and wonderful saleswoman on the sportswear floor. Hope, handling three to four people at the same time, threw her customers into a dressing room and piled the sportswear on them. It was "hard selling," but she got away with it using humor. The hours the woman put into that store! I never understood how in the background there were a husband and a child. Selling was her life, as it was for so many others in her profession at that time.

About twenty blocks south on Fifth Avenue, Lord & Taylor was one of my favorite shopping experiences in New York—thanks to Mrs. Lamm. Charlotte, who was becoming a dearer friend all the time, and I made a day of it, just as some people go to museums. We started on the fifth floor with lunch at the Bird Cage. In armchairs with connecting trays, we ordered "society sandwiches" of shrimp salad, cucumber, chicken, and date-nut bread with cream cheese; a salad that came with an ice-cream scoop of cottage cheese, egg salad, and tuna salad on top of greens mixed with beets and shredded carrots; or strawberry custard from rolling carts modeled on

Italian race cars. (The store's restaurant also served coffee, juice, or bouillon when it was cold outside to the shoppers who arrived daily at the store before it opened.) After lunch Charlotte and I went through the furniture department, then clothing and accessories with the savvy Mrs. Lamm, who put away expensive Ben Zuckerman suits for us until they went on sale.

The real treasures, however, were at Loehmann's. We journeyed to the site of a former plumbing store in the-middle-of-nowhere Brooklyn, where Mrs. Loehmann ruled her dressing-room-less empire from a chair overlooking women trying on the high-end fashion samples and overstock bargains right out on the open floor. Smoking from a long cigarette holder, Mrs. Loehmann brightened up her all-black ensemble—black silk stockings, black kidskin lace-up boots, and a black silk dress—with blue eye shadow and a bright pat of rouge on each cheek. With only the store's banquettes (in the same striped zebra material used by El Morocco) and gilt furniture to rest my purse and clothes on, I found many treasures, including a Norell checkered wool dress and a bolero jacket that still had the name of the model who wore the sample sewn into the garment. At ninety-nine dollars, it was expensive enough that I knew Sonny would murder me for buying it. Even though Loehmann's was known for its discounted merchandise, this was high couture—and couture, even at a bargain, is no bargain. I was used to a father who was thrilled to buy me beautiful clothes and still hadn't habituated myself to my husband, who, although his mother racked up huge bills at Hattie Carnegie, wasn't crazy about it when I spent money.

But if I released the Norell from my grasp, the dress would be snatched up in a second by one of the women circling like vultures.

This was a model, a one-of-a-kind that hadn't even been manufactured. (I wore it for an elaborate Easter brunch at the St. Regis hotel. Although it snowed that day, I was determined to wear it, and I did—and I froze.)

Accessories were absolutely irresistible at Henri Bendel after the fashion-forward Geraldine Stutz, an early proponent of Perry Ellis, Jean Muir, Sonia Rykiel, among many others, took over the shop and turned the main floor into the "Street of Shops." In the hours I spent poring over the little glass cases of jewelry, handbags, gloves, stockings, and scarves, I found a marvelous cat pin that was a real conversation piece. Made of mottled beige- and caramel-colored plastic with ersatz diamond eyes, the sitting cat takes up an entire lapel of a jacket. I thought that with a price tag of twenty-five dollars, it would get me my first divorce!

Treasures lurked all over the city. Mme. Isabel—a successful opera singer in Germany until she refused to join the Nazi Party and had to move to New York, where she survived by decorating sweaters—created a fashion of embellished knitwear. Queen Elizabeth was a fan of her exquisite cardigans adorned with fur, embroidery, beads, sequins, and ribbons. I liked to wear those divine tops with accordion-pleated skirts designed by Stella Sloat.

More used to life in New York, I turned from the quiet seriousness of my Chicago roots and dove into the local sport of style. There were bragging rights to be had as the first to stake claim to a trend or to find a new place. Although I didn't have too many friends, what they wore was very important. Each of us dressed to see what the other was wearing—and no one wanted to be outdone.

I wore a smart suit of red plaid by Davidow, which copied all the best French designs, for a shopping trip downtown. To a luncheon of cheese bread with egg salad and iced tea at Schrafft's, I chose a coordinated cashmere cardigan sweater set, a knee-length skirt, and David Evins pumps. For the same Easter lunch, I donned the Norell checkered wool dress, and the inspired florist Judith Garden, whose arrangements incorporating unusual materials and containers broke the mold of conventional formality, made me the most wonderful hat of gardenia leaves. A living chapeau: I adored its extravagance.

This is how we moved as a group. We didn't have a lot to do as married women, so instead we shopped till we dropped. A sweeping dress became an expression of one's ability, a jeweled necklace of one's worth. With an absence of other goals, clothes became our only markers for success. In other words, dressing became very competitive. And no one was more competitive than my in-laws.

My mother- and sister-in-law were the ultimate clotheshorses. Millie, an über-sophisticate, spent her life dressing to go out to restaurants and clubs. With her equally dashing husband, she led the nightlife in chiffon gowns by Galanos, Norell, Bill Blass, and all couture designers of the time. The combination of her stunning evening clothes and dazzling beauty turned even the most jaded heads.

Every spring my mother-in-law shopped for new hats with Mr. John, one of the most important milliners in the world. Florence also wore jewelry. *Real* jewelry. The era was about diamonds, not a great deal of color. She and her friends had diamond bracelets they called "stripes" that marked the length of their service to less-than-perfect husbands. Diamond and emerald drop earrings so heavy that they pulled on lobes and fifteen-carat diamond rings made up for a lot of bad behavior. I heard whispers that my father-in-law, who certainly spent more time at the racetrack than at home, had liaisons. I turned my head off to that, but Florence did have a *lot* of jewelry.

Many an afternoon my mother-in-law could be found at Hattie Carnegie in the East Fifties, where it was said that a lady could be dressed from "hat to hem" (she didn't sell shoes). Although Hattie, a native of Vienna, could not sew or sketch, she built a fashion empire on her own good taste. Her workrooms—where by 1940 she had more than a thousand employees making her custom clothing and ready-to-wear lines—became a breeding ground for designers. Norman Norell, Claire McCardell, Pauline Trigère, and James Galanos all began with Hattie, who created a style that was truly elegant and *très cher.* There were all manner of beautiful pieces, but her tailored suits, tight-waisted and cut high under the arm to make one look smaller and younger, were the thing. I sat through many fittings of my mother-in-law's suits at the store, and on one of these occasions Millie, who was very good to me, embarrassed her into buying me a gorgeous mauve tweed suit, which I treasured because it was my one and only.

Millie looked out for me like a big sister and worked all the angles as only she could. The Hattie Carnegie suit was wonderful, but the apartment she negotiated for us in the Park Avenue building she lived in was truly amazing. That Millie and her husband had an apartment on Park Avenue was a miracle of connections in itself, but when she told me she had procured an eight-room apartment on the other side of the building for Sonny and me, it excited me beyond anything that had previously happened to me in New

York. Apartments, particularly ones as gracious as this, were still as scarce as hen's teeth in 1951—and I truly wanted a proper home, like what I was used to, for our family, which now included a baby daughter.

Millie—a gambler like her father (and like the man she married)—traded in luck. Cardplayers who liked the high life, they lived under the code of what comes today could and probably will be gone tomorrow. Otto adored his kindred-spirit daughter and made it obvious in any way he could that she was the shining light of the family. Whenever they danced, he spun her around as if she were the only woman in the room.

In a stance perhaps born partly out of his father's favoritism, Sonny sided with his mother, who, despite indulging herself in her unhappiness through precious gems, furs, and couture clothes, was at heart conservative. (She built a secret nest egg by peeling bills from Otto's nighttime stash on the dresser, which took care of her in the end of her long life.) Both Sonny and his mother had a cautious bent that came from the fear that all they had could be gone, and quickly. They weren't entirely paranoid. My father-in-law was very much his own man and shared very little about his finances. He was a huge gambler and took many chances with the family fortune. As these types do, my father-in-law had to bet it all when he thought he had a winner. The business was always there for him to recoup any losses, so that no one ever seemed to suffer.

Even so, when Sonny and I walked into the sprawling and empty Park Avenue apartment, he demanded to know, "Who in God's name is going to furnish this?"

We had screaming fights about the furnishings and the

monthly rent of $225. Always the first to reach for the bill at the Colony or the Copa, he had enough money to be a sport but not buy furniture? Sonny said I was overextending him. I didn't care how angry he was. I was a twenty-three-year-old mother of a toddler, with another baby on the way, and as far as I was concerned, we needed the space.

When our first child, Kathy, was born two and half years earlier, I marveled at how such a tiny person could take up so much room. I shouldn't have blamed her; it was really the fault of all her accoutrements. Before she was born, I had an appointment at the layette department at Saks Fifth Avenue to assemble diapers, bibs, sleeping gear, and blankets—all of which was not delivered, done up in pink ribbon and piled into a bassinet, until the store got a call from the family that the new arrival had indeed arrived. (Many times I have duplicated this for clients who have babies by picking out layette items and folding them in a basket adorned with a ribbon and a sweet stuffed animal stuck in for good measure.) Kathy's Silver Cross pram was like a parked car inside the apartment. We dressed our carriages like beds, with embroidered sheets, monogrammed pillows, and blankets of wool, also monogrammed, navy on one side, light blue on the other. It took so long to get the baby all plumped up inside that by the time the carriage was down the elevator, it was time to turn around and come back.

I felt I deserved a real home, like the one on Park Avenue, since I had given Sonny a baby so close on the heels of our marriage, even though I'd been deeply conflicted. My unhappiness in New York made me concerned about having a child. If I brought one into this life, then I would never be able to escape. But I never discussed any of those feelings, and for Sonny my becoming a mother was a given. (Indeed, once I had Kathy, I thought my job was done. Perhaps because I was an only child, I wasn't too anxious to have another. But while Kathy was still an infant, Sonny told me, "Now you're going to have a boy." But what if I didn't have a boy? I wanted to know. "Then you're going to have another until you do," he said.)

As I suspected, motherhood had not been the bliss described in magazines. The low point came shortly after Kathy's birth, during a summer rental in Atlantic Beach with Charlotte, Charlie, and their baby, Jimmy. The day after Sonny and I attended a large party with swimming, dinner, and dancing at a Great Neck club, I awoke to a high fever and a complete loss of feeling in my right leg. Charlotte and Charlie didn't wait around for a diagnosis but evacuated immediately. It was most surely polio, which in the fifties was tantamount to the plague.

Nonetheless, a doctor with the stiff, high collar worn by men of his profession at the turn of the twentieth century, confirmed the bad news. I don't know how Sonny wrangled the specialist in infantile paralysis into coming (it was hard to get them near a case of polio), but my husband was good at that sort of thing.

The club we'd been to emptied its pool after hearing the news. Nobody would walk on our side of the street. I couldn't have cared less about any of that. All I cared about was having a spinal tap or being placed in an iron lung—and the new baby I had in the other room. While I can't take the unknown, once the reality is there, I become very strong. I turned my head off and glided through my illness, lying in bed for several weeks, during which Sonny took very good care of me. Confined to the same house with me for a month, he was extremely attentive. Unable to lift my head off the pillow, I only had him to rely upon, and though Sonny was healthy, he was very frightened. The combination of need and fear brought us closer.

Sonny wasn't quite as adept at taking care of a newborn, and the nurse we'd hired to help with Kathy had packed up and left like everyone else. My poor husband, who couldn't open a can of soup and maybe didn't know where the kitchen was in our apartment, fed her the bottle with the plug in the nipple and flushed her diapers down the toilet. Friends found us a wonderful Irish nurse who wasn't afraid to come in and rescue an ailing family.

My parents had no clue about my illness until I was well enough to return home to our apartment and they arrived in New York City for a visit. My father took one look at me when I met them debarking from the 20th Century Limited at Grand Central station, and although there were no lingering effects from the polio, he said, "My God, what happened to you? Have you been sick?" They got very angry with Sonny for not telling them, but they couldn't have done anything except worry if they had known.

Back in New York, I was determined to run as perfect a house for my husband as the one I'd grown up in. I was truly in love with Sonny from our first meeting. He crept into my thoughts at strange times. His hearty laugh (sometimes a phony one) and his voice, saying, "Hi. It's me," resonated deep within me. His presence alone elicited strong emotions in me. Once, while walking the dog, I was coming around Eighty-ninth Street just as he was coming out of the car on Eighty-eighth Street. The sight of him shocked me, almost like the screech of tires from an oncoming car, except this shock was a warmth in the pit of my stomach. Sonny truly excited me.

The perfect household began with the apartment on Park Avenue, and then there was the addition of Frieda, the cook. A very Germanic woman with very starched uniforms, she was like a general in the kitchen. The smell of her baking—blitz tortes, muffins, even her thick and crusty cinnamon toast—was not to be duplicated. During the day she wore a blue uniform and an apron purchased from the uniform departments at Bloomingdale's. In the evening, when she served dinner and was summoned to clear the plates by a colorful Murano glass bell, she wore a white uniform and apron. The children—not to open the icebox!—called her "Frau." She was supposed to help clean but, considering herself the cook, would only deign to dust the mahogany dining-room table—not an insignificant job, since it seated sixteen.

A nursemaid helped with the dishes at night and, depending on how well she got along with Frieda, shared her duties. A cleaning person came in twice a week, and once a week we had the services of a temperamental laundress, who wrapped the freshly ironed table linens in tissue paper before placing them in a chest of drawers. It was a full staff. Sonny, at home recuperating from a kidney-stone attack one day when the cleaning person and laundress were working, asked me, "Who are all these people?"

I tried to shop like my mother. I knew every person who worked at Empire, the greengrocer on Madison Avenue, and they me. The butcher, Holland Court, provided fresh eggs, legs of lamb, and huge beef tenderloins at Christmas. They would deliver to our apartment sometimes two or three times a day. My Frieda would call and order two pieces of calves' liver for the children's lunch, and if someone was added for dinner, they would deliver again. (Although rarely, I still treat myself to a visit there to buy Cornish hens; it continues to be the original family-owned business, with three Johns still calling me "Mrs. Halbreich.")

My house always had fresh flowers, company or not. The bills were huge! When we entertained, formal dinners for twelve or fourteen, I created special centerpieces. One of the most beautiful consisted of scooped-out cabbages filled with fruits and red geraniums. I also love my three-tier epergne, which I filled with frosted grapes (grapes dipped in egg white and sugar and put in the fridge to harden). I went all over the city to purchase beeswax candles in colors to match the table linens. Sonny's family employed a wonderful, dear man from the islands, Prince, as a chauffeur, whom we had wait table and bartend for parties in his immaculate white jacket.

I loved making a home, but I found taking care of Kathy and her little brother, John, rather boring, even though I loved them dearly. I particularly disliked going to the park and sitting with the other mothers. I found it maddening to listen to their talk of children's toilet habits and schools they hoped for. I said as much to the children's pediatrician when Kathy was an infant.

"I'd rather go grocery shopping or wax the floors on my hands and knees," I said.

"Let me give you a hint," he said. "Wrap Kathy up as if you were going outdoors. Take the carriage over to the window and open it. Rock her a couple of times. She'll go to sleep and will not be deprived of the outdoors."

I was not your light, gay mother who played games with them. My children were dressed to the hilt, though. *That* I liked doing.

Mrs. D'Jay, who made organdy smock dresses, came to the house to measure Kathy. My friends and I all said, "Not the big collars. Tiny collars are for tiny faces." Kathy, thin with cropped hair, looked beautiful and elegant in these very feminine dresses.

Two sisters on Madison Avenue ran a cluttered, noisy, and marvelous shop called Cerutti. Anita and Doris brought out velvet sailor dresses by Sylvia Whyte and good Trimfit socks while children ran around in their underwear, screaming and not wanting to try anything on. It was chaos, but out of it came great clothes. (Now Madison Avenue has so many sophisticated children's clothing shops that it makes my head spin. But when I look in the window, I don't know if what I'm seeing is for a six-year-old or someone getting married. Children today look like little replicas of their mothers.)

My mother knew a woman by the name of Florence Eiseman from Milwaukee who was starting in the children's wear business. With all the very elegant children's wear coming from Europe and New York, Florence was unusual. She understood that children don't have waistlines but "protruding tummies" and absolutely abhorred dressing little boys in miniature versions of grown-up suits. Instead boys had shirts and matching shorts for dress-up, and for girls she designed simple bodies accented with crisp grosgrain ribbon and graphic appliqués of fish, flowers, and trees that became her signature. Kathy and John became early Eiseman children, particularly because she did a lot of brother-sister outfits that I couldn't resist.

With a gracious and clean apartment, a vibrant social life, and well-scrubbed and well-dressed children, the Halbreich household was the model of 1950s impeccability. However, the man paying the bills wasn't a happy camper. Sonny, doling out a weekly sum for me on our dresser every Monday like it was a salary, always felt I spent too much.

Meanwhile, when it came to my clothes, I had become the "more" child. My first fur was a beautiful silky Russian-broadtail jacket, which was as fragile as lace and wore oh so poorly. The next was a blue fox jacket. But when Charlotte got a mink, I wanted one, too.

"My God, Betty. You already have a fur!" shouted Sonny, who was right but also belittling. The last thing I wanted to be was the nag in his life.

Clothes were not important to him; he had to be coaxed into buying a suit. However, they were to me, and it rankled me that he didn't care about that. He seemed to have plenty of money to be the huge sport whenever the dinner check came around, since he was always the first to grab for it. I didn't begrudge him this. His generosity was done in a kind way; the dark side was his fear of indulging me. Everything was for the outside world, and there was nothing left when he closed the door.

Just as I didn't understand that my shopping was an attempt to fill a gap, stretching activity to cover long but shallow days, I didn't understand why Sonny wanted to live more frugally than his parents did. I couldn't have a discussion with him about these issues. Once Sonny had spoken, that was it. Arguing with him was like arguing with a piece of furniture.

His parsimony was a revolt against his father, who would hand me a couple hundred dollars out of the blue with simply a "Here, honey," who bought me a diamond bracelet because, he said, "I know you don't have much jewelry," which made Sonny feel all of two feet tall. Even in the office, Otto didn't let up on his son, who, according to him, didn't do anything right. The walls were decorated with the biggest collection of stuffed fish anyone ever saw—stuffed marlins, swordfish, tuna, sharks—as a hanging testament to Otto's passion for deep-sea fishing and his rough tenaciousness. He was a taxidermist's delight! He was known for taking people, including his children, out on the boat and, no matter how the winds picked up, the waves grew, or the rain came down, refusing to turn around—just as he was known for breaking unions and making his son feel less of a man.

That was one of the reasons my father and Sonny were pals. Where his own father belittled Sonny, my father respected him. Otto was always saying he could have done a better job himself—I never heard him tell his son *he* had done a good job once. Meanwhile my father talked to him man to man. They had a profound connection, because my father was originally from New York, so he knew where Sonny came from. And just as Daddy disliked New York, so did Sonny, on a deep level, although he couldn't imagine living anywhere else. They also shared an occupation in retail, and Sonny trusted my father's opinion in business. But mainly they simply liked each other. Their close difference in age but specific familial relationship made them uniquely twofold, brothers as well as father and son.

Sonny definitely didn't have the same feeling for his father that he did for mine. Sometimes he responded to Otto's taunts and the two got into violent arguments. Neither man was very verbal (my father called Sonny "Mr. Zipper Mouth"), and more often than not Sonny just walked out and turned to his Rob Roys at the nearest bar.

Because his salary was dependent on his father, he was beholden to the man he disdained. In turn, Otto and Florence felt they owned us. We never celebrated anything—holidays, birthdays, babies—without them. They were even included in dinners out with friends, my father-in-law heading into the restaurant first to smooth the way by tipping the captain royally and Sonny following behind.

Still, I didn't accept their constant presence without a fuss. When Sonny asked his parents and his sister to come along to our anniversary dinner at the Colony, I pulled a long face that he understood immediately meant trouble.

"Forget it, Betty," he said. "They're coming."

I wanted to take the Donald Brooks dress I'd bought for the occasion—a tight, long-sleeved, black velvet top and the most extraordinary full skirt in organza with big flowers of white lace—that I loved only moments before and light it on fire. It was hard enough to share Sonny with every maître d' in town; now I had to also share him with his family—on our anniversary, no less.

At least Otto went out gambling with friends or on fishing trips. My mother-in-law, who was extremely needy and, like the rest of the shopping set, didn't have enough to do to fill good, valuable time, became a major bone of contention between Sonny and me. He felt so sorry that she had to live with an impossible man who did exactly what he wanted in whatever way he wanted, that Sonny not only defended her at all costs but also identified with her.

Whenever my doorman greeted me with the news that Mrs. Halbreich was waiting upstairs, my heart sank. I opened the door to find her perched on a chair in the den, alone in her Hattie Carnegie suit, her Mr. John hat, her mink stole, and her diamond stripes.

Florence, a very pretty, rather regal-looking woman with a broad New York accent, would have been even more beautiful if her mouth did not take such a downturn.

"Hi, Mom," I said, in what couldn't have been called the warmest welcome in the world.

My eyes turned back in my head as I heard Frieda setting two extra places at the table. Florence took it upon herself to come over; it was her son's apartment, after all. The excuse was that she had come to see "the children," who were invariably being bathed. She always chose the low end of the day, when the children were cranky, whiny, and not so happy to see her. They would rather see me, but now *I* was cranky from seeing her.

I had nothing in common with this woman sitting in the den reading a magazine. We had nothing to discuss other than clothes and jewelry, and I didn't want to talk about those either. It didn't matter. She was really waiting for Sonny to arrive; this was the bus stop. When Frieda brought her tea on a tray with some homemade cookies, it made me even angrier. I didn't like her and didn't want to make her comfortable. It wasn't very gracious, but I felt that she was the wedge between Sonny and me, whether that was true or not.

When Sonny, usually accompanied by my father-in-law, walked through the door, Florence lit up. She was so glad to see him.

"Hi, Mom," he said, giving her a big kiss.

It didn't take long for her to disparage her husband: "Why did you wear *that* suit?" Otto always wisecracked back in an equally ugly manner. I made an excuse to leave the room and call one of my friends from the bedroom. Five o'clock in the Halbreich house was no happy hour.

CHAPTER

Four

B*ut what would I do with the dining-room table?*

As I lay in bed, my mind raced around the apartment, accounting for the things I had laboriously accumulated after more than a decade of marriage and whipping up fear over what I would do if stripped of all of it.

Where would I live?

Despite the late hour, I was alone with my thoughts. Sonny was out God knows where and with God knows whom. Even if he did return before dawn, he wouldn't be himself. Drinking, started over lunch and stretched out until he tottered home, turned my charming, handsome husband into a slurring, unattractive, foul-mouthed man—a transformation it broke my heart to watch.

Even in a one-room with a bath, I could still take the dining table and the breakfront with the blue-and-white collection.

Sonny and I had found ourselves in so many bad situations that I thought often about leaving. But our home, or rather everything in it (the furniture from Chicago, the six-inch television set, one of the very first, which my father bought, the china I collected after first landing in New York), always drew me back. Possessions, that basis of my social life and self-worth, had taken a firm hold of me.

So instead I asked Sonny to leave.

The first time he didn't want to go. It was 1959; Kathy and John, ten and eight years old, respectively, were away at camp for the summer, which with its interminable days and shedding of outer layers was always particularly stressful on our relationship.

We spent Thursdays to Sundays at a cottage surrounded by mountain laurel on a lakefront in the Berkshires. Just as it had with our apartment on Park Avenue, money reared its ugly head as I set about making the cottage a home. Anytime I wanted to fix, change, or purchase something, I had to go to the source of the money himself, since I didn't have any of my own. And I was always met with resistance. When I found some great rustic kitchen stools that I simply had to have for the cottage, he fumed, "What do you need them for?" (That one I did win: The stools are still in the house now owned and loved by my son.)

Bickering through the renovations, however, wasn't the issue. What wore on my nerves was staggering through the summer constantly surrounded by a big group of friends who ate Frieda's cooking and sent shrieks of laughter into the bucolic setting as they drank and drank and drank.

Sonny was a true party person. He needed a crowd. To that end, bars, where camaraderie is always in plentiful supply, were his preferred setting. With the excuse that he was taking our schnauzer, Max, on a walk, Sonny frequented Malachy McCourt's eponymous bar near our apartment on more nights than he stayed home. What that dog knew on these very long walks? For sure he ate more pretzels than any animal had a right to.

Wherever we went, Sonny found a bar. On vacation in Mexico with his sister, also a fan of the high life, at the Villa Vera, an infamous Acapulco resort crawling with playboys and starlets, there was a bar smack in the middle of the pool. Sonny started drinking—and flirting—early and kept at it all day. He acted, to my mind, like a single man, loud and laughing, even as his long-suffering wife looked on from a nearby chaise longue.

Livid, I took to my room and refused to come out. I'm not a party girl and never have been. Listening to Sonny and his sister and their new pals scream with laughter next door until three in the morning, I became a basket case. In an expensive long-distance call that would certainly enrage Sonny, I implored my father to save me. "You have got to get me out of this!" I cried. "Daddy, I cannot endure it anymore."

My father and mother, both adoring of Sonny, always made peace even as they witnessed firsthand how his drinking poisoned our marriage. During one winter break with my family, Sonny arrived in Chicago just in time for New Year's Eve, a holiday I came to loathe as the night to cap off all party nights.

In the middle of a snowstorm, Sonny landed in Chicago inebriated and unable to speak. I didn't get the whole story, but during a trip to Philadelphia to see some friends there was a fight during which somehow my delightful husband had been punched in the voice box! "What are you doing to yourself?" I wailed while he sat on the floor with a bottle of scotch and drank until his bobbling head rested permanently on his chest.

I was furious over more than just the alcohol. I knew the men he had visited in Philadelphia, and they were attractive, single, with beautiful women always in tow. Someone had probably given Sonny a good shot for playing around with his lady friend.

When it came to women, my husband didn't need any help from his Philadelphia friends. Women were always attracted to him, and he to them. They flirted, he flirted. I often felt the fool, like right after Kathy's birth when a friend of ours asked about the origin of our daughter's name. "Oh, is Sonny naming his daughter after the showgirl he dated at the Copacabana?" she joked cruelly.

I didn't know how many of them there were, but I knew they waited for him at parties and met him at bars. Sonny's infidelities were thrown in my face. The outward, blatant flirting in my presence—was this intended to make me angrier and not go near him for months? In that way I suppose I helped push Sonny toward other women. But I had women calling at two o'clock in the morning asking for him. Try getting back to sleep after that!

I wasn't squeaky clean either. I threw the infidelities right back. Like my nana and my mother, I always liked men. From the time I was twelve, I'd had a boyfriend. For most of my young life, I was in and out of love, and yes, the boys liked me (no matter how many my father chased away).

At all the parties Sonny and I attended, there were men who paid attention to me. At first it frightened me, and then I hungered for it. To get back at Sonny and to be wanted. I had my liaisons, not with men who were going to rescue me but rather men who were attracted to me. As I became more reliant on them they would leave. That was heartbreaking, and I felt belittled. I was not made for that kind of lovemaking. The affairs only served to drive Sonny and me even further apart.

We had huge fights, where I tried to provoke Sonny by any means necessary.

"Where have you been?"

"What have you been doing?"

But I never got an answer.

Sonny's muteness was his greatest assault. He shut his mouth while I ranted on and on and on. Old Zipper Mouth. That I couldn't get a rise out of him angered me almost as much as my suspicions. Against his buttoned-up lip, I had nowhere to go. It was so unfair that I never got an explanation.

I picked up a radio, a beautiful gift from my family, and threw it on the floor. But it was like shaking a rag doll. Nothing came of it.

I escalated my attacks. At an Italian restaurant with a large group of friends, I had an impulse to hurl something at Sonny. He was in his cups, and I wanted to show that he wasn't the only one of us in the room. Many said that I gave Sonny a hard time. Everyone adored him, much more than they did me. It was the Malcontent versus the Charmer. So I threw a dessert at his head. At least it was now out in the open, I reasoned with all the maturity of a stupid child.

Sonny wasn't mean. He just never gave me enough of what I wanted, which was ostensibly more of himself. I longed for him to take me out to lunch and to a museum on a Saturday afternoon instead of drinking. I desired him alone, not with a big, boisterous crowd. I needed him to give without being asked.

Out of jealousy and rage, I succumbed to the sickness of dressing. Shopping was a mundane diversion from the unhappiness at home. I channeled a tremendous amount of energy into the habit, even though, or perhaps *because*, my expensive taste infuriated Sonny so. A particular golden sable I coveted created such a row that his mother intervened. ("Why don't you ask your father?" she said. "I thought my father had done enough," I replied.) No one had ever heard of a golden sable, but I'd seen a picture of the Duchess of Windsor wearing one and had made my mind up to get it by hook or by crook. A dear friend in the fur business, who loved me a bundle, laughed at my silliness and made me the beautiful coat. I loved that coat the way you would a friend. (It still hangs in my closet thirty-five years later.)

That I felt closer to my sable than to my husband should have been sign enough, but the attachment to the man was stronger than our affection. I transferred the deep dependence that my parents had fostered in me directly to Sonny. I was too fragile to imagine life alone.

Deep down I was angry at my neediness. So I severed the cord with my own children early. Although it took all my strength, I sent them out into the world very young. I literally threw both my children onto the subway at nine years old. (John missed his stop and wound up in the Bronx.) In the depths of my fear and feelings of inadequacy, I vowed they weren't going to grow up disabled, as I had become. They would be much, much stronger.

I was separated from John far too early, though, as we sent him away to school when he was still a little boy. His problems began when he couldn't keep up with his studies at his prestigious Upper East Side private school. He seemed not unlike the shell-shocked soldiers during World War II who could recognize a dog, for instance, but couldn't get the word out. John worked so hard as a child, running to a therapist most every day and having all sorts of tests. I worked hard, too, trying to help with homework. But, anxious myself, I felt I was doing more harm than good. Sonny, who saw a lot of himself in his son, had given up. "Stop," he said to me repeatedly.

"He's never going to college. He'll come into the business." I went crazy: "No!"

It was terrible for John. I finally brought him to Columbia Presbyterian for a day of every test imaginable, including scans of his head. It was just my little boy and me, him carrying my lunch tray for me in the Columbia cafeteria. After an entire day of wires, X-rays, everything imaginable, the doctor turned to me and his diagnosis was dyslexia. There was a man in Pomfret, Connecticut, who was a pioneer in reading disabilities, and so John entered the Rectory School when he was seven. We packed him up, shipped him out, and I took to my bed. When and where had I failed?

Sonny and I would bring the dog, Max, for visits and leave heartbroken. People at the Rectory were sympathetic, but I had a very difficult time. I wanted John home and everything normal. We got through it, and then he went off to another boarding school for high school. I hated the whole scene and believe he did, too, although he never complained.

During the holidays, however, when John was home and the whole family was together, I went all out. Being an only child and knowing loneliness at holiday time, I had grown up fantasizing everyone sitting around a food- and flower-laden table, beautiful packages under a tree—Hallmark kind of nonsense.

We celebrated every festivity. For birthday parties when the children were small I emptied the dining room to put down a grass carpet and filled small clay pots with flowers in the shape of scoops of ice cream. Frieda and I always worked hard at the birthday cake. She baked, and I decorated. We took a jelly roll and made it into a train for John's birthday one year. There were hired magicians, clowns. All the parents came. It could be an afternoon with as many as twenty-five to thirty people. There was always lots of screaming.

When it came to Christmas, my children would say I was a neurotic tree trimmer. It drove them bananas, but all their friends came for the event, even through the college years. On Easter Sunday everyone in the household loved getting his or her very own individual basket. We had dyed the eggs, but the general excitement was over the baskets themselves, from Woolworth's, silly things but fun.

I marveled over Kathy's eggs—splattered, painted, artistic, inventive, and visual, as with everything she did. She and I loved to make dioramas for Sunday school—such as the one we made for Sukkoth, the harvest festival. While we weren't a particularly observant household (we never attended the temple where Kathy attended religious school, and John never had a bar mitzvah), the shoe boxes filled with dried flowers and people we had crafted always won a prize.

I marveled over nearly everything Kathy did. From the time she attended nursery school, she was a star pupil. Never did we have to say to our tremendously smart and disciplined daughter, "Do your homework." Even during one of the city's major blackouts, we had to scrounge up every candle in the house so that she could study for a chemistry test, even though, as I kept telling her, school would be canceled the next day.

At school she was obedient, always on time, rarely sick, a prime student. Her defiance, which could be great, was reserved for things she disdained. From the start, Kathy was very willful. When we still had nurses for the children, a German doozy, who intimidated me, exclaimed that Kathy had kicked her in the stomach and was gone soon after. If Kathy, a notorious noneater like my mother, shut her lips tight, no one could wedge in a spoon. Once she went for an afternoon nap and woke up with the same piece of lamb chop she had defiantly parked inside her cheek during lunch. (Sweet, roly-poly John, on the other hand, was a nursemaid's delight and cleaned his plate.)

We all sent our children to the same private schools (if they could get in), the same Sunday school (they were happy to get them), and the same dancing school (Ms. Wolf's, and God knows what went on there). Kathy would not comply and become a clone. She dressed if you made her, learned proper manners, and pretended. On parents' weekend at the summer camp I sent her to in Maine, the director pulled Sonny and me aside to let us know what a strong personality we were dealing with. Kathy refused to get out of bed on the bugle call and had been caught behind the cabins smoking her first cigarette.

The director didn't need to tell me about this stubborn streak. Kathy and I had lots of disagreements that ended with my grabbing her by the arm to shake her. I would get so angry when she would not bend.

Underneath all that strong-willed studiousness was a very interesting and artistic young person. She liked clothes, but she liked the Metropolitan Museum of Art better (she wore the same school uniform from eighth grade through high school; she just kept rolling it up). At twelve years old, Kathy entered the Art Students League and was by far the youngest person in her live-model class. Sonny almost fainted when he picked her up one Saturday and saw a nude model and Kathy painting away.

At fifteen she got herself a job at a small folk museum located in midtown Manhattan. The following summer she went off to Chicago by herself for a newspaper job she'd gotten through my father's connections. Kathy came home flaunting eyeliner and a romance with a famous conductor, who had picked her out of the crowd at the Ravinia Festival in Highland Park.

I thought her father was going to commit all of us, since the summer of 1964 had been a hard one on everyone. One evening while coming home from the country, I bled so badly from my period that I couldn't get out of the car when we arrived at the apartment. Sonny had to run into the building to retrieve towels to wrap around me so I could go upstairs without showing the doormen the humiliating stain spread across my lower half.

My period had been getting progressively worse for a while, but now there was no ignoring the problem. The next day I was at a recommended gynecologist and a week later lying on a very narrow green metal table in an operating room at Mount Sinai. Moments before the hysterectomy, the young doctor told me, "Betty, we are going to do an incision you'll never see so that you can wear a bikini." A bikini? I was lying on the chopping block and he was talking to me about swimwear? I could have cared less; I just wanted him to get me out of there and on with it. "I've never worn a bikini in my life," I replied, "and I never intend to." Somehow being very willful, I didn't feel the effects of the medication intended to sedate me, so they put a very large mask over my face, and the next thing I knew, at thirty-five I'd had a partial hysterectomy. *Well*, I thought, *no more awful periods—or children.*

Three years later Kathy landed in Bennington (although her elite private school wanted her to go to Smith, she had to be a renegade), where she majored in art and English (Bernard Malamud, her adviser, wanted her to become a writer and said he wouldn't graduate her unless she stayed in the English department). By that time my daughter already had a full résumé.

Meanwhile I, with children out of the home and a husband hardly there either, had never worked a day in my life—per my father's orders ("It isn't nice," he said). So I thought that Ed Parnes, an old acquaintance of Sonny's who was opening a new division for the American designer Chester Weinberg, was just making small talk at a cocktail party when he offered me a job. I knew and liked Chester's clothes—he was ahead of his time, working in suede and bold prints as well as showing a lot of boots before any of that became popular. The new division, Chester Now, would attempt a lower-priced sportswear line that retained the avant-garde spirit of the more expensive couture. This was very early on in the evolution of secondary lines, when most designers did not cross over.

"Want to run it?" Ed asked.

"Run it?"

"Absolutely."

Either he was intoxicated or I was, or most likely we both were, because he meant it, and while I wasn't capable of running a cash register, let alone a business (I didn't do figures and still don't), I answered gaily, "Why not?" My courage sometimes showed up in strange ways.

In his office a week later, I was more honest about my ability. "Eddy, I have no idea what any of this is about," but he waved that off as a trifle, and I was hired. I didn't lie—I was terrible, and it only took about a month for Eddy to realize the mistake he'd made. He didn't fire or even admonish me. Instead he brought in Maria Scotto, an Italian ex-model who had worked with the designer Ken Scott. She was as fiery as her red hair, and the more aggressively she called buyers or added sales, the mousier I became. I didn't last the year with Chester Weinberg. (Forty years later, though, Maria and I are still close friends despite the difference in our temperaments; we love to chop and cook together in her kitchen in Bridgehampton, where she entertains and I sleep and eat her glorious pasta.)

I cared little about my lack of success at my first job. Seventh Avenue was just a temporary detour from my real life of twenty years on Park Avenue. As if to prove the point, each morning Sonny took me down to work and picked me up each night. There wasn't any leeway. If I were still clearing up or chatting in the showroom, I had to leave and wait downstairs like a child being fetched from school.

Having my husband pull up in a car chauffeured by Prince was part of what gave people the impression that here was a rich girl someone had taken on, a reputation that preceded me when I started working at Geoffrey Beene. The job was another stroke of luck during a cocktail party, where this time I met Bob O'Donnell, who had just left Neiman Marcus to head up a new secondary line for the legendary designer.

Mr. Beene decorated the three floors of 550 Seventh Avenue he occupied in the same silver and navy palette that extended throughout whatever he did, whether flatware or jumpsuits, for his entire life. The first floor was devoted to his couture, which was—and still is—the most beautiful clothing in the world. Born into a Louisiana family of doctors, Mr. Beene had spent a few semesters studying medicine at Tulane; the rigor and interest in the human body held over from this early discipline. He was a madman at construction. Trapeze dresses, architectural jackets, jersey, and silk—his clothes revolutionized fashion in the way that they draped a woman's figure and yet were instant classics in their timelessness.

The second floor was Beene Bag, his sportswear line, and the workrooms. In the early seventies, when I joined the company, nothing in fashion was manufactured abroad. Imports were not yet accepted, so Seventh Avenue was filled with craftspeople sewing, lacing, and beading the most beautiful items. The workrooms were my favorite part of Mr. Beene's company, because the pattern makers brought wonderful food: cookies I've never heard of and never seen again; thinly sliced cold meats; large hunks of cheese. One was transported to lunchtime in a small village in Italy when they laid out their daily spread on the cutting tables. Around those tables we celebrated every holiday, no matter how small, until Mr. Beene had a real tantrum about the constant partying.

The last floor housed Mr. Beene, a medium-priced line where I was hired as underling to head salesman Ernst Hamburg, a German gentleman to end all gentlemen. I had never seen a man more meticulous in my life. He was always brushing invisible flakes of nothing off his pristine suit. I knew that it was going to be an easy day when he came to work in his version of casual wear: a navy jacket and gray flannel pants that never showed a wrinkle. His shoes were polished so that you could see your face in them. Even his handwriting, always committed to paper with a gold pen kept in his breast pocket, was precise. Impeccable doesn't begin to describe the man. If he hadn't been Jewish, he would have been called a Nazi!

He was tough but wonderful, and we made a very good team. He showed the clothes, and I would get the coffee. People wondered why I let him push me around, but being ordered around was just what I needed. With my personal life growing more and more chaotic, the last thing I wanted was responsibility at work. Instead ours was an apprenticeship where Ernst taught me that it's truly possible to be a gentleman—or a gentlewoman—and be successful in business.

I watched as Ernst dealt with the buyers in his soft Germanic way, no matter how difficult or demanding they were. They needled for 20 percent off, complained about the hemline, wanted quicker deliveries, and left with only two dozen pieces after hours of debate. Until you got an order from somebody, you could choke to death. All the while Ernst showed the utmost patience, applying his precision to their maelstrom. As soon as the door closed, however, he let it be known how he really felt. Those clients would never have come back if they could have heard him.

While Ernst did the selling to stores like Saks or Neiman Marcus, he designated to me the small specialty stores across the country. Although a particular store might buy only four pieces, I found working with them extremely gratifying. They had a direct connection to their customers and knew exactly when something they bought worked or didn't. I never thought I would feel the satisfaction I did when they said, "Betty, that dress you sold us was brilliant." Not to mention when they reordered a piece.

We had to drag Mr. Beene out to meet the head of Saks or someone similarly important to sales when anyone like that was in the showroom. A private and mysterious man, he much preferred the company of his two beloved dachshunds in his office where the door was always closed. The chance of spotting our reclusive mentor on any given day was unlikely. However, we always knew he was "behind the door," and that was enough to strike fear into our hearts. He wasn't a communicative man but rather the quintessential designer hiding behind his bolts of exquisite cloth. Still, in his secretive way he knew everything and everyone (I always thought he ran a spy system). He would never tell you directly that he didn't like what you were wearing that day or how something looked during a fashion show. Instead the message came down with alarming alacrity from the powers that be.

Mr. Beene gave constant agita to everyone at the company, from the executives to the men in shipping, not because of his elusive style but because no one ever knew what he was going to do next. Mr. Beene listened to the press and fashion editors and then went on to do exactly what he wanted. That included creating dresses, coats, jackets that were way before their time and could never make it to the selling floor. (If they were presented today, the whole world would wear Geoffrey Beene.)

In his fetish for fabrics, he traveled to family-run European factories where he picked up bolts of rare and opulent cloth that upon his return he cut into the most divine pieces, which could never go into production because he had only that limited amount of material. The head of production tore his hair out. The business manager screamed. But there was nothing to be done about it; the styles couldn't be included in the new line. (Much later Mr. Beene opened a little shop in the Sherry-Netherland that became a marvelous outlet for his lavish, one-of-a-kind clothing.)

Although I worked for Mr. Beene in the smallest way, I swallowed the whole experience in gulps, including his clothes, which I wore religiously. I loved his beautiful dresses and wonderfully structured jackets. During my time at Geoffrey Beene, he introduced the jumpsuit. This was before the era of separates, and women like me didn't wear trousers. But I did wear his jumpsuit. They zipped in the back, which made going to the bathroom impossible, but made from his soft, supple jersey material they looked great with any one of my lapel pins. (Isaac Mizrahi later copied Mr. Beene's jumpsuit, except the younger designer put the zipper in the front, making trips to the restroom much more reasonable.)

I followed Mr. Beene in his revolutionary move to introduce pants, but that was the extent of my rebellion. Although the city was home to more radical elements through the sixties and seventies, I still lived a booked life. There were funkier places to go, but I didn't attend them. Sonny and I still made reservations.

Unfortunately, the midpriced line I was working for at Geoffrey Beene didn't stay at the party too long. After the division was closed, Ernst and I were invited to join couture, but that was way out of our milieu. The couture people were very vigorous sellers on the road with the clothes—traveling, doing trunk shows, and dining with the heads of couture departments across the country. They were too aggressive in their manner of selling for my mind-set. Plus, the idea of traveling alone and being responsible for large orders was too terrifying.

Again I told myself I didn't care. This time it was harder to rationalize. It was summer, and Sonny and I were off to the Berkshires for a very troublesome season. Without the structure and camaraderie of work or the company of my husband, whom I suspected was finding comfort in arms other than mine, I searched for an antidote for my loneliness. It's an old story, but I found my diversion one evening at a large party, in another man.

How easy it was to cross the line. Each time I knew it was wrong, as anyone entering into a similar situation does, but I plunged in, and when I came up, it was as if I had resurfaced from a pool to see blue, uncluttered sky. The fact that I was still attractive enough to excite someone thrilled me.

Rather than being all about having a sexual experience, I needed a man to talk to. Sonny was so gregarious in public, with his light, airy talk, but not one-on-one. He truly could not express himself. So the men I picked all shared two common factors: They were attracted to me, and they talked to me.

As for this man at the party, we talked about marriage (for he was married with children as well), work, lives, romance, longing. For a while the communication was enough to let me forget about everything else, but I soon discovered that sneaking around corners is not wonderful. We couldn't sit in a restaurant and have lunch or hold hands and walk down the street. We had to steal a few hours here and there, meeting at his brother's apartment or in a hotel room at 1 Fifth Avenue.

Trysts are for the lighthearted, and I'm not a lighthearted

woman. I began to want more than furtive meetings and late afternoons. But you can't get much more out of an affair. I quickly became too intense in my need and longing, and just as quickly my lover decided he couldn't see me anymore.

The old hurt resurfaced. Abandonment, this time in the form of a man whose tie to me was no bigger than a hotel key, fueled my desperation. Why did I set myself up for rejection again and again? Locked in a terrible loop, I became depressed and knew I had to find something to do with myself or I would fall apart. I felt I couldn't get out of bed in the mornings.

When someone from Oscar de la Renta's office called asking if I could come in and help out, I said yes immediately. The fit, however, was not good. I spent two months ineptly trying to sell Mr. de la Renta's famously ornate ball gowns. I tripped over tulle while his devoted clientele, social ladies of the highest order, acted as if I had just popped in from the Bowery to sell them a dress.

What made the job truly unbearable, however, weren't the dresses but the people. Mr. de la Renta swept in, swept out, and never looked at anyone. I don't care if you are making hot dogs—to create a work environment without camaraderie is not fair to anyone. Mr. Beene might have been the quietest, most behind-the-scenes human being I've ever known, with those who worked for him often arguing like a big family, but we had fun. There's no point if you don't have that.

When the people at de la Renta finally realized they didn't care for my work either, my dear friend Ernst contacted me to come interview with the Japanese designer Hanae Mori, and I went happily. Madame Mori, in the vein of Mr. Beene, was rarely seen. She glided in and out of her sumptuous whitewashed town house on East Seventy-ninth Street, but hers was a good group. I instantly picked up where I'd left off, following my old routine of soft selling from behind Ernst, only Madame Mori's clothes were flowing and ethereal, so different from Mr. Beene's architectural designs, in fabrics with the printed motifs of sea, mountains, and flowers of her native Japan.

I liked work (except when an ex-general and company executive came to America, and then we were in detention camp!), but home was so very bad. With Sonny growing ever more distant through drink, I threw on top of my accusations against him new, hurtful admissions of my own infidelity that I recognized were motivated more from getting a rise out of him than from any kind of personal passion. If that was my aim, then I failed miserably. He remained mum.

As far as I was concerned, I had failed miserably at everything. I didn't even know how to end my own marriage. My mother had always been the one to get rid of boys for me, but this I had to do myself.

I asked Sonny to leave. *Again.*

While the two of us sat in the den, I said, "You know what, Sonny? I think the both of us will be happier."

He didn't need convincing. This time Sonny was leaving without complaint.

"I suspect I'll be married within the year," I said defiantly.

"I suspect you will," he said.

The minute he went out the door, however, I knew I had made a mistake. Whether it was my parents leaving me home over Christmas or my college boyfriend breaking up with me, desertion was always my undoing.

I walked into the kitchen. The flower-patterned wallpaper from the fifties and the white wooden cabinets reaching to the ceiling were relics. The scene of bustling, careful preparations for many children's meals, dinner parties, and holiday feasts was now solitary and unused. Pots, pans, and all, left just as it had been when we were a family.

In the month after Sonny's departure, I swallowed nothing. I was so engrossed in myself and filled up on self-pity that I never gave a thought to eating. Not even my little family at Hanae Mori, where everyone worried about the great deal of weight I had lost, moved me from my misery. I looked at the job as filling time (completely unaware of how much I was learning and to what end it would come).

My worst fear—of being alone—was realized. And I had brought it on myself. I didn't know what to do with myself. I tried another liaison, this time with a doctor in the vein of my nana's particular fondness for men in the medical profession. But *unlike* Nana, I wasn't indulging myself in a pleasure but rather trying to hang on to something I had already lost. In my absurd attempt to replace Sonny with another man, I scared off the doctor, who was decidedly not interested in my particular case of the clinging syndrome. The breakup compounded my dejection, leaving me feeling lonelier than before.

Now, in the kitchen, I opened the middle of three wooden drawers, which was in turn divided into three horizontal sections: the first for small knives, melon scoopers, can openers, and other small kitchen equipment; the second for my sharpest carving, bread, paring, and other knives; and the third for gadgets, like biscuit and pizza cutters, that I rarely used.

My hand reached for the middle section and chose a small ordinary paring knife. I understood perfectly well where my actions would take me. I wanted to be in a hospital. I wanted to sink. *Sonny will feel sorry for me,* I reasoned. *And he will have to come back.*

I swept the blade across my wrist in the merest nick, a brushstroke really, not deep but a cut nonetheless. It would do. I did not want to take my own life; I wanted attention to be paid to me. Most important from Sonny, who would have to come home now and make everything fine. I picked up the phone on the kitchen wall and called Helene, a friend who also happened to be the wife of my personal physician.

"I think you had better come get me," I said.

She arrived so fast and did just what I wanted, calling her husband, who made the arrangements at Payne Whitney, a psychiatric hospital in a gloomy mansion-style building on the Upper East Side that overlooked the equally forbidding waters of the East River. We sat in a very small waiting room and talked, although not about what I'd done to myself. While she was doing everything to make me feel that "it was going to be all right," I could tell she was more frightened than I.

When I went into the admitting office, I knew full well what I was doing, and I committed myself. Once I heard the set of huge iron doors slam shut, however, I had a complete change of heart.

What have I done? What am I going to do? I have a dog to care for. Frieda will wonder where I am.

That slam woke me up to reality: No one was going to come get me. With the realization that I had literally locked myself in, fright turned to overwhelming anxiety.

After a doctor looked me over, I was taken to a room with eight beds, each covered in sad, gray bed linens. As the day wore into night, the other beds filled with women, ill, ghostlike characters out of a Fellini movie, until the lights went out on our silent group. The burning end of a cigarette made a little glowing loop around my bed as one of my bunkmates circled and circled without end. Every hour on the hour, an attendant with a flashlight appeared, shining his beam on each of us individually. However, what frightened me more than my circling roommate or the alarming hourly inspection was the communal bathroom. I had never shared a bathroom with anyone. Sharing one with eight strangers was horrid, horrid, horrid. I did not close my eyes that night. At midnight I was sent for. A pair of attendants fetched me from my room to be weighed by the doctor in the middle of the night as if it were Auschwitz. I weighed ninety-eight pounds.

The next day Frieda came to visit. Arriving with my own pillow and fresh pillowcases to replace the ones on my bed, she took one look at me and cried. *This is wonderful*, I thought. *I've reduced Frau to tears.* I didn't even know that was possible. When she left, her departure marked by the sound of the iron door clicking open and clacking shut, the outside world ceased to exist.

I quickly adjusted to the wrapped-in-batting feeling of life in the hospital. Sick people became my friends, horror stories replaced polite conversation, and time was organized by orderlies in white. None of us patients relinquished our problems so easily, though.

Locked up, I still found a way to hold on to my ability to control—through getting dressed.

The default style in Payne Whitney was disheveled. Most patients spent their day in robes, as if announcing their depression through the sad and nubby material around them. I had lost so much weight that I needed safety pins to keep my pants up, and my shirts were far from pressed, but that inner compulsion to get up every day and put myself together never left me. It wasn't vanity—rather the remnants of my sanity.

Others admired my clothing and didn't recognize it for the safety blanket it was. In group therapy the other patients poked their fingers at me and said, "But you don't really belong here."

Why? Because of the way I looked?

Dressing has always been easy for me. I have never in day-to-day living given a lot of thought to it. I guess it was what's known as a gift. "You always look so put together" was a common refrain. Feeling people looking, however, filled me with dread. Having my mother always telling me, "You're so pretty," made me jump, like a person being shocked by a loud noise. I don't care how pretty you are—if you don't feel pretty, hearing someone say you are makes you so miserable. With each compliment I withdrew more into nameless bad thoughts and buried fears.

Even in Payne Whitney, I had them fooled. During group sessions the other patients spit out, "You look and act normal."

"What are you doing here?" everyone wanted to know.

"I belong here, too," I said.

My insides were as debilitated as theirs. In reaction to the chaos I'd felt ever since I was a small child, everything had to be my way.

From the placement of a button on a skirt to the presents my husband purchased for me, inflexibility was my armor. Only the trait I'd developed as protection had turned on me—something I was forced to confront when Sonny finally came to visit.

When I first spotted him through the window, coming up the walkway to the entrance surrounded by all of April's growing things, I was elated. Although I was behind bars, the buds on the trees burst with green and my favorite lilacs were in bloom (anyone who came to visit always brought a small bouquet of spring). Regarding the man from afar, I could see that he was so different from the one I'd married. The laughing playboy was bloated and heavy-lidded. Nonetheless I was so glad to see him; he was going to get me out of this living hell.

I was led into a room with four doctors waiting and told to take a seat. Sonny then walked in. I got up to greet him and received a very cold greeting in return. He sat down, and I sat down. The doctors proceeded to lob a series of questions at him, each one ending in an answer that pained me as if my seat had become an electric chair. No matter how dire his responses, I clung to the hope that he was there to save me.

"What would you say is the future of this marriage?" a doctor asked.

"I'm ninety-nine percent sure it's over," he answered.

One percent!

Taking those bad odds, I humbled myself before him.

"I know we can do this," I begged. "I've learned so much here. Look at me. I'm a different person."

In typical Sonny fashion, he buttoned his lip—and broke my heart.

I was more adrift than when I had entered the hospital. The pain was everywhere. The sadness in Mother's big blue eyes during her visits was unbearable. I knew that as she gazed upon me, she not only felt the concern of any mother for a sick child but also saw something of herself. When my father died eight years earlier of a heart attack at the age of fifty-six, Mother was inconsolable and stopped eating. Although they'd had some beautiful fights, she worshipped him, and his dying sent her to the psychiatric ward of a hospital with a broken heart for almost a month. After she was discharged, Sonny and I moved her from the brownstone she loved into an apartment in a new high-rise around the block, a place she hated. It didn't matter that it faced Lake Michigan; her new apartment was too small for her taste. She had never lived in a one-bedroom apartment, and despite how charmingly the designer and Mother's friend Bruce Gregga had decorated it in blue and white, she never really lived there. When anyone who walked in gushed over the wonderful view, she said, "I don't live looking out a window at the view."

It was hard to have Mother, with whom I had become even more emotionally entwined after my father's death, witness my debilitated state in the hospital. But I experienced a wholly different kind of suffering as I watched my children—Kathy, a high-cheekboned, determined, and leggy twenty, and John, a wild-haired and gangly eighteen—laugh all the way up the same walkway Sonny and my mother had traveled to see me.

How dare they.

Visiting their mother in a mental institution should have been a more serious affair. Was this how much they cared? Maybe so.

Again I was brought into a room of clinicians. This time, however, I sat on a stool as if their plan were to rotate the specimen.

The doctors questioned my children on their feelings about their mother, and the answers were so brutal that I've pushed them out of my head. The pediatrician had been wrong; it was not enough to bundle them up and open the window. When I hurt myself in a pathetic attempt to gain Sonny's pity, I hadn't given them a passing thought. What kind of mother doesn't take into account her children's well-being in all moments? Apparently, everyone was agreed, not a very good one. But all I wanted was a life and some happiness. Now that my children were young adults, didn't I deserve as much?

I didn't allow the dynamic between my children and me to be altered by our awful session. (I don't like confrontation, and, clearly, neither did my children, because no one ever brought it up again.) But after six weeks in the hospital, I didn't feel any better than when I'd entered. I was no closer to keeping my dining-room table and breakfront together. Indeed, when a doctor announced I could go home—that very day!—I responded that I couldn't possibly. "I'm not ready."

Even my release from a locked mental institution had to be carried out my way.

The doctor assured me that I *was* ready and was indeed going home, so I asked to make a phone call, which I placed to Sonny.

"Could someone come pick me up?" I asked. "I'm being released."

A few hours later, I walked out of Payne Whitney, my suitcase and pillow under my arm, and the name of a psychologist to call in my purse, and I found Prince (already wearing his summer uniform of light gray jacket, pants, and matching chauffeur's cap) waiting for me with the car. He was alone.

I arrived home to find that in my absence Max the dog, who'd been suffering from cataracts, had gone completely blind; my sister-in-law, separated from her husband, had moved in, taking the varnish off my dresser with her spilled perfume and putting up pictures of her friends in my bedroom; and Sonny had found an apartment with a woman friend.

Not a day later, Prince was back. After being alerted to his arrival from my doorman, I went down to the lobby to find out the reason for the surprise visit. Silently Prince opened up the back door of the car. There sat a large broken box I recognized instantly. How could I not? My wedding dress was hanging out of it. Right after my wedding, I had given my mother-in-law my bridal gown to house in one of her many large closets, and twenty years later she'd sent the chauffeur to return it.

CHAPTER

Five

I awoke in the dark of early morning to the swimming sensation of sleeping alone. Sonny's presence lingered all around the bedroom, from the still-too-big bed to the tidy, washable liners he had made to cover the entire length and width of my dresser drawers to the checked gingham fabric from his family's company in which I'd cocooned the walls.

I searched for relief in housekeeping, making the bed just as soon as my feet hit the floor. Well, at least no one would jostle the straightened mattress, loosen the tight hospital corners, wrinkle the flawless bedspread, or flatten my plumped pillows, I reassured myself.

However, this morning I suffered from a particularly bad case of my chronic school stomachs. It was my first day of work at Bergdorf Goodman.

I opened my closets, where organization offered another moment of relief. How I'd lovingly tended to them when Sonny and I had first moved into the apartment on Park Avenue. There were storage boxes devoted to their accessories with quilted liners and hangers for all eventualities—even ones on which to hang fur stoles. I'd had the heavy wooden coat hangers monogrammed and those for delicates wrapped in cloth.

Without thought I chose a bottle green jersey Cacharel suit and a blouse in a red-and-yellow paisley pattern. Then I turned to the best part of my closets—the custom-built shoe racks. Running along the inside length of the doors, they occupied otherwise useless space and were much more visible than if my shoes were on the floor. Their ingenuity made me proud. From the slanted poles, each of which held a shoe, I chose a pair of neutral suede pumps that I imagined would be comfortable for a salesperson on her feet all day.

I moved on to the dresser, arranged as diligently, if not more so, as one in any store. The bottom drawer housed my alligator, cocktail, and beaded evening purses in individual Mark Cross cotton dust-bag covers—all beautiful but too small for a single woman, someone who needed to carry credit cards, money, makeup, and hairbrush when she went out.

In the middle drawer, my stockings were rolled into tight doughnuts (my own invention for keeping hosiery from its wish to be unruly), my underwear was hand-pressed, my nightgowns tied together with grosgrain ribbon in stacks, in the grand tradition of Isabelle the laundress. Although it was 1976, we female employees were expected to keep our legs covered, so I chose a pair of pantyhose.

Lastly I visited the top drawer, where my jewelry collection lived. Individual velvet bags opened up like little nests for my costume necklaces. Some pieces were in their original boxes, like a leopard pin that had once belonged to my mother. (I even had the card that went with it, addressed to her!) There was also an old jewelry box given to me by my mother-in-law, who'd had it monogrammed "B.H." instead of the "B.S.H." as was proper. From there I plucked a coral flower pin and the gold earrings my mother's friend had given me upon my engagement.

My state of anxiety didn't factor into my getting dressed. That aspect of my life was easy, in part due to my obsessive fastidiousness about putting things back in the right place. Even if I were *Who's Afraid of Virginia Woolf?* drunk, I'd still put my clothes and jewelry away with military precision before getting into bed, primarily because I found sleep impossible knowing that a single article I'd worn was out of place.

I didn't need to stand in front of the mirror; I knew my look. Its straight, clean lines spoke of an aversion to frivolity that succumbed only to a love of great accessories. Eclectic jewelry—chunky turquoise bracelets and larger rings, or my beloved plastic cat pin from Henri Bendel—was the signature on an otherwise understated template. My short hair and simple makeup were practical though proud.

Pulling on my clothes was no more a problem in this moment, as I tried to move forward with my life and start a new job, than it had been while I was hiding out from it at Payne Whitney six months earlier. The other patients in the hospital had been so impressed by my put-together appearance. If only they had seen how I'd fallen apart once I left.

When I returned home from the institution, there were no children or husband to direct me. I ruminated on why everyone—except for Frieda—had fled. Was it selfishness, the only child syndrome, overindulgent parents, a new environment, or all of the above? I went over the equation again and again in my cavernous apartment and always came up with the same answer: I was to blame for the failure of a marriage and a broken family.

The loneliness almost put me back in the hospital. I terrified poor Frieda, who arrived one morning to find me on the floor, crawling, screaming, and crying. She tried to no avail to get me to eat something as I got thinner and thinner. My sister-in-law was good to me; she came around regularly to take me out for walks. Making our way down the avenue we were quite a pair, the glamour girl and the skeleton.

I was beyond lonely, beyond desperate. If there was a word for my state, I didn't know it.

Upon my discharge from the hospital, I'd been given a referral to a psychologist and a bottle of pills, which I immediately flushed down the toilet when I got home. It was a stupidly dangerous thing to do, but I felt extremely threatened by the medication. I did, however, call upon the psychologist.

My first visit to Philip was not without its fair share of apprehension. We met on the ground floor of the brownstone on Eighty-fourth Street, although his office was on the third, because the building's service workers were on strike. As soon as I saw him— this tall, very, very thin, and definitely younger-than-I human being with long hair pulled back in a ponytail, I thought this was *not* going to be for me.

But he was the one to whom I'd been sent, and, like the Good Child, I always went where sent. Nursemaids, bedtimes, doctors, even husbands and a new home and city—I never questioned.

So Philip and I entered a tiny elevator that would have made even the most psychologically healthy person claustrophobic. (I wanted to rip off my spring cloth coat and head for the hills.) He closed the grate and, acting as operator-therapist, pushed down the lever. As the elevator shuddered terribly, Philip gave an apologetic smile. *I will kill myself before this elevator kills me*, I decided.

We made it to the third floor and entered his office, which had the coziness of a little living room with two good chairs, a couch, and a table with a lamp. More important, though, it was immaculate. I relaxed a bit.

Lying on the couch with Philip in a chair behind me so that I couldn't see him, à la the Freudian method in which he'd been trained, I noticed an avocado tree he was trying to sprout from a pit. Things that bloom talk to me. *That's never going to make it*, I thought, but kept it to myself. Instead I started in on the husband who wasn't my husband, the children who weren't children anymore, my apartment that wasn't a home.

Coming out of that institution was like coming out of a movie house in the daytime. Everything was very light and glary for a good while, disorienting me even when I traveled home to Chicago, where I ran into a friend from New York who was having lunch with the new executives from Bergdorf Goodman. I was lunching with my mother at the restaurant in the famous Drake Hotel.

I'd first met Corinne Coombe, a tiny, attractive, Chinese American buyer, when I was at Chester Weinberg and she at Liberty House, a chain of department stores throughout Hawaii. She had gone to work alongside her best friend, Dawn Mello, at B. Altman under one of the last of the great retailers, Ira Neimark. When Mr. Neimark became CEO of Bergdorf, charged with bringing fresh air into the conservative store, he brought along Dawn as fashion director and Corinne as general merchandise manager. The three of them, on a trip to Chicago to scout locations for another Bergdorf that never came to be, passed our table on their way out. Corinne, delighted to see me, kindly introduced me to the group.

Corinne, a very spiritual person, had shown me a lot of kindness since my return from the hospital. Just across the street from me on

Park Avenue, she and her husband took me under their wing. They checked in all the time and helped me to see a light at the end of the tunnel. In addition to making me dinner, Corinne insisted I come to work at Bergdorf. "After we left you that day you were having lunch with your mother, Mr. Neimark told me to 'get that girl to come to BG,'" she said.

"In fashion, misery is often confused with style," I said.

"Come and work at the store," Corinne said.

"Nobody's going to want me. I've been in a psychiatric institution."

Although I was still in the middle of getting myself together, for some reason Corinne thought I could be helpful and insisted I call Bergdorf's executive vice president, Leonard Hankin. With all my frailties, neuroses, and lack of experience, it was curious that jobs always found me. I never had to look for work or even make a résumé for that matter. My appearance, the way I paired a print or tied a blouse, gave the illusion of confidence and mastery. As frightened as I was, I heeded her counsel, made an appointment, suffered my standard stomachaches, dressed with care, put on the jewelry I'm known for, and met Mr. Hankin, a lovely gentleman from the old school. (Even with severe anxiety, another side of me pulls it together and says, *You have to. Let's go!*) He ran the fur department and other divisions I was too anxious to ask about. All I remember before I went blank was his asking, "What are we going to do with you if you come to BG?"

Corinne must have done quite a job lobbying because the store decided to take a chance on a tongue-tied woman straight out of an asylum.

And so, another round of school stomachs, dressing with care, picking jewelry, and going. One well-heeled foot in front of the other and too quickly I found myself at Fifty-seventh Street and Fifth Avenue, staring up at a façade of white South Dover marble, veined with city soot, that rose to a green-tiled mansard roof: my new place of work.

Bergdorf Goodman. Xanadu. Candy Land.

If there is such a thing as reality, this definitely wasn't its home. Surrounded by the Savoy Plaza, the Plaza hotel, and the Sherry Netherland, it was a plush corner of the world even during the '70s while much of the rest of the city was falling into dereliction and decay. With Bonwit Teller on one corner, Tiffany on another, and Henri Bendel just up the street, this was a land of old-fashioned luxury. The women who shopped at these places were not the sweater and bell-bottom set. They came to the store dressed with pantyhose, suits, mink coats in the winter, gloves, and proper handbags.

Inside, the French Renaissance interiors—marble walls lit by crystal chandeliers suspended from white cupolas decorated with oval painted miniatures—it all felt as if Marie Antoinette would pop in any minute for a hat fitting by Halston, the store's head milliner. My pumps made an unseemly racket on the inlaid marble floor as I crossed this hushed temple to what I hoped would be a new life.

The elevator doors closed around me and opened again to the fourth floor: couture. I stepped out into restrained elegance, where the display cases and racks were spare to the point of empty—and vigorously guarded by ladies in all black: *the vendeuses.*

These experts at selling very expensive clothes to the carriage trade eyed me in such a forbidding manner that I truly considered turning right around and heading back down the elevator. To say that the vendeuses were unwelcoming to newcomers was an understatement, and I clearly posed a particular threat. Among their dark uniform style (they dressed somberly so as not to take away anything from the customer), I in my green suit stood out like a peacock. In my world black was reserved for evening, not daytime employment.

My throat choked with emotion and my stomach went on a roller-coaster ride as I tried to hide on the floor. Not long ago I was on the other side, a shopper being waited on by the vendeuses. Although that was another life, I hadn't a clue how to find a place among these quintessential salespeople, subservient in their speech to customers and cutthroat competitive among themselves. I passed a stout woman whose severe updo matched her expression. Another, whose structured dress was the color of crow's feathers, pursed her lips in disapproval. If only they knew. Surely none of these women had ever taken to their bed for a three-day crying fit after their daughter broke a front tooth at the playground.

I held my chin up high, my pose for getting through this life, and found a pillar to tuck myself behind. I didn't have high hopes for my future at the store; I would be lucky to make it through lunch.

An unexpected tap on my shoulder nearly sent me through the roof.

"*Scusi*," said a tidy man with salt-and-pepper hair while bowing apologetically for my jumpiness. If *he* only knew.

"My intention is not to disturb you, signora," he continued. "My employer sent me over to talk with you. She does not speak English well. She is Signora Fendi." The man waved a manicured hand over to the other side of the store, where an imposing woman in the finest Italian cashmere and wool was surrounded by a fluttering team of people.

Of course I knew her. Anyone halfway interested in fashion knew Carla Fendi, one of five strong sisters who ran the empire they'd grown out of their parents' original Roman shop where as babies they had slept in drawers and as toddlers used its goods as playthings. The business was truly in their blood, and they had done impressive things with it. In the mid-sixties, they'd hired a young designer, Karl Lagerfeld, who created a brazen fur collection with its own double-F logo, for "Fun Fur." Through the rest of the sixties and early seventies, he imagined fur as no one else had—sheared pony-hair capes with oversize hoods in rust and extravagant black Mongolian lamb vests—so that Fendi became a necessity for the type who skied in Gstaad.

Ms. Fendi was in town to set up a new fur department at Bergdorf. Mr. Neimark had negotiated an exclusive deal with the store, which was quite a coup but also controversial. The Fun Fur from Italy was nothing like the rest of the stately fur department, where men came to buy their wives long minks or fox stoles. Amid her pelts sat Ms. Fendi with her walnut-colored skin and short, thick hair shellacked into an obedient helmet.

"Miss Carla Fendi would like to know *who* exactly you are, because you're dressed so well."

Ms. Fendi's compliment on my first-day-of-work outfit, delivered by way of a San Marco–style carrier pigeon, made me cringe. Husbands at cocktail parties, buyers at Mr. Beene's showroom, and mental patients were interested in me because of my clothes. It proved my hunch that I was nothing but a fraud. Ms. Fendi saw a woman with her chin up as if she owned the store, not the real terrified wreck who was in way over her head. So she liked my suit, my blouse, my jewelry. So what? It didn't help. With the suspicious eyes of the vendeuses on me, I had no idea what I was doing.

My instincts were right; I was a dreadful salesperson.

Years before, I'd confided in my mother that I was bored and wanted to work. My father, who forbade me to work my entire life (he didn't see room for a job on my pedestal), was no longer alive. I thought I would find a sympathetic ear with my mother, who always loved working. (My father encouraged *her* to work at a hospital shop, because its unpaid status gave it a dignified air—and it meant he didn't have to come home from the office.)

"Do anything," she said. "Just don't take clothes on and off of people."

In other words, don't become a salesperson.

Here I was doing just that—even if the clothes were costly couture coming off very wealthy backs. I had always listened to the advice of my mother as if my life depended on it. Was my job at Bergdorf nothing more than an act of rebellion at the less-than-tender age of forty?

My mother, however, was wrong. Taking clothes off and on people wasn't so bad. In fact, I rather liked it. I loved dressing the women who came into the store, either putting together entire outfits or showing them how to change what they had on with accent pieces. I found the way they glowed when they saw themselves in a different, more beautiful light peculiarly gratifying. I marveled that something so easy for me could mean so much to others.

What I detested was selling on the floor. As soon as the process of shopping became a commercial transaction, as opposed to a creative endeavor, I chilled to the whole enterprise. In the showrooms of Mr. Beene, Mr. Weinberg, and Madame Mori, I was working on a salary, so when buyers ordered pieces for their stores, it came across as a testament to their faith in the product and a belief in my ability to convey its beauty. On commission, which was the law of the fourth-floor jungle, each sale one had to enter in a ledger like some bookkeeper was a predatory act—and I was nowhere near as hungry as the vendeuses.

They were a mixed group from all nationalities and walks of life. (Some were quite eccentric: Miss Violet, in her sixties when I met her, was known for ice-skating in Central Park during her lunch hour when she started working for the store at fourteen.) What they all shared was an ability to sell. As a shopper entered the store, a woman sitting behind a glass cage alerted them to her presence over a public-address system. Hearing "Miss Violet, come forward; client is here" over the loudspeaker set my teeth on edge. But it didn't have that effect on the salespeople. For them selling was a mercenary sport that included cutting customers off at the elevator on the way to a colleague or hiding clothes for their clients in the most inconceivable and inaccessible places. They layered items of clothing on top of each other and then threw a coat over the whole thing, so that no one had a clue what was way underneath. Talk about hiding in plain sight!

I dodged the whole thing. I was never on the call system, and I did everything—including give my sales away—to avoid learning how to use the cash register. I'd never cared much for mathematics. The whole system made me feel incompetent and stupid. In those days one used a cash register and wrote down the sale in a sales book. I never did. I waited on people, showed them clothes, fit them, and, once the sale was complete, walked the receipt straight over to one of the other saleswomen, who was more than happy to do the arithmetic and add it to her sales numbers. There was a special room where the women wrote up their sales and made their phone calls to clients. I never had a section of that room. I wondered, observed, dressed clients, and grew to love those women who would kill for a sale. In the end they were like old relatives who tell all sorts of tales that no one is ever sure are true.

Not surprisingly, I didn't stay too long at the coldly exclusive fourth floor. By the fall I had a new assignment two floors down, in a new department devoted to Mr. Beene's clothes. The World of Geoffrey Beene, flanked by the fur department and Givenchy, was a beautiful store within a store and very Mr. Beene. Done in the designer's favorite silver and black, the nook featured a divine French window overlooking Fifth Avenue. It made for a perfect satellite to house Mr. Beene's revolutionary clothes and in which for me to hide out.

I suspect that Mr. Beene had requested me; he liked things that were familiar, and I was familiar. I couldn't be sure, however, because even though he came in regularly to dress the department, his private toy, he wasn't the friendliest or most communicative man. But it didn't go unnoticed that I knew his clothes on an intimate level. I had shared many meals and celebrations with the people who cut and sewed the airy jumpsuits, the long-sleeved dresses, and the crisp boleros with hidden spiraling seams that worked like magic on a woman's body. In his very silent way, he liked how I dressed and the fact that I wasn't the typical needy salesperson. Most important, he trusted me.

I turned the World of Geoffrey Beene into my world. Like me, Mr. Beene was a maniac about order, and he saw to every detail of his department, including the furnishings. A small obelisk in onyx pointed upward toward a rack of knit dresses. A lovely Jean Arp pencil work of small black shapes hanging on the wall mimicked the skins of two overlapping zebra rugs Mr. Beene had brought from home.

If the designer loved a pattern or form, it could pop up anywhere from a fauteuil's upholstery to an evening gown of silk panne velvet. The hunt for special objects to pique his imagination was a relentless pursuit. Dachshund statues, Chinese rock-crystal urns, American folk benches, or gilt mirrors with gold flowers growing through their middle all found a place in his world.

These things plucked from Palm Beach antique stores, Paris flea markets, country auctions, and Manhattan galleries under his singular vision came together like his cocktail dress of black velvet, lace, and plaid silk taffeta. Only a genius like Mr. Beene could make such a hodgepodge of incongruous parts play together in modern harmony.

The only chaos in my post was created by Mr. Beene himself, who could appear at the store with new merchandise, at any hour, at least a few times a week. Having cut these last-minute additions from his secret stash of unreproducible fabrics, Mr. Beene frightened most at the store the way he did in his own studio. His whims were the beauty, though, and the fun. And I made sure that women visiting the department understood Mr. Beene's work. His clothes had to be put on, since they were not hanger clothes. The entire thing was to get women to try them on, which was not always easy. But when it came to making customers look beautiful, I didn't mind becoming a little aggressive.

Whatever I was doing, women liked it. Customers came to spend hours visiting even when they knew there was nothing new for them to try on. The shop was ever changing, and this brought the women in, if only just to see what was new or how it was newly put together. The same merchandise was placed differently or accessorized in a new way, much as when a store keeps changing its window displays. The same women returned again and again, and the World of Mr. Beene turned into a salon of sorts. Those who shopped there got something from me and I from them.

Working at the store gave me a reason every morning to get out of bed, dress, and say good-bye to dear Frieda, upset that I had yet again skipped breakfast. No doctor could have ordered a better medicine.

There was camaraderie as well, since I continued to pass my sales along to the ladies as I had done on the fourth floor. No sooner was I done with a client than I walked the items over to a salesperson in Givenchy and had her ring it up. Anything to avoid the dreaded cash register. After I'd been at Bergdorf for about a year, Mr. Neimark cornered me in the fur salon and said, "Betty, there's no record of your having a single sale!

"What am I going to do with you?" he asked.

I honestly didn't know. It was clear that being on the floor didn't suit me. Even the World of Geoffrey Beene wasn't exactly right. Yet I didn't want my time at the store to end. I felt the tempo changing and wanted to be a part of it. There was something for me to do here, something for me to invent, a new and exciting challenge.

"We are fond of you here," Mr. Neimark said.

Even though I worked in Mr. Beene's department, when a client found a jacket and she didn't know what to pair with it, I couldn't resist pointing her to a skirt I thought would make an outfit—and while she was at it, there was the perfect pair of pumps in the first-floor shoe department. Women, craving the kind of direction I had to offer, returned to me over and over. The experience led to the realization that the store lacked an individual way for women to shop with help from knowledgeable people who knew what was in the store.

The practice of personal shopping was nothing new. It already existed at other big specialty stores like Bloomingdale's and Saks, adding a layer of luxury—the luxury of personal attention—to the shopping experience.

There were two ladies who shopped for clients throughout the store. The first, Madame Roux, a relative of Monsieur Givenchy (or so she said)—very coiffed, proper, well dressed, and French—spent most of her day in a small, neat office with a pen in one hand and a phone in the other. Her counterpart, Jo Hughes, who took care of the city's biggest socialites, always had the remnants of lunch down her front. Tony, a dirty little shih tzu, accompanied her everywhere, even as she tended to the heiresses of the time. Tony even went with his owner, whose temper was legendary, to lunch at La Côte Basque or 21, where he was apparently checked in the coatroom. That was personal shopping at Bergdorf Goodman!

In my time at the store, I had learned that I could put people together as well as I did myself. It wasn't just about showing them the best blouse to fit a large bosom. First I gained their confidence, and then I taught them how to tie a scarf.

"Betty," Mr. Neimark said, "what would you like to do?"

I had a sense, however dim, that this was my chance to create something. My gut feeling was as strong as my stomach was weak. This was an opportunity that would not come around again.

"Bergdorf needs a proper personal-shopping office," I said. "Take me off the floor and let me do something. I believe I can build a department around individual help."

Where did I get the nerve? Mr. Neimark didn't say no. He didn't say anything at all. My stomach lurched. What was I thinking, making such an outlandish request? He hadn't known what to do with me when they hired me, but then again no one ever has.

The answer to my request eventually came in the form of one of fashion's greatest tests, when out of the blue I was summoned to the Givenchy department by Mr. Neimark "to help a very important client."

"We want to see what you can do for her," he said.

I walked into Givenchy to meet the client.

Mrs. Paley.

Babe Paley.

The most fashionable woman in the world.

What in God's name was I going to do for *her*? The swan-necked wife of CBS founder Bill Paley, universally admired for her remarkable beauty and style, was the ultimate trendsetter. This was quite a trial all right. The powers-that-be were throwing me into the lion's den to see if I would come up alive.

After introducing myself with much politeness, I said the first thing that struck me: How did she get her thick crop of hair that magnificent blue-gray?

"I really have to ask you this: Everyone says you use Tintex on your hair to get that gorgeous gray color. Is it true?" I asked referring to the powder dye intended for clothes. It was said she used white Tintex as a rinse.

It wasn't true she said.

"Well, it's a wonderful, interesting rumor."

From then on we had a lovely time. I admired her bone structure. I also wondered to myself if the news I'd heard that she was in the first stages of cancer was true. I can hardly say I did anything for Mrs. Paley's style. She could have put on the stockroom clerk's uniform and looked like a queen. What I did do was make her comfortable and entertain her enough for an afternoon that I earned a chance to run my own department: Solutions. (I did not come up with the name, nor do I particularly like it. "This isn't a drugstore," I said when I first heard it. "That's where you find solutions." Nobody, in all these years, has ever owned up to naming this department. And whoever it was, he or she is long gone. I still rarely use the name, and I guess it is so much my place today that I forget. I have *never* answered the phone, "Solutions department!")

One solution at least was my salary. The two hundred dollars I earned each week from the store meant I didn't have to rely on a commission, or entirely on Sonny. Up until then I had been completely beholden to the man, who was still angrily paying my rent, my meat-market bills, Frieda, and Philip. For the first time in my life, I had a taste of independence. While Sonny continued to pay my rent and Frieda, taking my paycheck to the bank and opening my very first account was thrilling.

My "office" was the last two dressing rooms in a corridor of them tucked away around a corner on the third floor. Concealment is the hallmark of exclusivity, but this was taking it a bit far. I wondered how anyone was going to find me. However rough or hidden, the space was immediately redeemed by the most marvelous six-over-six sash window with a glorious view of the Plaza that opened up to Central Park, which stretched optimistically uptown and met the gorgeous limestone buildings of Fifth Avenue. Oddly enough, it reminded me of the window through which I had watched the trees bloom while at Payne Whitney.

If I thought I would disappear into my new department, I was sorely mistaken. Not a few days into the job, I arrived at work to find a plain unmarked envelope taped to the door. Across the heavy paper stock in a familiar elegant, low-slung cursive was my name. Clearly someone had found me.

As I walked into my office, I began to read the letter, which shockingly turned out to be from Mr. Beene. Barely a sentence or two into the letter, its content went from mystifying to terrifying. The silent man I knew to show very little emotion had had a ghastly reaction to my leaving his department. "How could you leave?" wrote a furious Mr. Beene. "When you were sick, I saved you from a mental institution. I bailed you out."

I gasped at this claim, which came as swift and hurtful as a kick in the stomach, shocking. A year ago it would have sent me into a permanent fetal position. But instead, a year into my analysis with Philip, I sat down at my desk and took out my own envelope.

Analysis can be very painful. For me, everything about it, even the hour I was given for my appointment, was difficult. The nine o'clock hour was never free in all the years I saw Philip. It was 7:00 or 8:00 A.M. that I'd have to run for. After the unsettling, tremulous elevator ride, I'd have to sit in his waiting room, where all the other patients were much younger than I. None of them looked anything like me.

The sum total felt like a test to see if Betty was going to make it. But I never canceled an appointment (even the day after a cataract operation). I was still worse than desperate when I went to see Philip. I wasn't behind bars, and I wasn't behind a locked door. But in essence I was still in the same place.

If it wasn't for the fear of getting so sick again, I certainly would have left after the first session. Reiterating and reopening yet again, for another person, the same old themes made me want to run home to polish every piece of silver that hadn't seen the light of day since my last dinner party before Sonny's departure or get on my hands and knees to buff the floors to a high shine although there weren't any little feet coming in from the park to scuff them.

We usually began with the marriage, and then he delved back into my childhood. We would leave childhood and return to Sonny. We seemed to be going over and over the same foolish territory like people lost in a desert rambling around the same dune. Philip was dig-dig-digging into my inner soul.

On the couch staring at the latest flower bulb that Philip was trying to coax life out of in a pot, I was in the midst of a familiar litany against Sonny, the old trying-to-keep-the-dining-set syndrome, when he tapped into a new font of meaning with one single sentence.

"Betty, get out of your dollhouse," he said.

Why in heaven's name would I do that? A dollhouse is perfection.

The one I'd had as a child, a Colonial house with papered walls and Colonial furniture, was the most important thing I ever owned. I loved it so and wished more than anything that I'd kept it, but I do not come from a family of keepers. When Kathy was young, Sonny and I put together a white Colonial house for her. He electrified it and wallpapered it. And I bought wonderful wooden furniture from Mrs. Thorne at the Women's Exchange in Chicago. Oh, it was very sweet. Kathy never loved that dollhouse as I did. But it wasn't for her, then or now. Sonny and I did things in that dollhouse together, not unlike when we took the house up in the New England countryside. That was all dollhouse living. Except it wasn't. In a dollhouse one moves the furniture around, but there is always a family—a mother, a father, children, a dog, some sort of contentment.

But I didn't know contentment. I had spent my whole life looking in, wanting to be there, and not being able to get in. I still fantasized that Sonny was coming back, even though by then he was living with another woman. Faced with abandonment, I regressed to a more comforting, if completely unreal, place.

The Dollhouse Disease? I suppose one could call it that. I was a carrier my whole life.

In all that repetition—you can't hurry the process of analysis or explain it—Philip shook my dollhouse upside down, scattering all its little appointments and inhabitants. It was hideous, and then it wasn't. I upended every little item in my miniature household to purge that which was very hidden.

All the while Philip was a tremendous strength to me in what he did not say. "You're doing better" or any of its iterations never came out of his mouth. He showed me how to heal myself.

The man helped me to grow up. Although in the adult world I was standing alone—totally alone—it was real, and unlike a child playing with her dollhouse, I had choices.

As I took Mr. Beene's letter and placed it in a fresh envelope with SOLUTIONS BY BETTY HALBREICH engraved on the back, I thought, *This cannot be rote. I've got to get on with it and start a new story here.*

Mr. Beene, who thought he had me stamped in the World of Geoffrey Beene for life, clearly did not like change. That was fine, but he had his facts all wrong. Yes, I'd been sick but he had nothing to do with saving me. Finally realizing I was worth saving, I was doing it myself.

"I'm going to tell Mr. Neimark," his letter threatened. "He needs to know what he's taken on."

Mr. Beene was absolutely right. Mr. Neimark should know what he had taken on. I knew from analysis how hard it was to understand my own motivations, let alone begin to unpack those of someone as mercurial as Mr. Beene. That didn't mean I had to suffer for his neuroses by cowering from the threat. I wrote Mr. Neimark's name on the envelope and sent it right up to his office without any accompanying explanation.

Mr. Neimark and Mr. Beene were friends with a long history,

and there was a good chance I would be dismissed from a position where I saw the possibility of doing great things for the store, the clients, and myself. Despite that, with the release of the letter I felt a lightness not typical in my overly toilet-trained personality. Out the window the summer sun gleamed against the white stone of the Pulitzer Fountain plaza and its central bronze figure, Pomona, the goddess of abundance. If Mr. Neimark wanted to get rid of me, so be it. (I never heard from Mr. Neimark on the matter and feel that since he knew Mr. Beene and his idiosyncrasies so well, he tore up the dreadful letter and forgot all about it.) Conflicts, like bedding removed from the closet after winter, are greatly improved with a good airing. With that I stood up to walk the store in search of any new and interesting merchandise that might have made it to the floor since yesterday.

So that's how you do it, I thought while exiting my little office. *You get on with life by facing it.*

CHAPTER

Six

The phone rang as if we were a police station. On one line I talked to a new person, a very reluctant mother of the bride, who needed a dress for her daughter's wedding. I wrote down "16" in my leather-bound datebook by her name when she answered, to the question of her size, "Twelve to fourteen." My assistant, Cristina, meanwhile, was on the other line, fielding message after message.

Tomorrow Mrs. Rodgers is bringing in the dress she bought last week. The seams are coming apart.

Mrs. Kleeman wants to locate a Victor Costa dress she saw on One Life to Live *today.*

The two of us, sitting on either side of the same Early American wood-grain table, worked to avoid knocking knees. I turned to the window, my salvation, for a little break. Gardeners, planting new Callery pear saplings on the side of the Pulitzer Fountain closest to my window, withered in the summer-afternoon sun. A few pigeons and people cooled their feet in the fountain's water.

The phone calls were only a small part of our day, which, like most of our days, was busy, tough, and without lunch. Clients, with appointments and without, had streamed in ceaselessly—each with her own pressing need. I thought Cristina, a nurse by training, was going to have a heart attack when not just the first and second wives but also the third wife of the same real-estate magnate called in succession as if bound by an uncanny sense of competition. Instead Cristina lit a cigarette, and so did I.

Nicotine got us through a lot, including the last "patient" of the day, as Cristina and I liked to call them. The rail-thin wife of a restaurateur, who ran a nationwide empire of casual dining eateries with big portions and modest prices, had a voracious appetite for fashion. She shopped a lot, but now, pregnant with her first child, she was in *all the time*. Every time she went up a size, she wanted more clothes.

With a thick black ponytail that ran the length of her back, she was so very beautiful that whatever I put on her, even in pregnancy, looked good. I put her in clothes current for the eighties. Thankfully, it was an era of big shirts and trapeze dresses, which worked well in pregnancy. I even got her into a full-legged jumpsuit.

Luckily, I was able to glean enough from the store's merchandise that she could continue to be tailored. This was a woman used to dressing every day in suits, day dresses, pantyhose, and proper shoes. For her to go from that to the offerings of maternity stores would have been unthinkable.

Pregnant women today are much more provocative. In that time a woman like this didn't walk around in tight dresses, leggings, or low necklines exposing huge breasts. Back then maternity fashion went to the other extreme. There were smocked tops as refined as a tablecloth with full pants that had a hole in the middle to accommodate the stomach. A woman looked like a penguin by the time she was done dressing. The other option, dresses with drawstrings that expanded when waistlines did, turned women into walking inflatable balloons. It was the most hideous dressing that ever existed. No wonder most pregnant women hid behind coats.

Many would have laughed, or been horrified, at the thousands of dollars of merchandise I gathered for my pregnant client, but I empathized with her thirst for clothes. While I was nine months pregnant with John, I went to my mother- and father-in-law's lavish anniversary party at the Hampshire House in a strapless, full-skirted red tulle evening gown that I purchased from Lord & Taylor several sizes larger than I normally wore. If I had to rely on clothing from a maternity shop, I would not have attended the event!

My understanding of my client ran deeper than a sense of style. Having lost her mother at such a young age that her father was not capable of caring for her, she was raised by a grandmother too depressed by her own daughter's death to be much of a caretaker to anyone. My client was a woman without a mother, but when the two of us were in my fitting room, I temporarily stood in for one. Every time she tried on a new piece, before she even looked at herself, she looked up at me in the mirror to see whether I approved or not.

"It's wonderful—and different," I said about a smock top with dramatic balloon sleeves and a gathered bateau neckline. "No one else will have it."

"Oh no, take that off immediately!" I said about a wrap dress that was a failed experiment.

In those moments she was at ease, which was no small thing. A nonnative of this city, like myself, she had been thrust into the most difficult, the most competitive, the most über–New York world through her husband's business. Gossips scrutinized her from head to toe. She deserved a moment of peace.

As I walked her out of the office and to the elevator, she had a contented smile on her face, as she always did when we finished a session. I felt as if I had done something rewarding for her.

Back in the office, Cristina had gone into the armoire that held the billings and other paperwork and come out with the bottle of wine we kept for when we truly had reached the end of our rope. It was also for many of our late-day clients who requested a glass—maybe to ease their consciences or for the camaraderie brought by sharing a drink.

No sooner had I sat down at the wooden table than the phone rang. It was my client who had just left, calling me from a pay phone!

"Should I wear a jacket or a sweater over the jumpsuit?" she asked.

"I would do a jacket."

"Maybe I should come in, then, and get another jacket."

Now, this was a very smart woman (she had been in the middle of getting a Ph.D. in economics when she married); she knew the answers to the questions she'd conjured up on her way out the door. Like Hansel and Gretel and the crumbs they dropped, she threw them out so that she could return.

"Put your feet up, dear. Call me tomorrow," I said.

I hung up and lifted my hard-earned drink to my lips, but before I could take a sip, Andrew Goodman passed by our office as he did almost every evening after the store closed. Although Mr. Goodman no longer owned the family business, he retained the title of chairman and a seventeen-room penthouse apartment on the top floor of the store. He reminded me of my father in the masculine way he smoked a cigarette, walked the store as Dad did in the department store he ran in Chicago, and dressed—right down to his brown English cordovan shoes.

"Busy day?" he asked, poking his head into the door.

"Yes, Mr. Goodman. Very busy."

I don't recollect how word got around about my little department. I don't even remember how I got my first break, but Solutions grew very quickly—as did I.

There was no advertising. Quite the opposite; my office was as hard to find as a speakeasy. People from my old life came to gawk. Friends from when Sonny and I were together couldn't imagine I was capable of holding a position, since none of them had nine-to-five jobs. A few returned to become clients, which was not a problem, because from the beginning I divided myself. When I took care of people I knew, I made it clear I did not own the store. This wasn't Bergdorf, Goodman, and Halbreich. The store was a wonderful façade behind which I could stand my ground and become a true professional.

Word quickly spread as I transferred my past life in clothes to my new department. I took the lady of leisure style off my back and put it on others, particularly women who didn't have only wealth but also big lives. With charities, multiple households around the world, and complicated families to run, they wanted to be fashionable but not look like everyone else. And they certainly couldn't be seen in the same dress twice—in the past I never would have either.

These women didn't have time to waste meandering through

racks of clothes. The actual act of finding what one is looking for is the part of shopping that proves so difficult for people. Stores make it their business to be confusing. Shuffling merchandise in devious ways, they want customers to go around in circles and to create the impression that there is new merchandise every month when really it's the same old stuff. To come in for a blazer and be able to go right to it, you would have to make shopping your life's work (which, of course, some people do).

I also found that many women were puzzled by fit and that I was much needed to help them with finding their correct size. Even salespersons had a hard time with sizing, which became a large part of my business. Fit is not in the forefront of most people's sensibility. No one knows how to use a three-way mirror to see the rear either! For me an ill-fitting garment is as grating as nails on a chalkboard.

Many people arrived in outfits that were ghastly in their fit and color, but they had to be convinced to part with them because of the clothing's label. If one buys a piece because of a label or a particular store and it is not becoming, that item is worth nothing. It can be the most wonderful dress in the world (and marked down to the best price!), but if it doesn't fit, it might as well become a mop-up cloth. Terribly costly mistakes like this are made all the time—and they come with a lot of guilt. (I know, because I have a dozen pairs of shoes in my closet that are so beautiful. Only my feet don't think so. I would like to wear them on my hands. Then I could absolve myself of the guilt I feel at all the money I spent on the shoes themselves and on the shoemaker who tried to stretch them.)

The women who came to Solutions wanted to be attractive and

stylish, but otherwise they were of all sizes, psychological states, and statures. An early visitor was Estée Lauder, whom I'd met some twenty years earlier at the hair salon not long after I first arrived in New York. While other women sat under the hair dryers, the future cosmetics company founder produced little blue pots of homemade creams that she applied to our faces. When Estée came to the department, she brought along her daughter-in-law Jo Carole and her granddaughters, Aerin and Jane. While we did Jo's fittings, the little girls in their snowsuits chewed bubble gum and begged to go home. (I think of this moment whenever I see Aerin, now the owner of a beauty-and-lifestyle brand, who is her grandmother reincarnated.)

More than a few female politicians—such as then–San Francisco mayor Dianne Feinstein, who towered at five foot ten, and the late Texas governor Ann Richards, with her famous immovable white hair that swirled like a cone of vanilla soft-serve—arrived for last-minute (usually that night) occasions. My office became an emergency room for serious cases of desperation shopping.

Betty Ford became a client after her own desperation-shopping visit. She and President Ford came in together with the Secret Service, who waited outside the door—not least of all because there wasn't any room for them in the office. Mrs. Ford emerged to show the president each dress we had chosen. In that act of a woman trying on dresses for her husband, they radiated a love I admired greatly.

After choosing a petite, dramatic dress for the evening event, Mrs. Ford left to get her hair done while the president, a delightful and attractive man, waited in my office for the alterations to be completed by my wonderful fitter Jeanne, who could work miracles with her scissors and needle.

When Jeanne came back down with the dress, it was immaculately pressed, professionally stuffed with mounds of tissue, and perfectly packed into a long garment bag that Mr. Ford instantly grabbed and slung under his arm as if it were a football from his University of Michigan linebacker days.

"No, no, Mr. President!" I said with no thought to the decorum one takes with a head of state and only of that dress, which I grabbed out of his arm. "If you're going to carry that dress, you have to take it by the handle like this."

While I showed him how to hold the bag properly, he turned to his security detail and said with a big grin, "Look at Betty! She's teaching me how to hold my very first dress."

My instruction to the president aside, Solutions was mainly about dressing. My clients included executives judged on their appearances in a way unimaginable to any man, those of social importance expected to be leaders of taste, and women who simply loved clothes. For all of them, fashion played a great part in defining themselves, and in that I felt a terrific responsibility. With the concern of a surrogate mother and the freedom of that girl who wore her cardigan backward during the war, I refused to create carbon copies of any trend. Instead I pushed the boundaries of a woman's individual style to help her establish a unique persona.

It was far more complicated than how well a woman looked in anything I put together for her. In the fitting room, I wasn't dressing only her, but I was also dressing for a mirror, a husband, children, in-laws, and a group of people at a dinner party. After they leave my clutches, clients go out into the world in the clothes I put on them and expect to be congratulated on how they look. If they don't, I get a lot of blowback. "I don't know, Betty, my husband didn't really like that dress." My answer to the problem of a dress that has been altered, tailored, and pressed, and so can't be returned is, "Don't wear it in his presence."

The accolades meant just as much work.

"Everybody who saw it looooved that dress," a client said.

"Well, then you can't wear it again."

To do this job right required a lot of legwork, and the only one helping me was my assistant, Cristina, who had no fashion sense whatsoever but a lot of smarts. As a nurse married to a doctor who'd moved to New York to do his residency, she had the wisdom to see that her life in her new city was too insular. She also had the strength to try something completely new. After falling in love with the store's Vanderbilt mansion, she applied for and landed a job selling Penhaligon's English toilet water on the ground floor. That's where I was lucky enough to find her for my own department. Cristina, thin as a reed, came to work sometimes looking like an unmade bed. If it wasn't a Brooks Brothers shirt, she didn't feel comfortable in it. But I didn't hire her as my assistant because of her style. (She is still my dearest friend, whom I would call in the middle of the night if I were in trouble.)

I've had a number of assistants over the years. When I interview, I never look at what someone is wearing. Well, that's not exactly true. If the applicant comes in all dressed up or as a mirror image of me, I know immediately she isn't right for the position. This job is not about clothes; it's about people. It's also a learning situation that begins at the very bottom. When you're working for me, you're working on the farm picking apples, which, translated to the landscape of personal shopping, means answering the phone and dealing with paperwork.

Regardless, I am a snob. I enjoy people with intellect. My assistants had all read a book and knew something about the outside world before they came to me. I don't need someone teetering on Louboutin shoes. I need someone to work with me.

Not only did I admire Cristina's courage in risking herself in a job that was way out of her milieu, but I also thoroughly enjoyed her wonderful sense of humor and her intelligence. She kept the receipts in good order (something at which I was a disaster). She also did her best to distract clients who popped in unexpectedly while I was helping someone else.

No matter how entertaining Cristina was, she rarely succeeded in diverting a woman who insisted on seeing me. I don't care if you're the king of England or the queen of Prussia; I cannot take care of two people at a time. Even if one of them is a simple alteration, I become absolutely unhinged running from dressing room to dressing room.

Once a wealthy woman, in from Mexico City for a few days, blew into my office looking for a very costly gown for a museum event because she had decided at the last minute she didn't like the one she'd brought from home. I was in the middle of contemplating the hem of a pant with Jeanne and one of my regular clients, so I asked the woman to come back a little later. I will never leave one client to help another.

"I can't be with you right now," I said. "Please, make an appointment, and I will be glad to help you."

The woman, however, didn't budge. She stood outside the fitting room where I had closed the door on my other client, literally pouting. All that was left for her to do was stamp her foot and whine, "I want it now!" If she was going to act like a small child, then I had to be the mother, tilting my chin up and clasping my hands below in an I-mean-business stance.

Maternal figures don't just comfort and nurture; they also set limits. In my business this is as essential as working a zipper. Far too often when I'm out on the floor I witness abrupt and irate customers treating salespeople rudely. It's an unfortunate truism that some believe that when they spend a lot of money, the sale automatically comes with a servant. Whenever someone like this takes out her frustrations on my co-workers or me, I often wonder if it's because she can't do it at home.

In my little domain, I always have a retort to plug up the mouths of the ill-mannered. I had a successful writer client who once brought a man with her to a fitting. She tried on all the clothes *for him*. But unlike Mrs. Ford, for whom seeking her husband's opinion was clearly an act of communication, this woman was parading around like a chorus girl. This was an act of seduction, during which I might as well have been invisible. At the end of the show, I asked her if she wanted to keep any of the items she had tossed around, to which she replied dismissively, "I'll let you know."

She didn't even afford me the dignity of looking at me while addressing me, choosing instead to make moony faces at her friend.

"If I do get anything, I'll need it sent by Thursday."

Later, when she had her secretary call, I insisted she get on the phone.

"You know," I said to her, "I hold my knife and fork the same way you do."

Deflecting the less savory parts of my business in an intelligent way diminished them and made room for the best part of the job, which was improving the lives of women through their costume. I dove into the task every morning by first walking through the store—back rooms and the floor alike—to hunt for a special item that might solve a problem or bring someone a bit of contentment. Part of this ritual was to keep me from clothing boredom. As I said, new clothes don't arrive every day, and I always hope to find something overlooked (or kept hidden for a special client by a clever salesperson).

I also tested myself with each pull. *Am I repeating myself too much?* If I noticed a favorite dress from the season in the lineup of too many clients, it was a signal that my taste was getting in the way of dressing these women. I take it as a solemn vow that each person is an individual—even when a client comes to me looking to transform her image, as so many do.

While reinvention is hard in any context, in the fitting room it can be excruciating. My ladies say they want something new, but once they stand in front of the mirror naked to the world, they battle physical flaws, real or perceived. In that moment they return to their security blankets (famous labels, expensive price tags, the color black) and rules they came in with (no bare arms, only vertical stripes, black and navy clash). Taste changes at best gradually. You can't move someone from a tailored human being to a fluffy dress with spangles. You may get her to give up the blazers and suits every now and then. *Maybe.*

I wanted the women who entrusted themselves to me to break out of their own molds and wear navy with black, go sleeveless, or break up ready-made outfits by pairing the designer separates with items from—*gasp!*—their own closets. But while they stood in such a vulnerable pose, how could I encourage my clients to be adventurous?

Through experiment, instinct, and experience, I developed my unique method of selling clothes. On top of the gifts I inherited from my fastidious and well-appointed childhood, I put the listening skills I learned in Margaret's kitchen to use in my fitting rooms and amassed a trove of information about my clients from their own mouths. To help women move their style forward while still retaining their identity and comfort, I took a triangulated approach—the classic threefer, if you will. I generally pulled three groups of items: those that were too easy, those that were too hard, and something in the middle. The line of attack worked especially well with people who when they came to me were as unsure of themselves as a fawn on new legs.

That was the case with a mother of four in from Charleston, South Carolina, searching for the right gown for a fancy ball back home. With red hair, porcelain skin, and a perfect figure, she could have worn anything; I chose three stunning gowns, all very different from one other. She instantly took to the most traditional, a peony-print chiffon with cap sleeves and a waist-cinching belt. Very lovely and sweet, just as I surmised this southern belle had been brought up to be. I went in a completely different direction and put her in a gray, sleek, defined dress of my choosing.

"Nobody else at the dance would wear this dress," I said to her size-2 reflection.

The dress was extraordinary on her. She looked like Jean Harlow. The three pieces of satin were utter simplicity save for the encrusted front. She said her husband would love it, but I could tell from the slight collapse in her bosom that she wasn't comfortable.

"You can't go to these things and not be comfortable," I said, unzipping her. (I tell all my clients that you should love yourself in something immediately; nothing gets better the more times you look at it in the mirror.) "If you can't dance, sit, or be comfortable with your friends, you'll blame me for it."

She put on the printed chiffon, which could have been her coming-out dress, and asked hopefully, "What do you think?"

"The truthful answer is: This dress is *not* how I envision you."

"But it's so easy."

"That's the problem. It's *too* easy."

She ended up with the second dress of my choosing: a fire-engine-red halter dress that wasn't as clingy as the gray but pushed her slightly out of her comfort zone. This delicate young mother wasn't willing to take the full risk this time, but I had rattled her chains.

If any of the salespeople on the floor had been present when I steered my client away from the printed chiffon, they would have sent me back to Payne Whitney immediately, for it was by far the most expensive of the three dresses. Working on salary as opposed to commission meant I had the freedom to offer clothes based on taste and feeling rather than the dollar figure on their tags. (When

I'm selecting, I never look at price; I already know that everything here is expensive.)

I didn't want to become an accountant. Still, I did keep an eye on how much my clients spent, although not in the way of most salespersons. Twenty years of living in this city of indulgences couldn't beat out the strong roots of midwestern conservatism planted when I was a child. I understood the pleasure of wearing something new. However, when luxury veered into excess, I put a stop to it immediately.

That's exactly what I did with the expansive wife of a Dallas developer who had made his fortune in real estate. She laughed easily through her fall-season shopping that resulted in two suits, some cocktail dresses, one long evening dress, three daytime skirts, a lounging robe and nightgown, a red python envelope purse, the most wonderful double-breasted cashmere coat with fold-up cuffs, and shoes for evening, day, and cocktail. Cristina was writing up the very long sales slips, and I had poured the fun, chatty "patient" some of our armoire wine when her face lit up with a revelation.

"Betty! But we aren't done. I need a fur coat!"

A fur coat? I didn't care if she lived in Alaska, let alone Texas, I couldn't. I just couldn't. A fur coat was the kind of big-ticket item most salespeople kill for, but it only gave me a case of the school stomachs. Memories of my old life returned as I pictured her unpacking all her purchases at home. Where was she going to hang everything? What was he going to say? No, no, no. Not on my watch. Closets can be too full. There *is* a point of saturation.

"Aren't you thrilled with what we've done?" I asked. "Because I am."

She had bought a new and extensive wardrobe for the season. Need, however, meant something incomplete. This wasn't about need. Nobody goes naked. "It's enough for now. There's always a tomorrow!"

She gave me a wide-eyed look (which is not an unusual response to the things I say). In my little corner of the store, I'm direct and truthful—two words not normally associated with the world of retail. I don't flatter or make nice-nice. There are many ways of selling, one being to repeat incessantly, like a trained parrot, "You look beautiful," even if it isn't true. I would rather have scrubbed the store's floors.

I became known for not having pulled up a zipper or buttoned a shirt before uttering, "Take it off. It's dreadful." My old friend Charlotte had only one arm in a dress when I ordered her to remove it at once.

"But, Betty. I haven't even put it on."

"It's terrible. I can tell in a heartbeat."

A no was as good as a yes in my book. I wasn't beyond letting a client walk out empty-handed. An appointment was a failure in my eyes only if the woman didn't walk away feeling better than when she came in. That was challenge enough with all that people have to endure.

In meeting this challenge, I became more than a master of fit and a guardian of color. I also learned how to read expressions and minds. When a client, a successful painter, didn't respond to the charcoal gray jacket with strong shoulders and the slouchy yet flattering black pants I put her in, I knew that something was wrong. Spunky and inventive, she loved to play dress-up with me. In this moment, though, she was somewhere else, and it didn't look to be a good place. After not much more than a "What's going on with you?" (it never takes a lot of prodding in my fitting room for the truth to pour out), she explained that she'd had an abortion. "I just don't feel like myself," she said. I knew what it meant to be unsteady as self-doubt made you unrecognizable to yourself.

I tried to send her home. Her intimate revelation rustled up something in my brain that I wasn't quite comfortable with: a dim memory of waiting for my mother outside on the porch of a terrible place with her sister-in-law, returning home to friends who took care of her, and hearing that word "abortion" in whispers. I was one of those kids with an ear to the keyhole.

My client didn't want to go home; she wanted to continue. So I took off the power suit and returned to the floor. I had no other choice. Remembering the friends who'd rallied around my mother, I pulled a wonderful jumpsuit, over which I threw a beautiful black taffeta coat with puffy sleeves that she didn't need. She brightened as we experimented past the clean, monastic lines she typically favored.

"I just hope you know yourself when you get home," I said.

The woman had come in not feeling well and left feeling much better (and poorer). No matter my own doubts about any situation, I never lose sight of my place in that fitting room: to leave my clients more self-assured when they walk out than when they entered.

To that end I respect vanity without catering to it. I always blame the dress rather than the person. Never "That looks awful on you." Rather, "The dress is awful." I say what I really think, not to be hurtful but to keep clients from feeling they don't look pretty in front of their mirrors at home.

I'm not in the business of stuffing closets with useless items—indeed, my motto is this: I don't dress closets. I don't come to work to create fashion plates either. My role is to offer people permission: to be catered to individually, to treat themselves to something beautiful, to be important, to feel better.

I gave permission to anyone I got into my clutches, rich or poor, important or unknown. I even gave it to Cristina, who grew up believing that looking in the mirror was not a good thing to do because her mother never did it. Underneath her casual uniform of a Brooks Brothers shirt, a pair of pants, and a sweater, I had detected a hint of interest in her reflection. So, like any good surrogate mother, I nagged her. "Come on, Cristina," I said. "You can do better." My commentary wasn't a put-down but a supportive promise. I wanted her to know that she could take care of herself without egotism.

The promise was delivered in the form of a coat I convinced her to purchase, which took no small amount of persuading. Even with her employee discount, the prospect of buying the luscious Italian camel cloth coat was unfathomable. "It's way too expensive," protested Cristina, a girl from Cheektowaga, New York, who couldn't imagine herself wearing designer anything. "You *have* to have this coat," I said firmly.

"Oh, God, I love it," she said when she saw herself in the coat that she still wears—for better or worse—to this day.

That was the magic word. Love. I wanted women to love themselves instantly when they put on a new coat, dress, or whatever. Having established that a human didn't need more than one outfit to wear and another while it was at the cleaner, what else was the purpose of buying all these clothes? To face the world and feel better. That was my challenge. Pairing a shirt with a pair of pants and throwing a sweater on top so that someone walked out with a new outfit didn't mean much. But when I watched a human being's face in that universal expression—"I really love this"—the feeling that she carried out with her purchase carried on in me as well.

Helping women with their wardrobes gave me some self-worth, which was a new feeling for me. Working also kept the loneliness I felt when I was home at bay. My old friends called to ask me to dinner or for weekends in the country, but they were part of couples with summer homes and more complete personal lives than I had. The store gave me purpose and a safe distance from which to watch everyone from my past go on without me. I was at work while the whole family attended the wedding of Sonny's niece at the Pierre just two short blocks away from my office window. I pictured them and all their diamonds trooping into the hotel, and then I turned the store into my own personal park where I walked miles without ever being alone. It was psychiatric heaven.

I never felt alone at work, and not just because of Cristina sitting knee to knee with me at the same table or the wide variety of women dropping into my department at any given moment. I had come to the store at a wonderful time of new beginnings.

Like me, the carriage trade was being transformed. Mr. Neimark gathered a young, talented, and experienced group of managers and buyers to overhaul the merchandise as well as the physical store. That included adding an escalator, during whose installation he liked to shout at me from the bottom, "I put the escalator in for you, Betty!"

The changes didn't happen overnight but were exciting. The escalator wasn't the only innovation; style itself experienced a major upheaval. Up until the late seventies, the majority of department and specialty stores carried predominantly American designers. The styles that were fitted on European models did not fit American women as well as homegrown designs did. Plus, there was still a belief that buying American-made products was the right thing to do. In the eighties, though, the store went in the opposite direction and devoted the whole of the second floor to new talent discovered abroad. These foreign imports included the exceptional tailoring of Giorgio Armani and Thierry Mugler's tight, curvy, and way-out dresses. The second floor was filled with the outlandish. There were Claude Montana's monstrous shoulders and military looks, as well as big plaids by Jean Paul Gaultier, who believed that the strange was beautiful, too.

Maybe so, but the strange wasn't an easy sell. The store became known as a vanguard of style; nonetheless it took a while for the customer to get used to this whole new avant-garde look. With more casual pieces rather than ensembles and more layering, it was the beginning of fashion as we know it today.

The new buyers and executives all had a sense of experimentation that I admired. I found camaraderie among these women, who were younger than me and very different from anyone I'd ever known. Some had children, some didn't. They were single, divorced, in relationships. But all of them had worked most of their lives.

The best-looking and quickest-moving of the bunch was Susie Butterfield, the store's publicity and special events director. I kept seeing her out of the corner of my eye, pushing furniture with the cleaning staff, rarely giving a smile, intent upon her job. PR work is never-ending, and you really have to stand apart from the others. I began following her when she was "touring the territory" and found we had a lot in common. Susie picked out the best and most expensive from nowhere, and we became fast friends. The parties she held for the store were legendary—people remember them still. (Her last hurrah, before she left after having a child, was a Fendi fashion show where she turned the Pulitzer Fountain into a runway for the models. The extravaganza was a grand exit.)

Before she left, however, Susie or one of the buyers would call at the end of a long, harrowing day to say, "Let's go have Japanese food." Off a group of us went to a comfortable little restaurant on the East Side that was nothing special but where they knew us. Not nearly as insular as my married friends, they weren't interested in the useless life of lunching, dinners, and dressing that had once made up the core of my existence. In these smart, ambitious women, I saw a reverse of my old self, the person on the other side of the mirror. Their confident example was an inspiration, their casual invitations to dine my biggest comfort.

Corinne, who was part of this close sorority, called at the end of one day to ask me out for a drink before her trip to Europe the following day. In the middle of our conversation at a bar near the store, a man approached us. He had a round, ruddy face, glasses, and white hair that must have been bright red when he was young. In his tweed jacket, there was a silk paisley pocket square, the only sign of dandyism in an otherwise elegant but conservative outfit.

"There's a man at the end of the bar who would like to meet you," he said to me with all the cool of someone with a gun to his back.

Corinne, truly a romantic, interjected, "Your friend? Well, what's wrong with *you*? This is my friend Betty."

I was absolutely humiliated. Still, not one to be rude, I made small talk with the man, whose name turned out to be Jim. Quite the sophisticate, I asked Jim if he liked movies. I couldn't think of anything better. Yes, he said, he liked them.

As we learned, the poor, newly divorced soul wasn't out of the house a week. That didn't deter Corinne, who whipped out a card on which she wrote my name, address, and telephone number!

Jim took the card rather sheepishly and called me the following day. I wasn't convinced. In Philip's office I explained why it was a bad idea.

"We're from two different worlds. He's Irish Catholic," I said.

"I don't pick men up in bars," I said.

Philip, always pushing me to break the Sonny habit, said, "You could step off the curb and meet someone, you know, Betty. Why don't you brace yourself and try it?"

I returned Jim's call and made a plan for him to meet me at the apartment after work. Then we could go from there to dinner somewhere in the neighborhood. I answered the door when Jim arrived, and the expression on his face was priceless. To begin with, he had never been in an apartment on Park Avenue, and certainly none that size. I put him at ease, for I was as frightened as he was. I poured him a scotch, and things became more relaxing.

If finding a different human being from Sonny was the medicine, Jim filled the prescription. Retired from a lifelong career in the insurance business, he was slow and methodical in everything. Where Sonny didn't care a whit about clothes, Jim loved to dress. He was a real Ralph Lauren model in his wonderful tweed jackets, great neckties, sweater vests, pocket squares, and argyle socks. Tall and stocky, he carried his clothes well. But what really impressed me was how well he kept them. He had twenty-year-old coats that looked as good as new.

Jim was impeccable, dependable, and lovely. The sweetest human being on earth—there were times I could have massacred him. While I was very quick, he was incredibly slow. In the time it took him to put on his shoes, I would be fully dressed, made up, hair in place, pocketbook organized, ready to go, and going out of my mind. I recognized, though, that the balance was good for me and began to learn tolerance from him.

When he found out I didn't have any insurance on my apartment, he set me up with a renter's policy. I knew nothing. Jim introduced me to a money manager and the concept of saving for retirement. Sonny, who'd left my weekly allowance on the dresser, never let me have a bank account. Jim went with me to the manager's office every quarter and patiently taught me how to build a nest egg. (I must say, to this day I really loathe doing my bank balance and writing checks—all due to my lack of mathematical skills.)

Jim showed me many things that no one ever had. I had never paid an electric or a telephone bill. He documented everything for me and then taught me how to keep manila envelopes to house them. He goaded me on to ask for a raise when I, too afraid to upset the applecart, was content to sit back and wait for one. (Good thing, or I'd still be waiting!) From childhood to child bride to a childish mother, I had always been taken care of. Always. That was a lot of growing up to do for a woman in her forties. But I had finally found a person who believed in my potential.

Jim made me more independent as we fell into a comfortable routine that began on Friday afternoons when he drove to Manhattan from his home in New Jersey to pick me up and shepherd me back there with him. We had the same fight every Friday at three o'clock. "Why aren't you ready? I don't want to go back in the traffic," Jim complained. And every Friday—in traffic—we returned to the simple condominium with a wood-burning fireplace that we put together.

My life in Clinton, a sweet town on the Raritan River with cherry-tree-lined streets, picturesque old mills, and a real Main Street, was blissfully isolated. In his cozy little apartment, surrounded by Early American finds, I spent weekends cooking for him, driving him crazy that he didn't vacuum or didn't make the bed right, and doing little else. He was not big on friends. He had a few that went way back, but Jim didn't require much in the way of a social life. Another only child like myself, he was content if he had a book in his hand (he relished detective stories, as did my father) and me by his side.

My weekend life was another playing house, which I just adored. I made Jim chauffeur me (I unfortunately never learned to drive) to an incessant stream of farm stands. "Betty, if I see one more strawberry . . ." he threatened. But he never refused me as I went straight into the strawberry patch, unable to pick enough of them, while he sat in the car reading the *New York Times*.

In that little apartment facing the pond, I made jam, pickles, and many of the foods of my youth. In the summer we had salads with fresh herbs and Jersey tomatoes and pickled peaches from the orchard served over ice cream. In the winter there were stews with sour cream and noodle pudding. We had his next-door neighbors over, because they knocked and asked what we were cooking—it smelled so good. His old pals came occasionally for an early supper of German potato salad and cold roast chicken or a brunch of eggs Benedict.

We made a good team. Jim learned to grocery shop. I told him what to get during the week, and, being frugal, he waited for the specials to buy the items. Jim measured all my baking ingredients, because I do not measure well. I put them together, and out came cakes, pies, and chocolate rolls. He loved to make biscuits or pancakes in the morning to surprise me.

Grocery stores, farmers' markets, and the occasional outdoor church sale were the extent of my shopping desires. I'd spent enough time in Macy's furniture department during my twenties to fulfill a lifetime of antiquing, and working all week as I did in the candy store, the last thing I wanted to see were clothes. Jim, however, did insist one time that we go to a mall. He thought I should have a pair of blue jeans.

Now, I have never worn blue jeans in my life; I hate the feel and the fit of them. By the time Jim took me to one of those enormous stores with jeans reaching to the heavens (too many not put back properly and thus even less enticing), most of the world was waltz-ing around in denim. We spent hours and hours at that store, where I must have tried on every single pair: straight, boot-cut, cowboy, and Indian chief. I still didn't buy them. They were too heavy, and the bulky way the button lay on my waist made me feel like a child with a protruding belly. It had taken me a long time to get comfort-able in pants, but this was going too far. I didn't buy the jeans (and to this day cannot and will not try them on).

While we walked the vast parking lot to our car, Jim, his new pair of jeans in hand, said, "Betty, everybody wears jeans."

If that was his sales pitch, boy, did he have the wrong customer. That word "everybody" did it for me. I heard my mother's voice: "Betty doesn't wear what everyone else wears. If everybody wore a head scarf, Betty wore the scarf around her waist." Jim taught me to buy insurance, save for retirement, and ask for a raise, but wear jeans? No thank you. And I abhorred *him* in them with equal pas-sion. Dear God, if he didn't look like a Boy Scout who'd outstayed his troop's welcome.

Out of all the marvelous things he and I did together, I think my favorite was our drives to and from Clinton. By the time I hopped into the car in the midst of snarled midtown traffic on Fridays, I was wound up from building an important business all week. The completely new feeling of making sales numbers, having women rely upon me, supporting my co-workers—being vital—turned me into a nervous wreck. Stretching oneself is always stressful.

From the moment that car door shut until I opened it again in Clinton, I never stopped complaining. No matter what I said, though,

Jim always helped me through, and by the time we got there, I was okay. He patiently listened to everything from petty squabbles to deep-seated fears. (Jim hardly ever lost his temper, but when he blew, I thought of the red hair of his youth.) He had a very good head on him and let me use him as the most solid sounding board anyone could ask for. I had finally found someone I could talk to.

Cristina described me as "wise out of the womb." I'm not sure my poor Jim, a prison to my ranting as we sat in bumper-to-bumper traffic, would have agreed. But I took on the mantle of Solomon at Solutions, where my ladies dropped by for advice that stretched way past the realm of shopping. Perched on the little love seat in my office, they asked about everything from coping with divorce to finding a good orthodontist. Coming to see me became an event.

I'm going to a dinner party tonight—should I send flowers?

I have a friend who needs a good divorce lawyer. Do you know anyone in Waukesha, Wisconsin?

Why do I have to put rubber soles on my ballet flats?

How do I get a grease spot out of French lace?

Do you believe my housekeeper doesn't iron?

Who's the best invisible weaver in town?

How do you feel about after-school playgroups?

They imbued me with remarkable powers: tentacles that reached all over the country, eyes in the back of my head, infallible resources, and superlative taste. I researched storage out of the city to house clothes for one of my clients who had so many possessions she didn't want to part with, and I negotiated the rate for her. I helped women line old pocketbooks, fix chipped china, or find a glass banana boat.

I kept a life in my personal book with recommendations for the best wedding-dress atelier (Mark Ingram, who'd once worked at BG), shoemaker, dry cleaners, ad infinitum. I don't know how often my own dear dentist was called on for an emergency toothache or a broken something-or-other. Requests for restaurant recommendations were so frequent that it was like a second job.

I like to make myself useful and therefore built a strong network of resources. Finding a resolution for problems involving the unknown, the difficult, and the rare was more gratifying to me than selling the costliest dress or handbag. Information, which women carried with them out of my office and far beyond, was power. I wanted to give my ladies fortitude in all things, and in that they felt better for just having asked. Like lighting a candle in church, coming to see me was a ritual of comfort.

Seven

I was aghast by what I found when I opened the garment bag that had been returned to my office—wire hangers.

Nothing in the store—or my closet—not even a cotton brassiere, hung on a wire hanger, those slippery harbingers of misshapen garments. I knew that the clothes, returned as if new, were used. A few weeks earlier, I had walked a wardrobe stylist for a photo shoot through the store to find clothes—a very new area of my business, servicing theatrical people.

Costume designers, an unknown entity to me when I began Studio Services as part of my department, needed a way to borrow clothes for a play, a movie, or an Estée Lauder advertisement—and return the pieces that didn't work. This was as novel to the store as it was to me. Loaning clothes was very scary, because one doesn't want them coming back with stains, or pins, or having been used. There is, unfortunately, a lot of sneakiness around clothes. (I once had a very devious private client who tore the buttons off a Chanel suit delivered to her home and called me to claim that the suit hadn't come with buttons—as if I would ever send a garment that wasn't in perfect shape, let alone without buttons! I pictured her having the extra buttons sewn onto a sweater in some kind of twofer.) Just to get the clothes out of the store, we had to go through security, credit ratings, everything short of asking for birth certificates.

The clothes from that early photo shoot came back on wire hangers, which told me they had been cleaned. It was a dead giveaway.

All I was missing was the dry cleaner's ticket. Wear-it-and-return was not a game I was interested in playing.

Although this was my first time in this game, I'd been on the playground for some time now and knew exactly how to handle the situation. I picked up the phone and put the fear of death into the stylist.

"You didn't use a very good cleaner," I said.

My office has always been known for establishing boundaries. I live in strict adherence to procedure and protocol and expect those in my orbit, no matter how briefly, to do the same. I came up with the plan of charging a fee of 15 percent, which was unheard of. That way if no clothes were kept from the pull, there was still a charge. I quickly established a reputation for being very tough, which was fine by me. I'm extremely particular about whom I work with and would rather turn a stylist down if something about it doesn't sit right with me. The wire hangers were an early lesson in that!

There were so many productions with big budgets, big-name actors, and big wardrobe budgets filming in New York in the eighties that I didn't have to worry about losing a few shifty stylists to my forthright manner. I suspect that some of them did stay away because of it, but then I was better off without them. Studio Services attracted the best in the business just as it became a very large and previously untapped source of revenue for the store.

The production designer Santo Loquasto and his costume designer, Jeffrey Kurland, were certainly counted among those at the top of their fields. I first met them in 1980 when they arrived in search of a high-end look for Lauren Bacall in a film called *The Fan*. For the thriller, in which Ms. Bacall played a glamorous star of stage and screen with a violent stalker, we went in for very extravagant clothes: Armani, Claude Montana, Chanel. The movie was a critical flop, but Jeffrey, Santo, and I, who share a love of beautiful fabrics and a wit that burns like acid, became family immediately.

Over the next fifteen years, Jeffrey and I shopped for some twenty-odd movies together. They included the films of Woody Allen, such as *Hannah and Her Sisters*, *Crimes and Misdemeanors*, and *Mighty Aphrodite*, none of which required clothes from the store. Unlike with my regular clients, who came to me for constant feedback, I didn't interfere when costume designers like Jeffrey were pulling clothes until I understood that my opinion was needed. Then I didn't hesitate to offer it.

I was prepared to do whatever I could to help Jeffrey when one afternoon he ran into my office in a full-blown panic. He was working on *Alice*, Woody Allen's film about an Upper East Side mother of two who spends her days shopping (familiar story line), for which we had pillaged the uniforms of the upper class (again Armani, Valentino, and Chanel—a *lot* of Chanel). As Jeffrey stood before my desk, it all came pouring out: They were shooting the scene where Alice, played by Mia Farrow, follows two gossips into the Ralph Lauren store on Seventy-second and Madison. Jeffrey dressed one of the gossipy friends, played by the veteran character actress Robin Bartlett, in a Beacon coat made from antique blankets and trimmed in burgundy fox by Ben Kahn, which at that time was the oldest existing American fur house.

"Sounds divine," I said. "Very à la Southwest. Perfect for Mr. Lauren's shop."

"The coat is good. I'm not happy with the jewelry," he said.

"I have a silver bolo tie and some earrings, but they're getting lost. Betty, I need jewelry."

"Sit down," I said, worried the poor thing was about to have a heart attack. "Do you want to eat something?"

I always fed people, both at home and in the office, but in times of trouble I found it particularly important.

"No, no," he said. "We are literally in the middle of the scene. I just hopped into a cab and raced over here. I'm desperate!"

Now, *this* was a fashion emergency. I had to help him, and quick. I just hoped I had the remedy.

"What kind of thing are you looking for?"

"Something turquoise. Chunky. I don't know. Something like what you're wearing." Jeffrey was pointing at the chunky turquoise, silver, and beaded Indian jewelry I had on.

Well, that was easy enough. I took the ring and the bracelets off my arm and handed them over. "You don't have time to go looking. Take these and go. Get out of here and shoot!"

Usually my most important offering to costume designers was not the clothes off my back but my knowledge of the store's merchandise. At that time Manhattan department and specialty stores didn't have studio services. Other than me, Connie Buck at Saks Fifth Avenue was the only one. (My interaction with Connie was very limited. I first encountered her when we both attended a costume designer's surprise birthday party. I went up to her and put my hand out to introduce myself—when you've had enough therapy, you put your hand out to everybody. She, however, didn't move a muscle.) It wasn't until a decade later, in the nineties, that other stores like Barneys and Henri Bendel started their own departments.

Naturally, costume designers shopped all over the city. But when they came to Bergdorf, carrying pictures and sizes on paper from which to pull multiple looks, they used me like a personal computer. The inventory was stored in my brain, and, better than a computer, I actually knew where the clothing lived. I guided Albert Wolsky to the white dressing gowns he envisioned for Meryl Streep in *Sophie's Choice* and Jeffrey to a less expensive version of the silk blouses he wanted for Mia Farrow in *Broadway Danny Rose*.

The people I worked with were very hands-on. Designers walked the entire store with me and dove into the stockrooms. They felt very privileged for having the opportunity to enter the store's back rooms and the chance to discover some tucked-away clothes not on the selling floor. They think you're giving them a gift, something special seeing it all hanging in depth. How many times did I hear, "Have you had this on anyone, Betty?" (Today I realize this is against the store's security rules; you aren't supposed to bring anyone who doesn't work for the store into the back rooms because management is worried about people stealing the merchandise. They let me do it because I have a good, long record.)

Compared to the psychological dance I did with my private clients, assisting professionals was a cakewalk. There was just as much troubleshooting to be done, but our rapport was full of the lightness of direct shoptalk.

"The actress will look good in this," a young designer said, holding up a dress.

"No way. That dress doesn't fit anybody."

"But I love the color."

"You don't wear color. You wear a dress."

I had the huge pleasure of knowing John Boxer, whom I met while he was working on *Raging Bull*. I was struck by how John achieved the iconic 1940s look that Martin Scorsese wanted by putting the lead actress, Cathy Moriarty, in playsuits and peasant dresses that could have come right out of my closet as a younger woman. But my favorite touch of all was a marvelous white crocheted snood he put on the actress's head, which I believe brought the headpiece back out of retirement for a period.

One evening John made an appointment to bring in the director Alan Pakula and the actress Candice Bergen, who were working on the 1979 film *Starting Over*. The fitting room was laden with gorgeous Candice clothes that John and I had spent the better part of the day gathering. We had everything down to the shoes for her character as the songwriter wife of Burt Reynolds.

The clothes went just fine on Candice, who could have worn a paper bag and looked absolutely stunning. But when we got to the shoes, an elegant pair of heels, she had a difficult time walking. She looked as stiff and scared on three-inch heels as if someone had just put her on stilts.

"I've been on horses most of my life," she said, shrugging apologetically.

Having grown up in Beverly Hills, the daughter of a famous ventriloquist, Candice, more brain than bombshell, had the luxury of circumventing the conventions of life she found boring—like wearing heels—until now.

"Somebody here in this store is going to have to teach this woman how to walk in shoes," Mr. Pakula said.

While he sat outside the office as if it were a stage or a runway, Candice, arresting in head-to-toe beige (including the heels) was hesitant to try the shoes on. John and I prodded her into taking the plunge, and she made it.

Months later Candice brought her beautiful mother, Frances Bergen, in to meet me. Frances, who had been a Powers model and was as gracious as she was extraordinary looking, wasn't the only relative Candice brought to my office. I also got a surprise visit from a tiny thing all bundled up shortly after the birth of Candice's daughter, Chloe. Although we don't work together much anymore, we have a warm relationship. Candice will call out of the blue to ask if I saw such-and-such blouse from the catalog and would she like it. I give her a quick no, and we go on to talk about real life.

Remembering real life was the key to what many called my talent in dealing with celebrities. I have never been awed by actors coming to the office. They're human beings, made up of the same matter as the rest of us mortals. I do not fawn over them; it would make me uncomfortable and, I believe, them as well. Instead I like to divert them while we're doing the fitting, just as I do with my private clients.

As Meryl Streep and I waited for a fitter to alter a dress for an awards ceremony, we talked about the loves of her life: her children. She told me how she liked to sew and was making Halloween costumes. How exciting it was for me to hear that. It was much easier to talk about real life—and not playacting life.

When the talented costume designer Albert Wolsky brought in Angela Lansbury, with whom he'd worked with on *The Manchurian*

Candidate, we nattered on about Ireland—where she had a home and Jim and I very much *wished* we did—trying on clothes all the time. I served a lunch that included fruit and wine on the white tissue paper I always laid out under plates in lieu of linen. We did get a lot done, and, more important, everyone was comfortable. (She just returned this past year after all that time for two outfits for a trip to Australia and an appearance on Channel 13. This time the entire fitting took only an hour.)

Before working on any of Woody Allen's films, I met Mia Farrow when she came in with Jane Greenwood, a cheerful and knowledgeable costume designer and a favorite of mine. We found a very simple Adele Simpson print shirtwaist dress, price $125, for a play the young actress was starring in with Frank Langella. Mia put it on and, turning to us both, exclaimed, "Do you know how many meals this would buy for the children in Biafra?" No, I didn't. At the time I didn't even know where Biafra was.

Jane also brought in Liza Minnelli for *Arthur*, who sniffled through the entire fitting. Although when I said to her, "Your cold sounds very bad. You should not be here today," she just looked at me strangely and huddled in the corner of the dressing room.

Stockard Channing came with William Ivey Long, a costume designer I was introduced to when he was fresh out of Yale by my young assistant and fellow alum Maren (who every day brought to work her lunch of a white-bread sandwich in a Wonder Bread wrapper). When we met, William appeared in a navy blazer, white shirt, striped tie, khaki pants (and to this day wears the same outfit). The John Guare play *Six Degrees of Separation* was my first time working with William, and before I knew it, we were fitting Stockard on top of my desk. I suspect it gave William a better perspective on the short actress.

Dressing actresses for real life was as easy as for a movie or a play in that they were used to looking at themselves with the objectivity of their profession and having a committee weigh in on their image. (Although in one way celebrities are no different from my private clients in their distortion of reality: They usually downsize themselves, too.) When the young, gutsy, and small Stockard came back later for her own clothes, I taught her how to show off her beautiful and shapely legs by putting her in short skirts and high heels. I had to elevate her in stature. Shoes can do that, even if they're modest heels and not the stilts that women are wearing today.

Great style, of course, has less to do with physical beauty than with high intellect. Joan Rivers, who for many years has come to the Solutions department, reinvents herself season to season, which only someone with great intellect can do. She is the definition of multifaceted, moving from QVC to a nightclub in Minneapolis to a program with her daughter at the 92nd Street Y, with the style of her clothes hinging on the gig of the moment. Although her onstage routine is filled with self-deprecating jokes about her appearance, she is a person who truly knows what looks best on her. Joan understands what fits and she knows what feats the right alterations can accomplish. And Joan isn't above suffering for style. I once watched her have a skirt taken in so much that she wasn't able to take strides more than a few inches long. It was, however, slimming and made her feel ten feet taller.

She is a chameleon, and not just with fashion. When I went to see her act at a small club downtown, right before she went up onstage, she looked as if she'd been out all night. The next moment, with the lights on her and the people at the cabaret tables roaring, she looked like she'd taken a rest cure. Joan feeds from her audience, which includes not just those who come to see her in a club but also people on the street.

Behind a closed door, she's as human as any person I know. Through countless fittings, we have talked about our families, our lives with men, people we've lost. It's a wonder how we ever got any clothes on her and fitted! The woman on TV's *Fashion Police* is not what one gets in real life. Sensitive and still remembering her past, Joan is generous to a fault. The fitters love and admire her, particularly Jeanne, who was truly dedicated. No matter the weather, sleet or snow, Jeanne rode the bus in from New Jersey every day of her life and wore out the chair in my office waiting for clients. She, who like me regarded rising to challenges as the hallmark of true service, rarely if ever said no—and Joan appreciated her for it. One Christmas the store hosted an appearance by Santa Claus, and Joan brought her young grandson in to meet him. Just as they were about to get their photo taken with Santa, Jeanne passed by. Joan pulled the fitter into the picture for a true Christmas family portrait.

Studio Services came to represent about half of my total sales for the store—and not because of my times spent with celebrities. The success of the theatrical aspect of my business was due in great part to the clothes feeding frenzy that was the soap-opera industry of the eighties.

Before the late seventies, when soap operas became breadwinners for the network, costume designers for the daytime programs were on limited budgets and mainly procured their wardrobes from large department stores like Abraham & Straus, which lent clothes to the programs, took them back, dry-cleaned them, then sold them to real people.

By the time those designers were coming to me, soaps were king. With big costume budgets, they used up clothes like Kleenex—though they certainly didn't purchase their entire wardrobe from me (no budget is *that* big). They were clever shoppers who used the entire city to clothe their characters. Carol Luiken, the costume designer on *All My Children* for twenty years, bought men's suits at an Upper West Side store called Foward that carried merchandise from bankrupt stores and factory rejects. A seedy store off Times Square, which sold electronics in addition to women's clothing, was perfect for the show's hookers. Carol—like Don Sheffield for *One Life to Live* and Bob Anton for *Search for Tomorrow* and *Guiding Light*—came to me for the female characters who were truly dressed in the latest fashions.

With dozens of cast members (not to mention extras) on television 260 days a year, there were a lot of costumes to create. The store's lingerie department got quite a workout, thanks to the many scenes set in the bedroom. The need for satin robes, provocative night-gowns, and lacy camisoles was insatiable. The costume designers used that department the way most people use a grocery store.

Shopping for soaps, we were defining the style of characters with five-, ten-, even twenty-year life spans (and often the characters were followed just as much for their clothes as for their story lines). While looking at dresses, we discussed them as if they were alive. What did this person do? Whom does she dress for? What does she think about clothes? In a funny crossover between my work with private clients and theatrical ones, I was creating costumes that were real wardrobes. Indeed, the costume designers established a physical closet in the studio for each character, filled with dresses, suits, purses, shoes, and—in the days when people still wore them— hats. (Once when he needed a cocktail hat for a particular scene, Bob Anton and I went to the counter of the hat department on the first floor, where he proceeded to try on the most lavish chapeaus in the store. Before you knew it, we had a very large group of people staring at this man with black curly hair and a bow tie adjusting women's hats on his head. Bob was completely oblivious to the crowd as he busily fussed with the veils.)

I spent so many years shopping for those characters that I got to know them as well as any client. Erica Kane, *All My Children*'s seductive powerhouse played by the gracious and gentle-spoken Susan Lucci, was the perfect Solutions customer. By turns a high-fashion model, a cosmetics tycoon, and a magazine publisher rolled into a perfect figure that made clothes so easy, Erica was truly fun to dress. Before she arrived at the store, the dressing room was prepared like a closet full of the most petite and glorious clothes. The newer foreign imports that many women found hard to understand were a cinch on her.

Carol Luiken—who could sew using a pattern and had a uniquely intellectual interest in period pieces—usually arrived to shop a little earlier than the store's official opening so that we could get a head start before the customers filled the floors. I dutifully took her to her favorite places—for Erica she favored the bright drama of Valentino and Ungaro—but I also steered her in different directions. (Even professionals benefit from a push down a new path every now and then.)

I have never favored a particular designer or label but rather go where my eye draws me. (Indeed, when I first arrived at Bergdorf Goodman, people shopped the store, not designers. Customers looked at scarves, cashmere, hats, and furs—not names on labels.) No one designer is consistently good. Some seasons a particular designer can be terrific, while the next he or she can be dreadful. Lines in themselves are not usually monolithic either but vary from piece to piece. That's why I stay flexible in my thinking and never write off anybody after a bad collection or slavishly follow someone after a beautiful season.

While introducing new ideas to clients or costume designers, I play the seductress, caressing the fabrics to illustrate their appealing feel and moving the clothes around so they are more alluring than a limp garment hanging from a rack. During one particularly good season of Christian Lacroix's, I suggested it to Carol for Erica.

"I don't know," she said. "His clothes are fussier than I'm used to."

I can be accused of many things, but fussy dressing is not one of them. Carol dutifully followed me; we had known each other long and well enough that she could trust that I wouldn't take her on a fool's errand. Once inside the department, I separated out the jackets, skirts, and pants, pairing them with basics that at once highlighted what was best about the look while also creating a simpler version of it.

"Why, Betty!" Carol exclaimed. "They said nothing to me until you touched them. What kind of magic do you have in your hands?"

There was no magic; I knew my merchandise from hours of poring through it every single day. I also understood the references these costume designers used while imagining their characters. When Carol was creating the look of a new character, she said, "I envision her as a Diana Vreeland type."

That is when my head kicks in and my memory bank spews out areas of clothes that aren't always visible.

I showed her a spare, collarless kimono jacket and a palazzo pant from a line of simply cut clothes. "Yes!" Carol said, eventually pairing the clothes she bought from me with ethnic jewelry inspired by the cuffs and other large costume pieces worn by the legendary fashion editor.

Usually my work on the soaps was less about esoteric creative concepts and more about making sure there were clothes on the actors' backs by the time the cameras rolled. More often than not, the costume designers came in with impossible needs. I heard "I've got a terrible problem, Betty" so many times that it could have been my middle name. I seemed to become the troubleshooter who got them out of jams such as needing three of the exact same outfit but in three different sizes for a scene shooting the following day in which a man is romancing one woman while he fantasizes about another in the same scenario (and the third was for the stand-in).

The insurmountable also involved finite resources. Everyone has a budget, and I always recognized the importance of that fact. Whether it's a woman coming to me for clothes for a cruise or a costume designer staging a Broadway play, I politely ask the price range and happily work within it. I have found that my respect of people's pocketbooks is appreciated, even if it means they don't find anything in the store. I've been known to refer them to another store—unthinkable to most in my business—where they would be more comfortable financially. To be embarrassed over the money situation is not in my realm of things to be.

Studio Services was no doubt hard work, but I found it incredibly stimulating. It was fun walking the store with these designers. They were college grads from Yale, Columbia, and other fine universities, and they opened my eyes to a wholly new aspect of fashion. While design and fit came naturally to me, I learned a lot about how clothes change onstage or behind the camera. Highly saturated colors bleed on-screen but work well onstage. Stripes, checks, herringbone, or any small, intricate patterns vibrate on television in what is known as moire patterns.

The technical aspects of wardrobe were easy enough for me, but there are philosophical ones, too. The designer hopes to bring something natural to the picture. The audience should not always be looking at the clothes—there *is* a story involved. One of the more interesting aspects of shopping for costumes was that most of the time it wasn't about hunting for pretty clothes. Yes, designers came to me for my taste and knowledge of the store. But building a character, even through clothes, is complex. The ones where some life truly comes through inevitably include humor—which I always try to bring when working with my favorite costume designers.

Not everyone, however, found me so funny. When the boutique owner, costume designer, and force of nature that is Patricia Field first came to see me in the nineties as she was starting on the wardrobe for *Sex and the City*, she arrived with conflicting reports about my humor—or lack thereof. One of the stylists from her clan had complained, "That Betty is so mean. She just won't give me the time of day." Yet simultaneously a designer who worked with her said, "That Betty, she is such a riot. I just love going over to see her. She makes shopping fun."

Was I a snob rejecting anyone who didn't look the role? Or someone who only relates to avant-garde types? Pat had to meet me to find out.

When she walked in for her appointment, she stood in stark contrast to the muted tones of my office's decor. Her Ronald McDonald–red hair (that matched her shade of lipstick) was capped by a crazy hat decorated with all kinds of slogans. A thin, mutilated T-shirt revealed a pair of lacy bra straps and her startling décolletage. The nails on her right hand were painted a deep purple, on her left a clear shimmer. Even I had to admit that the way she pulled herself together worked, though I couldn't have described how, exactly.

In her raspy smoker's voice, Pat talked to me about the four distinct women around which this new HBO show about being single in the big city revolved. The look, she said, was crucial. The style would have to be nuanced and not just another group of girls in miniskirts and high heels. This was a show for women, about women—and women care about style. Based on her description, I thought we would start on the fourth floor where there was one department I wanted her to see. Unfortunately, there was a lot of bad between the elevator and my destination.

"Who bought this garbage?" I said.

I hadn't even realized that my inner thoughts had escaped through my mouth until Pat and the two heavily tattooed assistants she'd brought with her started laughing. I guess they didn't think anyone in this store would be gauche enough to speak the truth—in their language, no less. I simply cocked an eyebrow and kept walking.

"Now I get what I'm dealing with," Pat said, sizing me up admiringly. "You're an archcritic.

"*You*," she continued, aiming a purple pointer nail at me, "are someone who needs to be amused. Like all creative types. Like me. I can see why it doesn't work out with you and everyone. We veer toward the people we think are going to give us the birdseed."

It was, as they say, the beginning of a beautiful relationship. From the outside you couldn't have found two more different people. She was a downtown party girl whose House of Field clothing line appealed to drag queens. I, an Upper East Sider, cloistered myself in the store during the week and in the quiet of the country on the weekends. But you can't tell a book by its cover. Pat was right: We were alike, and in more ways than just enjoying a good wisecrack.

Despite her bizarre appearance—and social life—Pat is extremely disciplined, as evidenced by the group she brings with her on shopping trips. Everybody who's come out of her barn has done well. (Today I work regularly with her protégés, such as *Gossip Girl*'s Eric Daman, *Smash*'s Paolo Nieddu, Jackie Demeterio of *The Big C* and the film *The Other Woman*, and Sue Gandy, who has been with Pat so long she can read her boss's mind.) It doesn't matter how many tattoos or piercings they have, they say "please" and "thank you," which is quite extraordinary in this business. Pat also doesn't resort to resting on labels but, like me, is guided by her taste. The style of *Sex and the City* was revolutionary precisely because it paired high-couture items with things one could buy on Canal

Street. Whereas on any other program before then, the classic Chanel jacket would signify high society, Pat changed its function into that of a jean jacket to go with a pair of Levi's and a ribbed white tank top.

It was exciting shopping for *Sex and the City* (although I must admit to never having seen the actual show: I don't have HBO). Pat never came alone; her group was paired off in twos—Eric and Paolo, Sue with Pat. We had the best time with clothes. It was like playing with dolls, because that's how the characters dressed. They were conjured up in the toy box of Pat's mind, where style meant an abundance of riches. If I thought I'd seen over-the-top, Pat went *over* over-the-top—and then some. She mixed prints as if she were blind, pairing a white skirt with bold black leaf shapes and a coat dotted with pink starfish. If we found a great dress, she found something to go over the great dress—and then something in the hand, around the neck, on top of the head. She flung a navy vintage nurse-style cape over a white button-down that went over an orange bustier. There was so much stuff-upon-stuff, and then whatever she bought she embellished in her workshop with even more. I doubt that a designer would have recognized his or her own creation when it appeared on the show.

This plethora of clothing took herculean shopping trips, for which Pat was more than willing and able. When we were on the floor, I always rued the fact that I didn't have a harness to tether her to us. She was in one spot pondering a pair of cuffed pants, then in another diving into a rack of silk blouses. We lost her more than once in the sweater section. The clothes she pulled heaped higher and higher in my arms until she got stuck on something—did this designer run small or true to size? Then the next thing you knew, she was trying the clothes on. Once she was so engrossed that she misplaced her own clothes in the store! Her two assistants and I had to retrace our steps until we found Pat's things lying forgotten on a chair.

I didn't mind the maniacal adventures with Pat. On the contrary, I found in them a release. Her big personality and fearless creativity were entertaining and an inspiration.

Entertainment was always walking through my door in the form of designers, who in years past came to the store for a day of meeting buyers and customers, then to my office, where we smoked and laughed and smoked. Those were marvelous times. (And, in hindsight, the most creative: We were going into a whole new, more relaxed, more provocative, and less luxurious look.)

I don't stick myself in front of the designers when they appear for trunk shows. I don't care for viewing clothes that way. They romance and dance around the collection, trying to whet your appetite to sell it, so I'm very scarce on those mornings. I like to hear the click of the hangers as I'm looking at the clothes for myself. However, when Isaac Mizrahi had his first trunk show at the store in 1987, I got very involved. I adored his clothes—American, colorful, well fitting—and I adored him. The lovably intellectual twenty-six-year-old, blessed with an unbelievable memory bank, spent most of the day in my office getting an education.

Many designers understand what it means to listen to their instincts, follow their muse, and make beautiful clothes. My contribution is that I can look at someone's work and say exactly who the customer is. Then out of all the people who come through my office,

I shepherd the clothes to the right ones. Isaac described what I do not as selling clothes but rather placing them. "It's almost like an adoption agency," he said.

I introduced Isaac's clothes to Candice Bergen, who looked perfect in the crisp lines and bold hues. Jane Pauley bought a raincoat, and a week later Liza Minnelli took a beautiful piqué coat. I called to inform him of all the purchases, because I knew he would be thrilled with the news—and he was. Back then, before the big-time marketing and hoopla that now accompanies a high-end clothing line, designers weren't the stars they are today. Finding out that an icon like Ms. Minnelli was wearing one of his pieces gave Isaac, just starting out, a much-needed boost.

I've had the marvelous luck to cull from and sell the unknown before everyone else jumps on the bandwagon. (I like the challenge within my own head.) Knowing the person who made the sketches, picked out the fabric, did fittings, and delivered a line makes me feel closer to the clothes—like meeting a long-lost relative. This was true of Isaac, as well as Michael Kors, first discovered by Dawn Mello. The Bergdorf Goodman executive spotted the designer while he was adjusting pieces he had designed in the window display of Lothar's, a store across the street on Fifty-seventh that sold trendy low-end items such as tie-dyed corduroy leisure suits to a high-end clientele. Within a year he was selling his own line at the store and gathering a coterie of people whenever he appeared. He was a true showman, and customers and salespeople alike flocked to him. It wasn't a shock to find out he'd been a child actor.

No matter how popular they became, Michael and Isaac never visited the store without stopping by my department—they didn't dare. They oohed and aahed, kissed and smoked with every human being who happened to be sitting there. (I like to find out what other interests designers have; most are very good at things other than designing. To create vibrant clothes, one must be multifaceted, a big reader, conversant in art, or otherwise inspired.) The visits were due in part to the fact that they knew that on my love seat they would have a good time (and be fed). But I also provided them—as well as many others starting out or trying to stay afloat in the industry—a unique perspective on fashion.

With my finger on the pulse of what women want, I communicate the practical application of a designer's invention. I can tell established designers when they are cutting their armholes too small for regular women or that the necklines of their latest collection do nothing to flatter a bosom. Consider it my contribution to the feminist movement.

The one battle we've all lost is the battle of the sleeve. For some godforsaken reason, designers today refuse to give the option of a sleeve—and women, as a rule, do not like their upper arms. You can work out from now to kingdom come (or so I hear), and the arms are either too muscular or too flabby. So give the option of a cover, I say. You can always alter the fabric of a sleeve—shorten to your liking or let the fabric down. But give an option. Today the designers feel the no-sleeve look is younger. Nonsense—it has nothing to do with age. No one else will take the step for a dumb sleeve!

Pants are another real doozy when it comes to fit. When Isaac started out, he made pants that fit extremely well. (Great-fitting pants are rarer than diamonds.) I put all my clients in them, and everyone felt wonderful. That is, until one day they suddenly lost their magic. Oh, no, no, no! I wasn't going to lose these gems without a fight. The next time we spoke, I gave it to him straight. "I don't know what happened, but your pants no longer fit anyone," I said. He was polite but defensive in his response.

I know I risked his not liking me. Isaac was on a roll; everybody loved him. Designers cultivate fit, so a critique like mine was devastating. Nobody else would call out a misstep to a fashion darling like him. The problem could have been anything from a different fit model to manufacturer. Figuring it out wouldn't be easy.

But he did. Isaac's pants returned to their former glory, and he thanked me for the help—in his own particular way. "It is like your mother telling you you need to lose a few pounds," he said of my criticism. "It's annoying, but it's true, and it helps."

I found that many young people sought out my truthful assessment of their work. William Ivey Long in his blue blazer and tie brought in the wonderful writer Wendy Wasserstein and sketches of the most extraordinary lingerie. He and the playwright planned to manufacture the lovely kind of lingerie that one found in films. Unfortunately, she was already ill and passed away before they could make a go of it. Word of mouth brings jewelry, handbag, and clothing designers; I do not turn anyone away. Rather than give them hope when I know there is none, I'm brutally honest. When I make a recommendation, however, the store reacts and will see the person, which is worth a great deal to any artisan.

Many designers over the years have taken my direction, with one notable exception. Mr. Beene, for whom I developed a deep affection, never would. He didn't take direction. *Period.*

A year or so after our awful parting of the ways, Mr. Beene

reconnected the thread between us by contacting my office. Immediately I knew the voice of his secretary, Joyce (who still works for the Beene industry). "Mr. Beene would like to have a cup of coffee with you tomorrow morning," she said.

I exorcised the fear and anger I had felt over the vicious note he hung from my office door and accepted. Anyone who does something like that, I reasoned, is very unsure of himself and lonely.

Our coffee date was delightful, even though he was the most discontented human being. Mr. Beene wanted to know about everything going on at the store—who was doing this and who that. As that first date turned into many over the years, I became his confidante, at least in the commercial aspect of his life. We gossiped about the store and his studio, but our past life together was never mentioned. That was fine by me, because I was here and secure. Mr. Beene didn't have the power to take away my safe harbor. I even felt flattered that the two of us had become true friends.

I went on to sell a *lot* of his clothes. Indeed, he became one of my favorite sources. Even Mr. Beene, however, had his good seasons and his bad. But I couldn't tell him to push a seam, lift a collar, or turn a bow. He wasn't good at evening clothes, although he didn't know it. His conviction in his product was unflappable. How he designed a piece was how it stood.

I didn't begrudge him his confidence. His suits, jackets, and less formal dresses were exquisite. The people I dressed in his clothes still own and wear them. Recently a client walked into my office wearing a Geoffrey Beene double-faced wool jacket with one fastening at the neck that was at once easy and architecturally masterful. The fabric, deep green plaid and cocoonlike, is of a quality that simply doesn't exist anymore. Her jacket was probably at least twenty years old.

I, too, wore his clothes. Every Christmas he generously sent me one of his samples, which couldn't be reproduced for one reason or another and had thrown his head of production into a fit of pique. I treasured my beige wool-and-cashmere seven-eighths coat and my green plaid jacket, because I understood just how rare they were.

Apparently so did Mr. Beene, who later on asked to have all the sample clothes he'd given me over the years for the archive he was building. Like a dope I agreed, and consequently most of my Beene clothes are in that archive. The man was a one-of-a-kind eccentric. Upon the publication of my first book, *Secrets of a Fashion Therapist,* in 1998, he loaned me a taupe taffeta dress to wear to a grand party given for me in a glorious apartment. I loved that Beene dress. Its narrow sleeves that went to the wrists, its trapeze shape, and its beautiful stand-up collar were to die for. I shall never forget it. But, like Cinderella, I had to return it the following day. If I could do it all over again, I would have fought for that dress.

I have the sneaky feeling that Mr. Beene, never Geoffrey, is up there aware of everything being written about him. He truly left his mark on my life—be that what it may. Sitting on my desk, right up there with my children's, I have a photo of one of our last visits together.

Eight

M r. Cronkite arrived at my office looking every bit as natty as usual—in his uniform of a navy blazer, a beautiful custom-made shirt, and a striped tie—but his expression was uncharacteristically unsure. Walter Cronkite's wife, Betsy, a client of mine for a long time, had taken very sick very suddenly.

The legendary newsman would come in every Christmas for her (he picked out a lovely tailored outfit for their boat trips or a cocktail dress for their busy social calendar). Meanwhile Betsy did the gifts for their girls, Nancy and Kathy. The pair, who shared a solid marriage for sixty-five years, couldn't have been more different in appearance. He was beyond immaculate, and she was like an old shoe!

I adored the way her Christmas lists were presented over the years, usually on the back of a long, narrow Con Ed or bank envelope. We ordered cappuccino for her and joked about how women adored Mr. Cronkite. Betsy pointed out how all the ladies at his book signings seemed to speak with a southern accent. Then it was down to work.

Her children were the main thrust. Treats for the girls always came first, and Betsy came next, if at all. She was the glue who held the family together. Clothes were the least important thing in her life; they were nothing but a necessity. She cared more about a funny old cat they had who was fed with chopsticks by a Chinese retainer. I always said to Mrs. Cronkite, "You should write a book on the family." She had the letters she and her husband had sent to each other during World War II, when they were both war correspondents.

Betsy didn't give a nickel for day dressing. However, she had to play the part of Mrs. Cronkite in the evening. She would bring me the Adolfos she'd had for centuries, and we would alter them, get them up-to-date—if possible. She poked fun at the cocktail-party circuit until we eventually found a dress. When I saw the end result, pictures of her in the paper "all done up," I smiled to myself, thinking of the person in the dressing room.

Now that she was ill, Mr. Cronkite took out the list of gifts for the girls, one that, instead of being scrawled on the back of a Con Ed bill, was neatly written on card-stock stationery. The contrast came as a jolt to my system.

I brought the selections to him and his protective longtime secretary, whom he had brought along. (It's a waste of time to cart people through the store; they only end up bewildered.) He had extremely fine taste, so we gave short shrift to the looking part. He would choose, ask my advice, and among the three of us we put together beautiful Christmas packages.

When it was time for him to go, I rode the elevator with him down to his car. As we approached the exit door, he turned to me and in his most recognizable, beautiful voice, said, "What will I do without Betsy?"

They had been married for more than half a century; his fear and sadness were not only palpable but also understandable.

"Mr. Cronkite," I said, "you will be pot-roasted to death."

When someone crosses my office threshold, I take in the whole person and not just the items on the shopping list. I dive into the problems of day-to-day living, which include dealing with birthday gifts for a new daughter-in-law and suitable clothing for sad occasions such as funerals.

With each of my long-standing clients, I had first entered the dressing room a stranger. But after years of putting on and taking clothes off of women's bodies—as they grew bigger with children, aged, lost weight after divorces, or were ravaged by illness—I became a confidante and sometimes like family.

In the simple act of disrobing, a woman bares her soul, and I am there as a witness. Stripped of her clothes, she is very exposed. It is my job to make her comfortable with me and ultimately with herself. Although I'm not used to it, on occasion I have been locked out of the fitting room. I keep knocking on the door until finally I get one foot in. "Now, look," I say. "It's much easier if I'm here to zip you up, unzip you, and try the clothes on." Usually that works, and embarrassment gives way to an encouraging intimacy.

I have never taken advantage of this vulnerability in order to sell clothes. (I have one client who tries her clothes on with her back to the mirror, facing me. Trusting and preferring my opinion over her own reflection.) Rather I honor it by being a good listener, which I consider the most important attribute I bring to my work.

I'm always listening. In the dressing room, just the two of us, I hear about children, husbands, mothers, vacations, homes, associations, food, likes, and dislikes. All the while, my work of assembling a wardrobe, doing alterations, and squeezing into shoes provides a comforting diversion to the woman in front of the mirror.

Such a comfort it is that I fill a lot of people's free time. I had one lovely little lady who visited many times during the week, because her apartment in the Hampshire House right around the block from the store made the trip terribly convenient. I often saw her coming around the corner of the Plaza, arms full of clothes to be fixed or just to be looked at by me to confirm whether they should be thrown, given, or packed away.

I listen not just to stories and requests but also to the unspoken fantasies of the women I serve. While a publishing executive and longtime client of mine wore my patience thin by picking out narrow item after narrow item, despite her big hips, I finally asked, "Why do you keep doing this to yourself?" She didn't answer, which was fine, since my question had really been just rhetorical. I knew the answer: She had a new gentleman friend. I could just tell. She was trying to change her entire life, including her pant size and birthday. When I tried skirts on that would fit but whose label she deemed not trendy enough, I received a resounding "No!" She wanted a younger image for sure.

"If I tore out the label, would you like it?" I asked, although I knew the answer to that, too.

Even more important than having a keen sense of fit and color is the ability to discern another person's deep desires, which I can only do in a one-on-one situation. That's why I'm constantly trying to push others out of my fitting room. They—say, the new boyfriend—can be there in spirit, but unfortunately they are usually there in body as well. The classic example is the woman who brings two friends along so that I wind up needing to sell an item to three people instead of one.

Friends and boyfriends are one thing, but mothers and daughters are another. I *always* separate them—if I can.

When a mother of two from Greenwich, Connecticut, first came in, she opted to bring along her husband, who worked at a prestigious law firm not far from the store. She was a conservative beauty with a perfect figure, which left me wondering what she needed from me, since she could have worn practically anything in the store. With her husband enjoying a comfortable chair and a snack, I was free to engage in some fitting-room talk, and before too long I understood she was going through a midlife crisis. With her youngest starting college, she was looking for a new direction. I sensed her hope: Perhaps if she paid more attention to her style, other self-improvements would follow.

Her husband was so appreciative and applauded the looks that were very different for his wife. (Many men are frightened by change—particularly when it comes to their spouses.) We had fun, and she left with a number of life-affirming purchases.

My new client had such a good time that she returned a week later with her daughter. The mother needed a gown for an upcoming charity event benefiting a local hospital. All the clothes suited her, but we settled on a navy blue backless gown in jersey with a bugle-beaded waistband. She was a lean column in the forties-inspired dress with lightly padded shoulders, long sleeves, and a narrow, full-length skirt.

The eighteen-year-old wasn't so sure. She had been critical of every dress, and now her nitpicking eroded her mother's confidence in her final choice. ("Why do the sleeves have those little gathers? . . .

Is the belt *supposed* to look like that? . . . It's the same color as our school uniforms—I'm just saying.") It was also wearing on my nerves. We were already fitting the dress, and I didn't care to start from square one.

"Do you know the word 'basted'?" I asked the daughter.

"No."

"They are the loose stitches the fitter is running through your mother's dress, so that we can see if the alteration will be correct."

The girl's eyes were dancing over some dresses hanging immediately outside the dressing room, which meant she wasn't listening to the words I was saying. This wasn't a case of a fraught mother-daughter relationship, rather it was one of the narcissism of youth. What the daughter really wanted to do was get on with it and see something for herself.

I excused myself while Jeanne, the fitter, rapidly worked her needle and thread, and I ran to the floor, where I grabbed the first two very slinky dresses I could lay my hands on. The daughter was pleased—for the first time all afternoon. When the fitting continued a little longer to get the drape of the open back just right, I went back out to the floor for even more dresses and a pair of shoes for the young woman. Her mother didn't buy anything for her daughter in the end, but that was okay. The expensive playthings served their purpose to distract the teen during her mother's fitting.

When the woman called later in the week to check on the arrival of her dress, I said, "Will you do me a favor?"

"Oh, absolutely, Betty. Anything," she said.

"Next time you come in, would you mind leaving the children at home and bring your husband back?"

I didn't have anything against her daughter, whose behavior was nothing unusual. I didn't love the make-work these family outings created for me. Very often the accompanying friend or relative is really interested in something for herself rather than for the person being accompanied. Competition among women is quite fierce in the sport of dressing. All day long we size one another up in restaurants, on the street, in the elevator.

I'm tolerant, up to a point, of daughters, who are *supposed* to disdain mothers so they can grow past them. But when it comes to mothers who want to outshine their children, I have a much harder time. After presenting clothing I had pulled as a birthday present for a client's daughter, I was nonplussed by the woman, who began to try them on.

"You told me she is built differently than you are," I said, dismayed.

Her daughter was on the bigger side, with a huge bosom, while this woman was a wisp with no bosom at all.

"I'll try them on anyway," she said, ignoring me.

That meant she was really trying the clothes on for herself, not for her daughter. During the next hour and a half, I felt as if I were watching Ethel Merman playing the conniving mother in *Gypsy* until my client had her fill and announced, "I have to go. It's lunchtime. And you know I always have a lunch date."

"I know," I said.

Thank you, Lord.

"How about a handbag?" I suggested in a roomful of dropped-on-the-floor clothes. "We don't have to put the bosom in it. Let's go down and do a handbag." And that is exactly what we did.

Just like friends or family members, my clients can irritate me. They rake me over the coals, treat me like a handmaiden, and take advantage of the years we have together. In their litanies of complaints and woes, they are repetitive, redundant, and even ridiculous. It reminds me of the lunches at Schrafft's and how my friends and I would bicker or tear into the women who weren't seated with us at the counter. Sometimes I do believe that my clients are losing their minds. It's a wonder I haven't lost my own, because when it comes to their problems, I've heard it, and heard it, and heard it. And still I love most of them. I know that I am deeply attached to them all.

I see so much that could be taken care of in their lives. Hard things, unfair things. The lust for clothes is a brilliant defense mechanism (particularly if you are a person of means). The displacement of love, affection, and attention onto a pair of shoes or a dress has built an entire industry. Like all good defenses, however, they are best used in moderation and only when one understands a little of the motivations that lurk beneath the surface. That's where I come in with my midwestern insistence on restraint in spending and my religion's penchant for talk. Yes, when I close the fitting-room door, the doctor is in.

"Betty, you would make a great lay therapist," Philip told me.

"Well, I would certainly be less expensive," I replied.

He laughed. Over the years of many mornings spent lying on the couch, being repetitive, redundant, and ridiculous, I had developed a huge rapport with this man. Because we were never allowed to tread on the details of his biography, we bonded over our shared love for plants and flowers. He was always cultivating something under that lamp on his table. When I saw that a plant he'd been milking along didn't make it, I brought him bulbs: heavenly fragrant paper-whites that a child couldn't kill or rewarding African violets that thrived on little light. We both liked to watch things grow.

To have someone who knew me as well as Philip did was very confidence-building, which made our final meeting deeply bitter-sweet. As much as I had relied on our sessions, I had to end them now that I was firmly ensconced in my "fitting room." I wanted to see if I could do it on my own. When I retraced my steps, I recog-nized that he'd taken a woman out of an institution and helped her go on to *do* something. Something challenging. Something good. Something satisfying. I was thankful to him for everything, includ-ing his parting words.

"Betty, I'm very proud of you."

I was thankful to my clients as well. I say that no one "needs" any of the things I sell, yet this business is run on need. *I* really want to be needed. This would probably come as a surprise to many because of the way I work. I never call people to say I have some-thing they might like or badger them to come in. I found it insult-ing when I received those kinds of calls as a younger woman. We would be about to sit down to dinner when the phone rang. "This is So-and-So from Store X. The most darling dress just came in, and I thought immediately of you." You have to wait until people want something.

If someone wants to work with me, however, that someone mar-ries me. And, like all spouses, they often tire of me. After years of our working together, they disappear, and I never call to ask where they are, because they always come back. (When they do return, however, I admonish them never to disappear again.)

I still have my very first bride as a client. She came to me not long after I started the department, when her mother, very well dressed in Issey Miyake, arrived anxiously. Her daughter was getting married in less than a month, and she said, "We haven't found a dress!"

Her daughter was right out of the Social Register's most desirable. Blond, stunning, and straitlaced, she was scared of me for only as long as it took me to escort her to the bridal department.

For the very special Washington–New York affair, she dressed in a Scarlett O'Hara–style dress with a gloriously large skirt. Her mother was so generous, purchasing her a wardrobe of couture clothes, for which My First Bride was the perfect hanger. That season instead of veils they were doing huge, huge picture hats. As we clustered French flowers around the wide brim of her hat, I thought of the magnificent arrangements at my wedding and my own mother's generosity at Chicago's Saks Fifth Avenue before I'd left for another life in New York. In My First Bride, a very particular young woman who could have graced the cover of *Vogue* when she was fully dressed for her nuptials, I saw something of myself. Her mother told me all those years ago, "If my daughter believes in and trusts you, then you have a friend for life."

Her mother is long gone, but the memory remains even now that my bride has three children in their late twenties. I dressed her for pregnancy (during the last one she was so huge that we kept bumping into each other in the fitting room), parties, graduations, and funerals.

She and her wonderful husband constantly invite me to the theater, to dinner, and, most important, celebrations. However, the greatest testament to the enduring commitment her mother predicted is My First Bride's weekly phone call. By God, every Sunday at one o'clock, the phone rings and it's she. I think she feels as if she's calling her mother. I hear all her nonsense. The doorman doesn't bring up the dry cleaning, and the housekeeper doesn't move the furniture when she cleans. The man painting her apartment asked her, "Why are you so mean to me?"

I wanted to call him up and say, "It's because she's nearsighted." All my nearsighted clients notice if a hem is a quarter of a centimeter off. Nearsighted people have a different mentality; because they can spot one stitch that's off in a seam, they are hard to please. I know because my mother was one. "You are the quintessential Princess and the Pea," I tell her.

Still, she is the most devoted friend anyone could hope to have. Her standards for her friends' happiness are as high as they are for her clothing alterations and apartment renovations. She wouldn't even stand for my missing out on one Sunday of the Real Estate section when it didn't come with my delivery of the *New York Times*.

"It's my favorite section on the weekend," I complained during one of our Sunday calls.

"Didn't you get it on Saturday?" she asked.

"No, I did not get it on Saturday, and I didn't get it on Sunday."

Early that evening the doorman called on my intercom: the Real

Estate section was being sent up. She had dropped it off on her way in from the country. The gesture was absurd, because (1) I could have found the section from any number of sources much closer by (like my next-door neighbors) and (2) I really could have gone one weekend without reading about New York City real estate, since I was never going to move out of my apartment!

On some level, though, grand gestures are always absurd. That is what makes them so appreciated by the recipient. It is the unnecessary, even the frivolous, that makes for the most thoughtful acts. Finding the best nursing home for one's ailing mother is duty. Delivering weekly bouquets of astonishing flowers to her room to remind her of the garden she tended for many years—as one of my clients does—is inspired.

In my business I have witnessed how the superficial cover of clothes can become essential in trying times. The ease and joy of slipping on a pair of fresh new shoes eclipses a balanced checkbook or other more noble pursuits when one faces the darkest challenges.

For my beyond-brave client Mona, clothes, at some of the sickest periods of her illness, distracted. With her wonderful laugh, clipped hair, and love of tight pants and with-it clothing, Mona, a prominent philanthropist, was the ultimate entertainer. No one refused a chance to feast on the always delicious and abundant food in the coffered-ceiling salon of her apartment on Fifth Avenue that boasted the Metropolitan Museum as its backyard. Even the highest echelon of New York's social elite felt grateful for the invitation. Meanwhile I used to joke with Mona about how she hosted a cast of thousands for a charity, said hello to all, and then disappeared out the back door.

Her true métier was human relationships. A practicing psycho-
therapist, she was devoted to her son, daughter, and grandchildren.
It wasn't unusual to find Mona walking through the crowded shoe
department carrying one grandchild under her arm, pushing another in the carriage, and still looking at shoes!

After she was diagnosed with ovarian cancer, we began to play a
game of needs. "I need," she said, "shirts that button down for my
chemo, sweaters that are full, colorful, and soft, and gathered skirts
and pants for my extra pounds from medication." She even dressed
for appointments with her doctors, who admired her spunk and
tenacity.

I admired her, too—particularly because I had not been nearly
as jolly with my own bout of cancer. I wanted to inject humor into
what was a very tense situation for Mona, but it was a challenge for
me, as I remembered my illness in the early 1990s.

I first noticed the strange spot on my right breast while at
Jim's house one weekend. I don't know how I detected the small
bump in the bathroom mirror while getting ready to go to bed,
since I'm not big on mirrors—or lights, for that matter. (I like to
work in the dark!) I called Helene, my internist's wife and my
friend, whom I relied upon in various states of alarm. Just as she'd
had her husband arrange my admittance to Payne Whitney, where
she accompanied me after my suicide attempt, again she had him
set everything up so that in my terrified state I could glide easily
into professional help.

The specialist was up the street from my apartment, so there
was no putting it off. The office had a huge waiting room occupied
by at least twenty-five miserable women. It was excruciatingly long,

so whether or not you were sick when you went in, you were a basket case by the time you left.

Unfortunately, this problem was not all in my mind. While examining me, the surgeon, one of the most renowned doctors in the field, worked in carpet slippers.

"Yes, it was something," he said.

I walked back into the waiting room, where Jim, scared and anxious, was waiting for me. As we walked the two blocks home, I looked up as if someone or something could see me. It was spring, and the tulips along Park Avenue's median swayed with merry color. I've always been ill in the spring: polio, a hysterectomy, a mental breakdown, and now cancer. Right there I vowed that "I shall never put another cigarette to my lips again." Anything to help me get through the operation.

"Now, Betty . . ." Jim said cautiously. He wanted me to quit smoking but worried that in my dramatic fashion, I was making a promise that I couldn't keep and over which I would later be angry at myself.

Just like my mother, her mother, and her mother's mother, I had been smoking ever since I was thirteen years old. My grandmother smoked until her dying day, and my mother continued to smoke until she was eighty-four.

"No!" I interrupted dear Jim.

I would have made a deal with the devil, I was so petrified. (From that day forward, I never did put another cigarette in my mouth. That's not cold turkey—that's cold everything. When I found cigarettes hidden in a candy dish two years after I quit, I wasn't the least bit tempted. I never felt like smoking again.)

The next stop was to see the surgeon. My sister-in-law, more nervous than I, volunteered to take me to the surgeon. When I was with Sonny, Mildred had become like a sister to me, not only because we were together constantly (for a long time we lived in the same building on Park Avenue) but also because we spoke freely with each other. She was a completely different type—Mildred lived in a very fast lane—but still I could talk to her, particularly about her mother, whom she found equally impossible. And although she was close to her brother, she knew what my problems with Sonny were and was very understanding, since she had two failed marriages herself.

As we sat in that office together, she was so worried that I ended up comforting her, which was a welcome distraction from my own anxiety. The surgeon was cold and to the point: It would have to be removed, and the sooner the better.

Within the week of his terrible proclamation, I was in Mount Sinai Hospital and on the operating table. The noises surrounding me—hustling and bustling, chatter and orders—made me feel like I was in a supermarket. Then the lights went out.

I awoke to more hovering in the recovery room. As soon as I could fully open my eyes, I looked up at the nurse and said, "Take me to my family." While I suffer so much with fear beforehand when things get very bad with me, I always muster some inner courage and find the strength to move forward. The nurse eventually did as I asked and brought me to my family, that being Kathy, John, and poor Jim, who was white as a sheet. He, too, was no great fan of hospitals. So the sight of me bandaged from neck down to rib cage must have been quite a shock. (When they left the hospital,

Jim was so upset he forgot where his car was parked, and they all spent a good deal of time in Mount Sinai's parking lot.)

I had a private room and a nurse. (In those days one could afford it.) I survived the surgery; however the night nurse, who must have been in her seventies, nearly killed me. The horror of her pulling me up to change my pillows or turn me by the hair while I was in so much pain! The next day brought yet more horror: I had an allergic reaction to the surgical tape in the form of an agonizing rash all over my upper body. The surgeon who discovered it promptly took two hands and yanked off the tape. The pain was worse than the operation. Who had time to agonize over what had been removed?

Frieda made up for the torture by taking good care of me at home. She coaxed me to eat, although I couldn't get a spoon to my mouth because food was a turnoff. Corinne and her husband, Roger, checked in on me. All my new and old friends were considerate and kind. I did have Jim, but illness was not his strong suit. It really frightened him. Two weeks later he picked me up on Friday—back to our routine—and I was glad to rest in his small apartment with the windows open so I could hear the mourning doves at daybreak. Still, I felt alone; illness can do that.

Sonny had crept into my head while I was in the hospital. When I got the nerve to call him, however, he was cool and I felt devastated once more. His only offer was to have Prince, the chauffeur, come pick me up at the hospital and take me home.

The children were concerned, but they had their full lives. Sonny had been wrong about John, who went off to a small college, graduated in only three and a half years, bought a truck, took a dog from the pound, and headed out west. He worked in kitchens and did all sorts of odd jobs. When he came back east, he worked on a goat farm making cheese and then earned a teaching degree from the University of Massachusetts. John went on to get his master's degree in education at Columbia at night. Would anyone believe it? How we anguish and never know what the end will be. Sharing my love of nature, farm stands, and home, John had grown into a super dad of twin girls who would give up anything for his children.

Kathy never changed from the little girl who was always her own self. Although Sonny nearly had a heart attack after walking in on her painting a nude at her Art Students League class, that didn't end her career in the visual arts. At fifteen she was the youngest person ever accepted by Skowhegan, an artist's colony in Maine, where she painted with adults.

Her life has been full of achievements. After her graduation from college, Kathy stayed in Bennington to work on the *Bennington Banner*, a fine newspaper. Then she took a job in admissions at the college for a while, which led to a job at MIT installing new galleries. During this time she met her future husband, a very Germanic lawyer from Grosse Pointe, Michigan, with quiet, piercing blue eyes, reddish hair, and a beard that was already turning white. They married and had a son, Henry.

The Walker Art Center in Minneapolis beckoned when her son was barely two, and Kathy became one of the most outstanding art directors ever. She developed a fine reputation, known for her innovativeness, good judgment, and extreme honesty. People in the art world began to turn to her, not for controversy but for the new. She gained prominence in her field without seeking the limelight. Her standing in the art world was earned not only by being intelligent but also a good listener. It is hard for me to look at photos of her in handmade smocked dresses and realize that lamb chop did not go down. She was and is some pack of her own person.

Neither she nor John had to worry about the kind of mother who worked full-time, and that's the way I wanted it. My biggest gift to them was the freedom from worrying. When they were little, I was a crazy mother who overly bathed, overly dressed, and overly chastised them for manners. A lot of it stuck, but just as much went right down the sink. Now that they were grown up, I never nagged, "Why don't you call me?" If I wanted to speak to one of my children, I picked up the phone and called them, as in any other adult relationship. The relationship I had with my own mother, where I had to speak to her every other day, was from a different era that I let be.

I didn't want to encumber their lives with small talk. But when the important things arose, I knew where they were. I didn't worry that we didn't spend every holiday together. When we did, it was wonderful. Kathy, now the cook of the family, took over birthdays, Christmas, whatever. That is my treat. I am very proud of my children, and they're proud of me. "We are cuckoo," Kathy said of our family. "But we would rather be cuckoo than sane."

And so I felt independent enough to go to my daily radiation treatments during the week alone. The doctor's office was always filled and became like a club. I saw the same patients during the week, although, sadly, some didn't make it over the long haul. The people who worked there were caring. In a dark room, I was painted on the right side of my chest where the very large, extremely frightening machine took aim. The radiation was meted out in small doses, and the technicians were very careful. I was quite fortunate in that I didn't suffer burns the way many patients did. I would leave the radiation appointments on Seventy-fifth Street and walk slowly home. There wasn't much else I could do.

I had a very difficult time facing my mirror; I felt so disfigured and so lopsided. It took me weeks to look at what they had done—a mastectomy—and then I was revolted. From then on I never looked—and dressed with my back to the mirror. To bed I wore heavy T-shirts so that Jim would never see me in that condition.

Instead of my image in the mirror, I carried inside my head the image of a woman I'd helped in the beginning of my career. I had pulled a whole wardrobe for the client, a member of a prominent American family often in the press, and was ready to zip up the first item when I turned around to find her in front of the mirror, deformed and shocking. I hadn't been forewarned about her double mastectomy; apparently this was her way of announcing the news. The reveal was aggressive and angry, like the scars running down her chest, made all the more provoking because she was typically a guarded, private woman. Who could blame her? I kept marching forward through the awful revelation by concerning myself with how to solve the very different fit in her clothing—and make her comfortable even if she was less concerned than I believed.

I'm tough and don't give in when it comes to most things, including my own recovery. Reconstruction was never my plan. No more hospital, thank you. I have never been a great patient. I'm terrified of everything medical—including dentistry. As I say to my dentist, whom I've known from the first day he came into practice, "I love you as a person, and I hate what you do for a living." My method of preventive care is to wish things away.

My mind-set after my breast-cancer surgery was to get back to the store as quickly as I could. When I returned six weeks after my operation, management was surprised that I was back so soon. "Why are you here?" they asked. "Shouldn't you be taking it easy— at home?"

"Why?"

Little did they know, I needed them more than they needed me.

During the first day back at work, my footing was unsure. Everyone was delighted to see me. A dear fitter, Rose, who'd visited me in the hospital and brought me homemade cakes and cookies, was there to welcome me. (A few years later, she herself succumbed to breast cancer.) My greatest comfort, however, was my routine. I looked at my datebook, which was blessedly filled with tasks needing my sole attention.

Jane Trapnell and Susan St. James, Kate & Allie—11-ish.

Betty Buckley has an audition and needs to come in today for something to wear.

Mrs. Rockman called to invite you to a baby shower for Sue Jacobs, July 17.

Mrs. Peters, black with beaded item, Novarese tunic dress came in.

Sue Ekahn came by with info on her couture lingerie. She will call in August.

Kathy from Mona office to purchase Filofax and gift certificate for Chris.

A special-order green dress with lace came in, and Mr. Beene is interested in knowing how it fits. Call him.

Sylvia Weinstock called about having a drink and Mother's birth-

day cake: lilies of the valleys and violets? When was the actual date in June?

Candice Bergen and Bill Hargate for Murphy Brown *tomorrow.*

Rita Ryack called, may bring Lauren Bacall next week.

How safe I felt behind my desk contemplating a day of serving others! Until that moment I hadn't fully realized how much the office was my stronghold.

I looked out my window at the Callery pear trees that were always the first to bloom. Their showy white flowers burst like fluffy clouds around the fountain. From that view I tracked every leaf and flower that blossomed to tell me how the seasons were progressing. Since I was very small, I have grown everything I possibly could, collecting carrot tops, grapefruit seeds, and anything else for my most precious possession: a greenhouse the size of a dollhouse.

Yet ironically, with the love I have for everything green and flowering, I had always fought anxiety and depression with spring's arrival. I preferred the dark of winter, when my home is more welcoming. Summer's very long days are too unplanned. Vacationing is not my strong suit.

After six weeks away from the office, where time is structured and I'm at my highest comfort level, I understood that for me this was truly my "safe harbor." All those years in the outside world, I was afraid to take a step. In this very insular place, I confronted so many people's insecurities and sadnesses that it forced me to become more articulate and resilient.

During my sessions with Philip, I had a recurring dream that I was standing at my office window holding a gun. A rifle, no less! I had never held a gun in my life. This went on for years, and Philip and I sifted through many involved interpretations. Why was I standing at this window? Why was the gun pointed out? We never resolved what it meant. I'm not a big believer in giving every symbol a neat meaning. It's just like dressing: I turn away from anything that's overdone. I did, however, wonder what exactly I was protecting.

CHAPTER

Nine

The phone rang early in the morning on January 2. It was Jim's daughter.

"Betty, are you ready to hear this? My dad died today."

No, I wasn't ready. Who is ever ready? When Sonny and I were together, I used to lie awake at night worrying that I would get this call about him. Little did I know that bad news comes early in the morning.

While death is always a shock to the system, Jim's was particularly so. Just the day before, he had driven me home from the Bridgehampton home of my former Chester Weinberg colleague and now dear friend Maria, where we had rung in 2008. Celebrating the New Year with Maria and her husband, Bill, had become a tradition for Jim and me. We always arrived the day before their annual New Year's Eve black-tie celebration, so that the boys could watch football, go to the grocery store to pick up last-minute forgottens, and nap. Meanwhile Maria and I chopped, sorted, sautéed, and bickered about the placement of the flowers. (When she cooks and entertains, I am definitely the sous-maid.) After guests arrived at nine o'clock, we feasted on a traditional Italian New Year's menu, including homemade lasagna, torrone, champagne, and *cotechino e lenticchie*. The idea with the last dish of sausage and lentils is that the more lentils you eat, the better luck you'll have. Jim had seconds that night.

It was a good swift death, which was wonderful for Jim but

awful for me. One day he was my male companion of twenty-nine years, the next he was gone. Jim loved me, but more so he tolerated me. I gave him a hard time up until the day he died. In Bridge-hampton when Jim went up to take a nap, I nagged, "Why are you doing *that*?" I knew very well why he was taking a nap; his energy level was different from mine.

Despite all those years together, during which Jim put up with me and in turn I cherished him as my best friend and confidant, we never once talked of marriage. That's because our relationship—healthy, mutual, strong—was never the love affair I'd had with the man I was married to. And Jim knew it.

There wasn't the sexual attraction I had to Sonny or other men. However, something better came out of it. When I met Jim with his very soft way, I bent. I was ready for someone to take me over and teach me how to be a grown-up woman. Sonny had never trusted me with anything but a weekly allowance, and my mother and father had raised me in a world where you didn't discuss money. Jim taught me how to address my checks to the IRS, found me Scott, a lovely local man who helped me build up some savings, and showed me how to discuss business matters with my superiors at the store—or at least to pick up a phone and try. (Scott is still my trusted adviser.)

My mother never quite understood the relationship. Not only was he not rich enough for me, but we weren't from the same back-ground. My daughter, on the other hand, always thanked him for being there for me.

Jim was a real, true friend who understood and accepted my craziness. In the spring when I spied bushes of lilacs or lilies of the valley, he pulled up the car and lowered himself behind the wheel so no one could see him while I picked and pulled to my heart's content. Never enough. Often an angry owner would appear to scold me, and I would apologize, run to the car with my bounty, and drive off. Jim never begrudged me my thievery.

Before Jim's funeral John and Kathy drove me to his apartment in New Jersey to pack up my things and some of the belongings we shared. There I found evidence of the last moments of his life—how he had made the bed, perked some coffee, and vacuumed. He knew when I came out two days later there would be an inspection. The only mar in his meticulousness and sign that he felt ill was the imprint of where he had laid his head on the plumped pillow.

Despite my grief I sanely collected the clothing he had adored. He wasn't sophisticated, but he and his friends had dressed to the nines. If they had two coins to rub together, they managed to have the right tie, blazer, loafers, fedoras, the works—even argyle socks. He and his friends—especially Eddie, who looked like someone out of an English menswear ad—would dress just to have lunch in an unassuming restaurant in the sticks.

Although Jim always looked straight out of Brooks Brothers or Paul Stuart, he purchased pieces for his wardrobe from everywhere. He could go to the outlets in Flemington, New Jersey, and come back with the best. Before I met him, I had never been to an outlet store in my life. Yet I, too, learned how to shop there with taste. After Jim's funeral I dispersed the treasured clothing among his friends: the beautiful neckties and Jim's Borsalino to Eddie, the sweaters and socks to John and Bill.

Just as Jim and I didn't discuss marriage, so Sonny—who never returned to the Park Avenue apartment again—and I didn't once broach the subject of divorce. When my mind quieted down and I had established a career, I was still not able to put him on the back burner. Sonny was *a* burner for sure—but not really in the back. He didn't support me, but I was still his wife. I was *somebody's* wife and hoped never to cut that thin, formal line between us.

Obviously Sonny didn't either, or he would have said, "Betty, let's get this over with." I have no idea whether he wanted to maintain a connection, as I did, or if he simply didn't want to remarry. The woman he was with, the very same one he went to live with after he left me, was content with the arrangement. Even as the effects of Parkinson's disease began to ravage him, she was very good to him. Sonny and I both chose completely different human beings the second time around.

I saw my husband at various occasions throughout the years, such as John's wedding to Nancy in 1987, when he and Jim met for the first time and Sonny hideously asked, "What kind of car do you drive?" (Jim, in full control, said blandly, "A hatchback.") Sonny, already in his cups, didn't look like Sonny, at least not the Sonny I had known. From a very handsome human being, he had become a bloated and blown-up man who was obviously doing bad things to himself.

Despite that, and despite the fact that I never forgave him for not standing up for me with his family, I loved him until that day in 2004 when John called me at Jim's apartment in New Jersey to say, "Dad's passed away." Sitting on the little couch next to Jim, where we had been watching television when the phone rang, I thought of how Sonny had suffered through illness in a way that no one should suffer. In his very last moment of tenderness toward me, he acknowledged what I had accomplished at work. "I always knew you would be something," he said. My husband was not a bad person— weak, but not bad.

His passing cut the thread that neither of us could, and I wept at the finality. Suddenly anger and disappointment were hopeful feelings when compared to the nothingness left by death. Jim did not deny me my sorrow, for he understood the grief I felt as Sonny and all my complicated emotions toward him disappeared into a void.

Now the void had swallowed my Jim. How my life changed after he died so suddenly. When you lose a husband, you go back to many things: your first date, the sexual experience, children, building a life, and in my case the crumbling of a life—so many sad times as well as happy ones.

However, Jim left me intangible yet real things. Through his kindness and honesty, he influenced my inner strength. Losing Jim was like losing my best friend.

Until Jim met me, he had lived a very cost-conscious existence, with never much money left over for theater, restaurants, or any other of the plus things in life. The resources of my network served us as well as it did my clients and allowed for things Jim would never have done alone—namely, travel. One summer we rented a gorgeous stone farmhouse in Tuscany from a friend of Maria's, where we closed the shutters every afternoon and kept out the heat. What fun it was to do all of Tuscany—the hill country, vineyards, small restaurants where we sat outside and ate food fresh from the earth that day—using a Chianti map!

People I knew through the store assumed I would hunker down at some tony hotel when I traveled. On the contrary. Jim and I preferred housekeeping, be it in Italy, Ireland, London, or New Jersey. In Tuscany we ate one meal a day out and went home for either lunch or dinner. Once, while shopping for fruit early in our stay, I was picking out plums when the vendor became agitated. In Italian (*"Non toccare il frutto"*) he demanded I put down my plums and proceeded to hand them to me one by one. In an Italian supermarket, three women giggled at me to my face while I went through the checkout counter. I finally realized why: I had my T-shirt with a logo inside out. Why they thought that hysterical still boggles my mind.

We rented an apartment in London, not long after my cancer treatment, in a building where my cousin's British ex-wife lived. We were thrilled, because it had a lovely garden and was located in Camden Town, which was very funky at the time. But everyone, and I mean everyone, was very unsociable to us. The only person who ever greeted us with a hello was the milkman, and we didn't drink milk. Jim and I rose above it and had a great time all the same, sitting in the beautiful parks, smelling the roses, and being real tourists.

Our best travels, though, by far were the magnificent summers we spent in Ireland. I had a young assistant whose parents rented us a house in Durrus, a village in County Cork known for its wonderful locally produced food (which meant more farm stands for poor Jim). We rented a car and for nearly a month traveled the country's breathtakingly harsh coastlines, verdant hills, and towns with ruined castles and little houses with thatched roofs covered in flowers. The sweet peas, in abundance during our trip, were completely unlike their scrawny American counterparts. Oh, the colors!

Jim kidded me about my eating smoked salmon in Ireland; I

literally could not get enough of it. Every pub we lunched in had the exact same menu: egg, egg salad, ham, ham salad, salmon. It became our theme song, and I always chose the salmon. We gorged ourselves on egg yolks the color of oranges, thick slabs of bacon, butter and clotted cream the likes of which I had never tasted, and dark, nutty Irish soda bread one could eat by the loaf. Whatever cuisine we chose for our evening meal came with three kinds of potatoes. Even Italian.

Jim's Irish humor blossomed in pubs full of blarney and all through the Auld Sod. The locals milked a brew all day while they talked and talked. By the time the bartender pulled them a second beer, you could be in another country. When he went for the local newspaper (he was addicted), he would be gone for an hour or so, talking to the locals about fishing. He came back with promising tales of what they were going to catch and bring us. Not one fish did I see.

The place felt so familiar and comforting to me, a nice Jewish girl from Chicago, as well. I was back with the people who had raised me, after all. We talked about buying a home there.

On our last trip, I tried to connect with one of John and Kathy's nursemaids, Rita, who had left us when the children were early school age to return to marry. When John was seventeen, he took himself to Ireland, found Rita and her family struggling to make ends meet on their farm, slept in their barn with the animals, and loved every moment. Rita, however, passed away the year before my trip and, much to my sadness, left behind four children. When Jim and I arrived to meet them at the local hotel for tea, they were already waiting for us in their church best with their father. They had brought along a framed black-and-white photograph of their mother, in her white uniform and coat, with John and Kathy, both in their English Sunday coats, taken long ago atop the Statue of Liberty.

When you age, death seems to creep into early morning phone calls, the hands of small children, and, in my case, a leather-bound datebook's growing number of names and numbers of people who no longer exist. Although the list is long, I never scratch anyone out of my directory book in the office. You do not delete names because a person is gone. The loss is painful enough after years of caring for them. When I see their names in my pages, I think fond thoughts of silly things we did, of lost packages, hems too short, suits that made them feel unconquerable.

Doris: How I had admired her patrician stance since we summered at the same beach club when I first arrived in New York. Everyone did. In all her years, I never saw the woman—who raised three sons, all very successful in business, and lived through the demise of her husband—lose her strength, dignity, and graciousness. She had a wonderful woman, Elaine, who took care of her needs when she became older and frailer. Together they laughed, went to movies, ate meals. After a bad hip operation, Doris carried a silver-headed cane, which she despised, flung in all corners of the dressing room, and often used to swat me with during fittings.

Mrs. W: A most forbidding woman from Virginia, who led a very active life and bought tailored clothes of the season like she was a dictator. Cristina and I were called up to the president's office to defend ourselves against some complaint she had against us that I no longer remember. Not much later she fell on the marble first floor, broke a hip, sued the store, and wouldn't let it go. Then the president saw the real Mrs. W, and we were vindicated. (Twenty years later a new young customer came to me with the same last name. I asked her if she was related, and, by God, it turned out that Mrs. W, whom she called "a monster," was her husband's step-relative.)

Estelle: A dear personal friend of mine became a client because her husband, who picked out her clothes, fell ill but still wanted her to "look pretty." She switched her dependency from him to me; I had known her from my previous life and worked hard at keeping her looking just as her husband, who had great taste, would have liked. She bought very lovely clothes until she, too, became ill.

When her children asked me to go through her closets after she died, I revisited all the clothes I'd introduced her to. Only now, as they went from objects of desire to pieces of nostalgia, they took on a new and painful meaning. The Bill Blass dresses she'd once accessorized looked forgotten; the Givenchy pantsuits that had framed her elegantly seemed as important as a dishrag. Her girls asked me if there was anything I wanted from the vast amount of clothing. Yes, a Geoffrey Beene navy-and-white dress, which I still wear. Even more than Mr. Beene's remarkable construction, it is the human connection that I treasure.

My work with clients often does not stop at the grave. Having watched many children grow up in my fitting room, I always make myself useful to them in any way I can when a parent dies. For dear clients I have been known to help in the disposing of extensive closets, as I did with Estelle. I write condolence cards with insights they might not have into their parents. ("Your mother always took risks in fashion," I wrote to the daughter of one extremely reserved and bookish woman I draped in scarves, camel coats, flannels, and tweeds.) I also dress children for the most difficult day they will ever pass.

My client Mona fought up to the very end, but eventually cancer won. When her death was imminent, a good friend of hers called to say that her daughter, Gila, was coming to New York with her young children, having grabbed the first flight from her home in Boulder, Colorado. Would I get something for her to wear for the funeral and the days to follow?

Sifting through the racks, from the outside I looked like anyone else in the store. On the inside, though, I was stricken. I had known Gila—an accomplished psychiatrist and mother—since she was twelve. While I looked for a simple dress and a coat to go over it, I couldn't indulge my sorrow. I turned away from black, for Mona would not have approved. Too, too sad. Instead I worked around navy skirts and tops. The coat served a great purpose, as it not only completed the outfit but also made it reserved rather than heavy. For receiving at home, I did pants and easy sweaters, throwing in a bit of soft color in tops for cheer. Gila did not come in; she was grief-stricken—as was her brother, Ari—and had two small children. I organized and labeled the pieces of the wardrobe so that she could choose from her apartment, where I had everything sent. I watched her speak from the podium in the temple, wearing what I had chosen. Amid all the sorrow, I was happy that a bit of me was up there with her.

A couple of months later, I received a call from Gila—she was coming to New York for a family wedding and again needed help. I was so pleased, even though without Mona the visit would be bittersweet. But I was ready to play surrogate and relive the fun experiences that belonged to the past, down to serving the tea sandwiches her mother had adored.

Gila and I had the most delightful time, laughing and keeping up a running dialogue under the subject line of "What would Mona say?" She was adorable in everything. During the fitting I watched her exorcise a lot of grief. The clothes she took were bright, and much more current (Mona would approve!) than her usual. Her mother was included in every cucumber-and-butter sandwich, every pair of jeans, and every joke—so much so that we actually felt her laugh in that fitting room.

I was happy with Gila's visit. Coming to the store was theater, an adventure, a way not to be sad. Although her grief was still there, she put it on the shelf. What replaced it was a woman, a very adult person, who could look in a mirror.

I understood her loss intimately, because with the passing of my own mother I knew what it meant to mourn the death of a vibrant, fun woman adored by many. While she had always been a standout from the crowd, in the years between my father's death and hers, Mother really came into her own.

Once she no longer had a husband to tend to, Carol Stoll started a whole new life that centered around her beloved Oak Street Book Shop. Not long after my father died, she went to work at the bookstore, which she quickly took over and transformed into a Chicago institution during her twenty-three-year tenure.

Mother had always loved books. There are photos of her as a child carrying a book, and she was always a huge reader—as were my grandmother, my daughter, and I. But what she had going for her more than her passion for the written word was her ability to sell. Mother was what they call a natural-born saleswoman.

Her talent for retail began with the impeccable taste she had in everything from table linens to literature. While my father was still alive, Mother built a wonderful gift shop for the Weiss Memorial Hospital in Chicago with her innate merchandising ability. Unlike the other ladies who *devoted* their time when they were not wintering in Florida or playing golf at the club during the summer, she and my father didn't go anywhere or play anything. So Mother ended up with a full-time, completely unpaid job at the gift shop, and she loved every minute. Under her reign this was a place to buy not tacky Mylar balloons or stuffed animals with cloying sayings but beautiful handbags and lingerie that all the doctors purchased for their wives.

As owner of a bookstore, Mother swiftly turned it into a lovely clubhouse whose location bore the imprint of her fine judgment. She understood Oak Street's appeal way before Joan Weinstein opened up her famed fashion boutique, Ultimo, down the block. The street that went from spottily chic to a premiere shopping destination known for its luxurious local boutiques was made up of nondescript little stores on the lower level of brownstones where young people lived inexpensively when the bookstore moved there. Across the street there appeared to be a bunch of old row houses. But behind the façade was an elegant mansion owned by Colonel Leon Mandel, who also owned Mandel Brothers, the Chicago department store where my father was president. The town house he shared with his beautiful Cuban-born wife, Carola, boasted a swimming pool on the main floor. It was a very secret sort of thing, but mother, who knew everyone and everything in Chicago, went all the way back to her school days with Leon.

Mother gentrified her brownstone by planting window boxes on the iron fencing in the eight steps up to the bookstore's landing. Every spring her Martha Washington geraniums and white petunias brought irresistible charm to her little corner at 54 East Oak Street. If passersby touched them, which they often did, she poked her head out the window and yelled. That was *her* garden.

From that window where she sat seven days a week, she had a view of everyone on the street—and they of her. From behind her hundred-year-old cash register, which terrified me, she knocked on the window when people went by to urge them to come in. If she'd had a hook, she would have used it to haul in customers.

Her desk was unbelievably cluttered with clippings, receipts, always a potted plant of some kind, and an ashtray full of cigarette butts. She lived on black coffee and cigarettes until she quit smoking. Behind her was a board where she kept photos, messages, and coffee mugs engraved with the names of all her special customers: Norman, Gardie, Irving, David, Gene.

In her bookshop she cultivated a whole coterie of successful men (never a woman in the bunch). It included Norman Wallace, who played piano in the Chicago supper clubs; businessman and supporter of the arts Irving Tick; film critic Gene Siskel; and playwright David Mamet. These members of Chicago's intellectual elite debated with, confided in, and absolutely doted on my mother. Gardner Stern (Gardie), a married man with four sons who was the handsomest human being in the whole world, visited her every day after he retired.

Through a narrow room loaded with books—on either side and down the middle, stacked as high as the ceiling—past a small room housing works of drama where students from Northwestern sat reading for hours, there was a tiny single-burner kitchen where coffee brewed all day long. She served so much Hills Brothers coffee and Sara Lee coffee cake that I used to say to her, "Mother, your profits are all in the refreshments."

People called the Oak Street Book Shop an old-fashioned store, but Mother ran it exactly as she lived: with graciousness and personality. (At the luncheonette around the corner where she had breakfast every morning, which was, of course, coffee and coffee cake, they always put out a real place mat and a cloth napkin when she arrived; Mother did not approve of paper napkins.) She was equally good at teaching the rudiments of living well. That was a part of her important relationship with the renowned photographer Victor Skrebneski and designer Bruce Gregga. (They also had personalized mugs.) My mother met them when they weren't much more than young hippie guys from mundane childhoods in North Chicago, the industrial suburb that was home to many Eastern European immigrants. She was Victor's intellectual and aesthetic muse as he rose to fame snapping portraits of the likes of Andy Warhol and Bette Davis and discovering Cindy Crawford. Bruce, who got his start as a stylist and set designer for Victor, became popular among some of the influential and hip new young entrepreneurs.

In return, Victor and Bruce entertained and kept Mother safe as she started this new life of work, dinners, friends, and travels without my father. She became more flamboyant in all things, even her fashion. She wore feathers, a haircut with bangs, and sequined evening dresses. (After a night at some grand party, she couldn't unzip her sequined gown, so she slept in it until the elevator man arrived at seven o'clock the next morning.)

Mother, who dressed beautifully from the time I remember, loved clothes, hats, and femininity. She looked like a lighter, prettier version of Diana Vreeland. Her taste was her own—no one could sell anything to my mother because it was new or the thing to wear. She bought Ungaro's print dresses and coats and adored feather boas. No matter what the circumstances, she was up-to-date, and with very little effort. Whether a new dress or a pin in the right place, she had more flair than anyone else in her group of friends. They worked at it, and she was born with innovative taste. For that reason her friends always asked her to go shopping with them, where Mother employed a secret code for delivering verdicts in front of sales staff: "Thirty-four" for "Good" and "Thirty-six" for "Awful, take it off." I have often wondered if any of the salespersons caught on to their trick. Shopping was a true activity.

Carol Stoll moved with the times. She took herself down the street to Ultimo. In the appropriately avant-garde interior of tented batik cotton, red-lacquered Chinese furniture, and a chandelier of stag horns and a ship's figurehead (all designed by Bruce Gregga; Chicago is quite a tight society), Joan introduced my mother to the new, younger, trendy way of dressing. Still a size 6-8, Mother looked good in the new European designers like Jean Muir and Sonia Rykiel. Victor favored her in an Emilio Pucci black dress with a shocking pink geometric print. She went all out to make herself very chic, and she succeeded.

The one thing that did not suit my mother was getting old—

does it anyone? Like me she didn't look in the mirror a great deal, but she had a certain vanity about her. She never told anyone her age—not even me. I was always quite unsure of it, until her death, because it never mattered. That is, until she had to close her bookstore after the rent tripled to an untenable sixty-five hundred dollars a month, and she seemed to grow old overnight. She was like a balloon with the air leaking out.

"Every morning I've gotten up, I couldn't wait to get here," Mother told the *Chicago Tribune* in the last days before the shop's shuttering. That wasn't public-relations nonsense, but the God's honest truth. She never took a day off, not even when I visited her in Chicago. I went from the airport to the bookstore, where I sat all day long watching her greet patrons and roll her eyes. (Mother had very large, expressive blue eyes that she used to great effect.) I was lucky if we went to dinner at a proper hour.

Without the Oak Street Book Shop, suddenly there wasn't a reason for her to get up at all. When she closed the store and got rid of her car, her running days were officially over. (She still kept a car in the garage in her building long after she stopped driving. Proud of the fact that she had been driving since sixteen, she didn't want her freedom taken away. But my Jim finally convinced her to get rid of the expense, which she did by selling the vehicle to the garage's porter for five hundred dollars—a nice tip!) With no more arguing about bestseller lists, driving to the grocery store, rolling her eyes in the bars with the young, she became uninterested in life and took to her bed.

Although her health started to deteriorate, she never went to a doctor. She knew the best doctors on a social level, and they all loved her, but she practiced her own medicine: a lot of aspirin. "Everyone should practice a little Christian Science," she used to say. After her independence went, all the ailments that were on stall opened up: her eyes, her back, even eating became a huge problem.

Before she really went downhill, she had friends in the building who would look in on her, but she was ashamed of her appearance. Her dear friend and hairdresser Jim Foley came when she allowed it. His coiffing of her lifted her spirits, and for a few days she did feel a little better. She hated how she looked and declined invitations. As she retreated, all the pains she had endured crept up.

I felt so bad that I couldn't be there to look in on her. We spoke many times during the week, but it wasn't enough. My job and a hatred of flying meant I didn't get there as much as I would have liked. She always assured me she was fine; the women we had hired were fine, too. She became Mrs. Fine-Fine and never complained, even though the days were long and her eyesight didn't allow her to keep up with her beloved reading. She suffered alone, but didn't she want it that way. She wasn't going to lose her dignity and wanted to leave as those who lived on had known her: vibrant, intelligent, and witty.

We had a memorial for her with flowers she would have approved of after she died on October 21, 1998. In the days leading up to it, I set about cleaning her closets as I had done for many clients. The clothes I found were things she hadn't used in a very long time. It was like going through a stranger's closet. She had packed herself up and gone years before. I gave away almost everything except for her monogrammed handkerchiefs and many scarves. Monogrammed handkerchiefs were something Mother loved. We all had an abundance.

At Rosehill Cemetery, which was as pretty as a park, we eulogized Mother around a giant array of flowers instead of a coffin. Somehow the florist found peonies and roses in pinks of all kinds, very feminine and not funereal. She would have liked that. It was the ultimate centerpiece.

Just a small box, and she was buried next to my father. My son John put it into the ground with stationery and bookmarks from the store. Before we left, Kathy turned to me and said, "Now you can really start to live, Mom." I don't know what possessed my daughter to say that. My mother didn't stop me from living; that was *my* choice. I hid behind her.

We had been attached at the hip for a lifetime. In trips to the butcher, the baker, the greengrocer; lunches at the Pump Room; visits to Nana; breakups with boyfriends that she negotiated; my doomed marriage, so unlike the love affair she had with my father; my choice for a second act in Jim, who was decidedly not accomplished or glamorous enough for her taste; and afternoons in the bookstore watching her trade witty barbs with Chicago's most intelligent men, I was always in her shadow. My mother and father glorified me in a way that unintentionally diminished me. In telling everyone how beautiful I was, they created a hothouse rose. They would have done anything short of murder to see me married to the richest man in the world and living on a yacht, in a penthouse, and more. They made me a fairy princess that I really didn't want to be.

I thought she was much smarter than I was. She was certainly much more assured. (The *Chicago Tribune* reported in her obituary that "she once told Lawrence Sanders . . . that his last book was so bad he must be in the cocktail hour of his life." Then, just as I had goaded my first assistant, Cristina, into cutting her hair, Mother had told the novelist, "You can do better than this, Larry.") With her silk violets, gardenias, or roses (according to the season) clutched at the neck of her dress, she rolled her big blue eyes in her dramatic Fanny Brice way and told it like it was. And people think *I'm* a character!

There was *one* way in which we weren't so different: work. When Carol Luiken, the *All My Children* costume designer, called my office "a salon of the grand order," it made me think of Mother, coffee and cigarettes always close. She, too, ran a grand salon, no doubt about it.

We were identical; we both listen to the world's problems. As I'm dressing my clients, I learn so much about them. As she sold her books, and her patrons smoked their cigarettes and drank their coffee, she did the same thing. She was a super salesperson, soft and very savvy. In the same way that some people say I have a hand when fingering a supple glove-leather jacket or the beaded trim of a shift, so that they see the garment in a way they never would on the rack, Mother had a very sensuous way of selling.

I witnessed her in action at the bookstore, patting a hardcover like it was a sweet small child's cheek and saying, "Oh, *this*? This is the best, the best."

When she got into people's heads, no one could resist her. Like me, she was really a schoolhouse psychiatrist. Both of us always got behind the diversionary dress or novel to the heart of the matter—except with each other. There we had no ability. Despite our closeness and deep devotion to each other, I never got any answers out of her about the secrets of our family, ever.

When Mother was dying, I mustered the courage to ask about

the story of her first marriage and my biological father. All I knew was that he had moved to California while I was in my teens. When Kathy was born, my husband received a call at his office from him, asking if he could visit us at home. My immediate reaction was the same as when I was little—no—and I never saw him again. I only became aware that he'd died during a trip I made to Chicago to see my mother, when we went back to the South Side and visited the grocery-store owner I'd loved as a child. He told me my father was gone.

After I asked her, all that my ailing mother would commit to was that they'd met at the University of Chicago and that her parents were the ones to force her into it. I don't believe it, but I'll never know. That and so much more went with her to the grave.

If by "start to live," Kathy meant start telling it like it is, then she was right about what she'd said to me at the cemetery in Chicago. I inherited the full length of Mother's tongue after she passed away. I thought of Gila replacing the image of herself after her mother's death and the white-haired woman I now saw when I looked at my own reflection. Indeed, there were many times while standing in front of the bathroom mirror that I said, "Good morning, Mother!"

I have always known my own mind, but with the death of my mother I lost any inhibitions in expressing it. Although my job was ostensibly sales, I couldn't help but rail against the disturbing direction of fashion that mimicked the larger trends in society of disposability, ostentation, and inflation.

In the 1980s clothes still had craftsmanship. There was pride in quality and much more luxury attached to everything, from the fabric to construction. At the same time, dressing was much simpler and more normal: a jacket, a dress, a skirt, and a blouse. A little more than a decade later, everything was layered, provocative, cloned, mass-produced in Third World countries—and exponentially more expensive.

Walking through the store, I felt like Alice after she's fallen down the rabbit hole. The shoes grew taller and taller (an orthopedic doctor's dream), the dresses shorter and shorter, the prices bigger and bigger, the evening wear glitterier and glitterier. I didn't care how over-the-top it all had become—I refused to betray my sense of elegance. I would never entertain the paint-your-soles-red style of dressing. My clients did not attract attention with their fashion through shock value but rather through that classic American idea of dressing that I feared was quickly disappearing.

More than ever women came in concerned more about brand names than whether a garment fit over their rear. I didn't want them to love a suit because it was Dior but rather because it looked good. Whenever a client begged to know, "Whose is it?" I wanted to yell, "Who cares?" As I witnessed customers Prada themselves to death or go Oscar wild, in typical fashion I went contrary to the crowd and began almost to ignore the labels altogether so that when someone invariably asked, "Whose is it?" I would have to pull their collar like a naughty schoolchild's and read the tag.

The old-time costume designers joined my lament. Whenever they came to the store, they complained bitterly about the garments that lined the path to my office. I didn't disagree, but I didn't have the luxury of completely disdaining the clothing around me. I could only sell what was carried. If I grumbled incessantly, I would be a codger reminiscing about the good old days and out of a job. To stay sharp and ahead of the season, one must bend.

Clothes that looked like they might fit were deceptively small. One day while I was in the middle of my morning rounds, the lovely young manager of a boutique stopped me to point out a new squarish dress that she thought would be good for my clientele.

"You think that's for a client of mine who's larger, don't you?" I asked, arching an eyebrow.

"Well, it's . . . it's such a pretty dress," she stammered, clearly nervous. I appreciated her enthusiasm for her boutique but wanted to teach her something about fit, which very few salespeople at the store understood. In general, women don't understand fit, but current designers don't make it any easier. Clothing, which now revolves around 0s, 2s, and 4s (which most of the world is not), runs smaller than it used to. What was once a size 12–14 is now an 8–10.

"May I show you something?" I asked the manager.

I picked up the sleeve of the dress, which went to the elbow. To the uneducated eye, it did look like an easy-to-wear, square, silk dress. However, the designer had cut from shoulder to underneath the arm in such a narrow way that it would not have accommodated a woman with a full arm. It didn't matter how boxy the body of the dress was—no woman I knew could get her arm into that armhole. For some reason designers had come to believe that a small armhole and a narrow sleeve made the garment young, and all brands were fighting for this bizarre conception of youth (a big mistake, since no one can be all things to all people). Very tight and very short seemed to be everyone's idea of young. No one I knew ever wore clothes like that when I was young.

Part of the problem stemmed from the fact that many fashion stars in this new era were young men (mostly in their twenties), who didn't have the first clue about real women. Among the biggest offenders of fit was the trend to cut the waist of pants below instead of on the waist. The uncomfortable, short crotch created problems of both the physical and mental variety.

"Tell me what sizes you think they bought this dress in," I asked the poor manager, who would surely never point out anything to me again.

"Well, I think up to a forty. . . ."

"Exactly."

That was the other problem: Many of the buyers, who had no rapport with anyone other than a computer, thought 0s and 2s made the store young and hip. They weren't thinking about what anything looked like on anybody. In a store filled to the brim with 36s, 38s, and 40s—4s, 6s, and 8s—what was I to do with my 12s and 14s? Nothing, because unlike in the old days, when a garment had hems and side seams so that one had something to let out, everything now was mitered and finished. In the obsession with squeezing out a buck any way possible, there was not an extra scrap of fabric to be found.

My poor clients. While fashion was supposed to boost the self-esteem of women by cloaking them in beautiful things, it seemed to me that its new aim was quite the opposite. Lovely older women were punished for not spending every waking minute in the gym, wasting away on a juice fast, or endangering their lives with liposuction. It wasn't much easier for young women in an age when they're all so mindful of being trim that they practically live in exercise clothes, which leave little to the imagination. In my day one boarded an airplane in a suit, gloves, and a hat. However, last time I went to the airport, I mistook it for a fitness center.

All the rules of appropriateness have gone out the window—and not only in dressing. Just as women wear T-shirts and flip-flops so that they look like they're going to the beach when in fact they're off to their places of employment (let me say, no one wants to see your feet at work), so people use the elevator for their office. I will never get used to everyone plugged into mobile phones in restaurants, the ladies' room, the middle of the street, or anywhere else for that matter. I attribute much of society's downfall to the cell phone, a device I abhor. The iPhone that the store gave me has never left its charger on my desk; it's a wonder anyone can find me.

A particularly egregious multitasking client was conversing loudly and intimately as though the fourth floor of the store were her living room, while I tried to read her nonverbal cues like a domestic. When she snapped her fingers and pointed at a cashmere shawl, I decided I'd had enough.

"I think we have to touch base here," I said, interrupting her conversation. "I don't really want to hear about somebody in Hungary who purged a husband or a castle or whatever. . . ."

She looked confused. She didn't realize how offensive her actions were. She figured the rest of the world does it—and she wasn't wrong.

"I'm selling clothes," I said, "not writing a column."

Everyone who loves clothes, without exception, believes that what I do is the living end. I love clothes, too, but I began to suffer from the candy-store syndrome. Surrounded by sweet stuff all the time, you gag on it after a while.

I still came to work earlier than anyone else and threw myself into the daily task of becoming a handmaiden who shortened dresses, found multiples of a new favorite silver platter, and any other errand my clients conjured up. I was at their disposal even as age lined my face, turned my hair white, and made my feet worse than they already were naturally.

It wasn't pride that spurred me to work even as I paid the senior-citizen fare for the bus to and fro. No, I was compelled to be of service, fulfilling the needs of others because I actually thought it was the right thing to do. It was a holdover from my upbringing as the responsible good girl who took proper care of her sweaters and straightened her picture frames every evening before bed: I could not rest until the completion of a project. Satisfaction is a very difficult concept for me. I don't know what it is to sit back and say, "Well done!" There's too much on the next page, and tomorrow rears its head with another problem to be solved.

This relentless pursuit of perfection meant I stood out from most of the sales staff just as much as I had when I'd landed among the vendeuses of old. I didn't approve of much of what I saw on the floor. One salesperson wore a pair of five-inch stilettos—with the price sticker still on the sole—in which she couldn't even walk properly. Another in a microminiskirt who—to my absolute shame—chewed gum like a cow its cud and dragged the dresses she was carrying for a client so that they cleaned the floor. When I watched two saleswomen loaded down with shoe boxes disappear into one of the register rooms, I followed and caught them taking off their shoes!

"You work, not *shop*, here," I admonished them.

I also did not approve of what I *didn't* see on the floor—namely the buyers. Gone were all the members from the original group of women who'd befriended me when I first arrived at the store. Real buyers who were always on the floor, they knew fabrics and took a hands-on approach to their job. The new buyers had their offices off base on Madison Avenue, where they liked to hide. When I encountered one young woman who after months on the job still refused to do as much as make eye contact with me, I said to her, "I don't even know you. Why don't you say hello?"

"I'm shy," she said.

Shy? She didn't look shy around the other buyers as they tapped away on their cell phones and click-clacked away on their high heels. Whenever I tried to get someone at the store on the phone, I was always told he or she was "in a meeting." I told one person who couldn't have been in a meeting for the entire month I was unable to reach her, "Find a word other than 'meeting.' It's getting worn out."

What happened to decorum? As far as I could tell, it went out with wearing gloves on a plane.

At one point Barneys called me for an interview after I had gained some sort of fame in my position. (Newspaper and magazine reporters love me, partially because I know how to feed them one-liners to liven up the same old dull fashion stories, but also because I know how to answer the phone!) During the entire interview, the head of the store had his feet on the desk.

"Well, it's a done deal, Betty," he said with the soles of his shoes staring up at me. "Prepare to be here in a month."

"Sorry," I replied, standing to leave. "I don't work for anyone who puts his feet up on the desk."

Perhaps I was a codger. I vehemently mourned the death of good manners, devotion to quality, joy in hard work, obligation to others—and I mourned the deaths of those who'd embodied these qualities that appeared to be on the verge of extinction. Of course, one of these spirits was Mother, who'd read as many as she could of the seven thousand books housed in her little shop in order to recommend with true authority and lost her will to live when she ceased to be needed. But there were many more. Too many.

Jeanne, my beloved fitter who'd died of cancer, worked up until the very end. A mighty mouse, she missed Bergdorf immensely when she had to take a leave for her chemotherapy treatments. Work was her life. During our daily phone chats, she listened intently to everything happening at the store: who was in, who wasn't. I was very careful in my words. I didn't want her to think anyone had replaced her, which of course no one had. No one ever has. They are still expert artisans in their trade, but their work has changed as well. They are rushed and pressured from above.

Frieda was another one. Her standards were more exacting than those of anyone I'd ever met. She would push the silver tray around to serve dinner only if there were no more than four people. If we had more than four guests, then she insisted we employ Prince to serve while she stood back with her hands clasped over her starched uniform (which, incidentally, she didn't do herself but sent to the laundress). Waiting for approval, she didn't budge until someone said, "Frieda, that roulade of beef was very good," or "Nobody makes profiteroles like you, Frieda." Then she would beam and march through the dining room's swinging door to offer yet another helping.

She was some bird, but she stuck with me through thick and thin for more than thirty years. Although she wasn't happy when the household split up, Frieda, an unlikely romantic, was so pleased when Jim entered the picture. She had her own relationship with a married man a step above her, or so she thought. She would hurry through the dishes and run to meet him or go to his summerhouse on the weekends—where I suspected she cooked and cleaned for him, too.

When I noticed she wasn't herself and was finding it difficult to walk, I thought maybe she was drinking. Then one morning I saw in her room that she had placed a chair next to her bed to pull herself up in the morning.

Not long after, she came to me to announce she was leaving. She was going to her apartment in Astoria for good. (She had that walk-up apartment, her security, all the years she was with me.) I was upset, but I understood. We kissed and hugged. I said I would see her soon. But I never saw her again. They found her in the apartment less than three weeks later—on the floor. She had saved me the incident, but not the pain.

Worse than any joint pain or wrinkly neck is waking up one day and realizing that nearly everyone you've learned to love over a lifetime is gone. It's a ubiquitous and familiar tragedy that becomes particularly unjust when it happens to you.

Despite the authority with which I ran my business and got people dressed, I was vulnerable. I was never an independent soul and felt at the mercy of all this loss. I missed my phone calls with Mother and the funny little notes from her that had punctuated my entire life. I considered my humor a poor substitute for hers. Neither the store nor the neighborhood was as gracious without Corinne.

Without Jim my weekends and vacations were torturously long. I wasn't comfortable doing things alone and so found myself spending much of them cleaning already clean floors and organizing my already organized closets. Looking into the fifty-plus years' worth of clothing I had accumulated since arriving in New York, it struck me that no one had ever helped *me* get dressed. What was going to happen with the demise of Betty? I had an idea to label the clothes I wanted to wear when I went and how to put them together. This way all that my children had to do was go to the closet, throw me into the clothes—sans shoes—and then into the inferno.

I thought I had learned to be alone. But *this* was true loneliness, and I had a lot more learning left to do.

CHAPTER

Ten

Things that grow speak to me. When I open my office door, orchids—tall, florid, pink and lavender trophies gifted to me from clients and designers who are amazed at how I keep them flowering season after season—greet my morning arrival.

Despite their loveliness, they were not to be outdone by the view that is their backdrop. The Callery pear trees have grown so large that they obscure nearly all the other treasures framed in the window by my desk: the Plaza, the Pulitzer Fountain, Fifth Avenue, and Central Park. They've dropped their showy white spring blossoms and now fill the entire window with summer green.

Settling in for the workday, I put out the water and change into my walking shoes. Long ago the store took my feet. They are my nemeses, that I liken to a headache. Then I beat it right back out the door. At eight-thirty in the morning, it would be at least a half hour before the sprightliest salespersons amble in. I like this hour; sometimes I see shipments of new clothes when the truck that delivers them arrives. Usually, though, I find new pieces that have been returned or previously hidden. There's a whole game here that I like to call H&H, for "hide and hold." A few weeks after any sale, out come clothes I have never seen. *Never.* And I am *always* looking. It's the oldest retail trick in the book.

This kind of behavior makes my work harder, but I don't shrink from a challenge. There is nothing new under the sun, yet finding the new is my task. Luckily, God gave me a third eye that allows me to see things that others do not. At least when it comes to clothes, which I have always loved and worn well with little effort. So when I do my walk, which I do every morning, I see a lot. I pretend that everything is new in what has become a game, a routine, a distraction.

I start today's rounds in the stockroom, as is my habit. I don't like to take from the floor and mess up what the stock clerks have worked hard to put back in good order. In the back room, however, nobody returns anything properly. After greeting Lester at the desk (I say hello to everyone), I proceed to the floor-to-ceiling rolling racks of clothes, where I find colors all mixed up and sizes in no particular order. The awful sight, which for me is as grating as nails on a chalkboard, compels me to take on the role of stock lady for a few minutes as I put garments back in their place. A black leather schoolgirl skirt jumps out at me, but not in a good way. Certain pieces I play with, and certain ones I don't. This one was a don't. Moving through the racks only reveals more of the same from the floor. Still, I roll each one back and forth, because thoroughness is part of the game. Three-quarters through I notice something bright and unfamiliar: a darling bougainvillea-print ruched sheath dress. The flowers have caught my eye.

"Have these been counted in?" I ask Lester, holding up one of the suits.

"Brand-new merchandise, Betty."

I look through the sizes and say a small prayer. The dress was designed by a Frenchman as unforgiving as his culture, which means I need a 48 to fit over my client's ample hips—and the store does not buy many in that size, no matter how many customers wear larger sizes. But I've gotten there first and so find the one and only 48. I promptly sign it out with Lester. (I feel a bit like a bandit when this occurs.)

My mission this morning is to see if there are any last-minute treasures to add to what I've already pulled for a new young lawyer client with troublesome hips—and there's still the matter of a T-shirt to go with my long-standing client's palazzo pants. I've discovered over the last few weeks that there are absolutely no T-shirts in this store.

I make an executive decision to skip the fourth floor, aka la-la land. Whenever I do go there, I riffle through the evening and couture collections and usually leave. I don't believe in special orders. By the time the gown—which is not in stock for purchase but is ordered according to the customer's size, color, and other specifications— arrives, the client says, "Is this really what I ordered?" After such a long time, the customer loses interest or has purchased a dress somewhere else. Plus, I'm not a big glitter fan, and these days the dresses positively drip in it. A beautiful gown should be like a painting not a disco ball.

By the time I arrive at five, I feel as if I'm thrift-shopping, the way the store crams all the merchandise together. But I never discount the lower-priced lines. I think nothing of pairing pants and a sweater from the fifth floor with a thousand-dollar jacket from the second. I simply go where my eye takes me. However, I often need to hide the price tag from my clients so they don't pre-judge the garment. People who can afford expensive clothes natu-rally prefer them.

While making my way through the maze of garments, plucking and pulling every now and again, I bump into Vivian.

"Hi and good morning. Is it almost Friday yet?"

"Hi, Betty."

Vivian, who sees to it that the floor is in order and restocked with proper sizes, is the only one who comes close to the thirty-eight years I've been working at the store. During her thirty-five years, she has been through everything and everyone. She has raised children and grandchildren—and she's still here. After exchang-ing a few "It isn't like it used to be" work complaints, Vivian and I part ways.

It's quiet. Deep into July it will be quiet all day.

That doesn't bother me. Even on dull days such as this one, when everybody is in the Hamptons or upstate, I can find something that needs accomplishing. The store is my playhouse. Every time I show up to the office, I reinvent the game. If I were simply holding up a dress and saying, "Do you like it?" I would be a drudge. But I relish work and hardly ever take a sick day. By 7:00 A.M. I have risen, dressed, and made my bed as if someone were coming to do an in-spection. I make lunch to bring to work and for my cleaning woman—a proper plate of cold veal, a salad, and fruit or whatever I have available—because otherwise she will not eat. At home every-thing is dusted, wiped, and organized within an inch of its life be-fore I'm out of the apartment by 8:30 A.M. (My friends kid me that there is no day of rest. On the weekends I turn into a human scour-ing pad, rearrange what has already been arranged, iron as therapy, and wax a floor on my hands and knees. Although it is becoming a bit difficult to rise again from the last position, I do not give up. I wonder if all the glamorous persons passing through my office would be surprised.)

On the sixth floor, I hit the security code for the stockroom as quickly as I dial my son's phone number. I know all the security codes for all the store's back rooms by heart. Whenever people com-ment on how much they love the store's windows, I always say, "I'm sure they're beautiful, but I don't know, because I don't look at them." I live internally—in the back rooms. I'm not a mannequin dresser; I dress real people.

"Good morning, Mozelle," I say to the tall stock clerk standing and talking to another woman.

"Hi, Betty."

"Are you on vacation?"

"I'm at the men's store."

"That *is* a vacation."

I don't find anything to go with the pants, but I do find a spe-cific striped top in a large that another client of mine coveted and I was unable to find, either on the floor or in the computer, a week earlier. It's hanging on the side along with many other garments on hold.

"How long has this been on hold?" I ask Mozelle.

She looks at the pink memo slip attached to the hanger and re-plies, "Fifteen days."

Disgraceful.

"Oh, come on. How is anyone supposed to do business here?"

As I walk back out, my crankiness is abated by the hush of the empty store, a privilege of access that in all my years here has never lost its thrill. The clothes placed on the correct racks and shelves, the floors freshly swept, and the neatly folded shopping bags waiting like elegant writing paper; it is everything I imagined as a little girl wondering what Marshall Field's was like when nobody was around.

My father was exactly the same way—a real retailer. He didn't just work at Mandel Brothers but saw the old Chicago department store as an extension of himself. So did my parents' friends who called the house to ask, "Can Harry bring the toaster to the repair department?" And he did gladly. He didn't mind being pulled back to his work for whatever the reason. He knew every nook and cranny of that store just as I do this one.

I take a gloriously empty elevator down to the third floor and pass a young woman in thick black glasses returning from the morning sales meeting as evidenced by a half-eaten bagel on a paper plate.

"Is that Jil Sander?" she asks, pointing to my green suit, which for the last twenty years comes out of my closet every spring for a pressing, then is pressed again and returned to the closet in the fall. I paired it with a tie-dye print shirt in black and lime green that I won after selling so many of them last season.

"No, it's O.L.D.," I say, and keep walking.

I have to wear clothes—and I do love them—but I've seen *everything*. Unlike my father, whose diabetes didn't allow him to indulge his sweet tooth to the fullest so he dipped his finger into the maraschino cherry filling whenever he visited the chocolate department of Mandel Brothers, I am satiated with clothes.

I bump into the buyer for Armani, which has been appearing newer to me recently. I think we're going back to that tailored look, because we have nowhere else to go. At this point everyone is walking around looking like they're going to the beach. My only problem is that no one can make Mr. Armani young again.

"We aren't sizing correctly," I say, stopping the buyer. "There are some size-forty-eight people in the world."

"We do have them."

"Very few."

He jots down my comments with the seriousness of a physician taking notes on a case. We'll see if it comes to anything. In the meantime I grab an aqua blazer as a last-minute idea for my lawyer.

On my way to my office, I pass Kenneth in front of a new display. A real old-fashioned buyer in a young man's body, he is hands-on as he does the floor, repositioning the clothes and talking to the salespersons. I admire him immensely. Everyone else is too busy on the computer to take a look at what's going on in the real store. After we exchange greetings, I glimpse the display in front of him. One mannequin wears a drab black dress shirt buttoned all the way to the top with a gray A-line skirt, a thin black leather belt, and the most monstrous pair of black platform prison-matron shoes.

"Heil Hitler!"

Being eighty-six years old gives me license to say almost anything I like.

The second mannequin has the Lady Gestapo outfit with a pencil skirt in leather, a black dress shirt, a motorcycle jacket, and those same terrible shoes.

"I remember World War II," I say. "There's so much leather, they must have killed every cow in Germany *and* Poland!"

Kenneth laughs. "Oh, Betty."

"Don't 'Oh, Betty' me."

I turn the corner and run smack into André, the head carpenter overseeing the latest round of renovations. Stores are constantly renovating, because they, too, need to convince customers that there's something new to be found.

"Hello, my dear," I say, delighted. "Thank you so much for fixing my door."

"Anything for you, Betty."

André launches into the subject of his eldest daughter; he worries about her finding someone. I tell him that every pot has a cover, adding that, "I'm going to the Berkshires soon, and I'll bring back that jam you like."

Sometimes my A.M. rounds feel like early morning therapy sessions, but I love it. Only a few days earlier, I encountered an engineer who wasn't his usual jovial self. Why? As it turned out, he's getting a divorce. With his three little children away, he was going to therapy to deal with it. I held the elevator door open, and we talked until I got a smile out of him. "You aren't going to lose your children," I said.

In my banter with André, the engineer, the fitters in the workrooms at the top of the store, I'm reminded again of my father, who roamed throughout his store, including the hosiery department. He made an elderly lady selling stockings feel like a glamour girl!

Work keeps me firmly rooted in the present. It's important to have someplace you need to be in the morning. Plus, there's nothing like a "much-needed" dress that doesn't arrive on schedule to the apartment of a very important client not habituated to waiting that keeps an eighty-six-year-old woman on her toes.

Yet I recognize how my job also ties me to the past. I cannot let go of the old routines no matter how outdated or outmoded they may be. For example, I would never in a million years dream of going out in public barefaced. I have to put on lipstick and mascara even to travel half a block for a loaf of bread. How do I know I won't meet Prince Charming on the way?

The customs ingrained in me from my earliest recollections are permanent, for good or for bad. Although I live alone, I don't eat standing over the sink. Buying, chopping, and cooking food, on the very same Roper with six burners that I've used ever since first walking into this apartment sixty years ago, gives me fulfillment. Unlike in my mother's dotage, when her larder contained only champagne, coffee cake, coffee, and peanut butter, you can walk into my apartment at any time and find plenty to eat for breakfast, lunch, cocktail hour, and dinner. Just as in the "old days," my tray is set for every meal with a cloth doily and a napkin, china, silverware—the whole nine yards. I've always felt that if I fall into any other habit, everything will take a downward spin. I am, as they say, overly toilet trained.

It's the same with my clothing. As soon as I get home, I undress, brush my clothes, put them on the proper hangers, and give them an airing before they return to the closet—which, containing a lifetime of garments, is a Narnian portal to times and places that no longer exist.

My clients often ask for advice on how to get rid of clothing. I always say to keep the beautiful pieces: embroidered, beaded, or one-of-a-kind looks. They are usually sumptuous and feel new when revisited. Treat them like lovely antiques. Most often the decision whether to keep or lose a garment hinges on size. Bodies change over the years. If you're a size 14, the size 8 in the back of ye olde closet will never make it on the new you. Toss!

My biggest piece of advice for closet cleaning, however, is this: *Do as I say, not as I do.* I find tossing my own clothing so very hard, like parting with a favorite toy, or memories of what happened when I was wearing that dress. Many things raise their heads to this sentimentality. Every item seems to have a label attached, and I don't mean Dior, Givenchy, or Galanos. Rather, my mother bought it for me, or it was worn with Jim during our last New Year's Eve together.

I'm my own worst enemy. I even had trouble bidding adieu to my wedding dress—the one that began a failed marriage and that my mother-in-law returned to me the day I got back from the mental hospital. In order to let it go, I had to find a home for it, which took me many years. I tried everything and everyone to rid myself of the big white burden. It had little meaning yet represented something momentous. What's in a dress anyway, worn for a couple of hours and rarely worn again? Enough that I spent a year convincing the Weisman Art Museum at the University of Minnesota, home to a large period clothing collection, to become the final resting place of my wedding gown and veil.

I can afford to collect because I have the luxury of twelve closets. (Closet space is the one benefit of living alone.) That kind of storage space, which simply doesn't exist in buildings anymore, is as anachronistically luxurious as the clothes they hold. (But, my God, do I need a Kenzo from my daughter's wedding twenty-seven years ago or evening shoes I can't get a toe into but are too beautiful to toss?)

Being very compulsive and single, I can arrange, rearrange, and do whatever I please. The closets in my bedroom, a world unto themselves, have shoe doors constructed in the 1950s by a closet shop—the kind we used in that era for custom hangers, poles to reach high places, custom-made molding and quilted cotton lining for the shelves, all done in the color of your choice. My beloved shoe door that holds about a dozen pairs suspended by the heels leaves the floor bare so dust bunnies do not gather.

The first closet, originally Sonny's, has one long rod where I hang pants, each pair on its own pant hanger. Skirts, next, hang the same way. Long ago I found brace dividers that slip over the pole, with each divider holding three blouses, shirts, or cardigans, so that each garment does not get creased. On this gadget I hang all my shirts by color: white, colored, stripes, then prints. Above the rod there are two shelves that house handbags. The top holds large bags, baskets, or summer leathers. The lower has smaller handbags and clutches with two quilted boxes on either side for out-of-season items such as summer T-shirts or winter sweaters, depending on what month it is. All are very easy to reach.

The second closet in the bedroom, which has yet another shoe door to accommodate the shoes I wear every day, has one shelf in the back that houses absolutely *nothing*. Imagine that luxury! It is too high to put anything on, and I don't need it for storage. Long ago I used it for hats, which I always hated and so never needed to reach. This closet holds my dresses. (I wear a lot of dresses if I can find them. If not, I constantly wear my old favorites Geoffrey Beene, Issey Miyake, early Michael Kors.) From a lower rod hang seasonal jackets—lightweight summer in the back, a bit heavier cottons in the front. I keep sachets on hangers often to divide: pants, sachet, skirts, sachet, et cetera.

If any of the clients I had admonished over the years for being the "more child" could see my bedroom, they would surely tell the physician to heal herself. For beyond the closets are three dressers, sitting side by side, where the goods inside them look as if they're about to be sold, so exactly are they placed.

The first dresser is filled with curios: old belt buckles, Mother's oversize silk flowers that I often pin on my lapel in the spring, change purses from my grandmother, a fan of black ostrich feathers that belonged to my great-grandmother, a handmade satin Geoffrey Beene belt, a scarf constructed of ribbons.

On to the second dresser, which houses scarves folded and stacked end up, like index cards in a library's filing system. The second drawer is lingerie: nightgowns, underpinnings, and petticoats from my original trousseau. I tie them in bundles with ribbon and, just like Mother, throw in an empty perfume bottle for good measure.

In the bottom drawer are summer pantyhose in bags and turtle-neck T-shirts in all colors that my adorable household person has given me over the years. I often wear them under sweaters. Cotton is kind.

The third dresser is my playground. The bottom drawer holds the evening bags that are no longer practical for me as a single woman to use without the availability of a man's pockets to stuff—including a very rare minaudière of real gold from Venice that was a fiftieth-birthday present from a mother who wanted me to have the world. I had some old diamonds I've never worn, so we threw them on the closure. I've never seen another like it.

I can't tell you the jewelry I have that's lying in gutters and taxi-cabs, yet there is still enough left over to fill the other two drawers of the dresser. Lucite trays hold wonderful pins, earrings, bracelets, and necklaces long and short—all laid out in a very organized way. Attached to everything, a story. There is the wild brooch of citrine, diamonds, and rubies in art deco swirls that my father brought back from a business trip and Mother hated. She told my father, who never bought her jewelry, "You must have done something quite terrible." My big malachite cat that I bought as a young married woman perusing the shops at Henri Bendel stares out at me with its rhinestone eyes; every time I wear it, one of my clients says, "We have to make copies of this!" One year Kathy decided she loved but-tons and turned a bowlful—military, Chanel, horn—into a bracelet that I still wear in the dead of winter. In my little jewelry pouches, I keep individual necklaces from the talented Meredith Frederick that have become a signature of sorts.

In the holy of holies, my battered blue jewelry box with B.H. in gold from my mother-in-law, I keep three gold watches: Mother's, Sonny's, and one that was a gift to me when I turned sixteen. I also have Margaret's church amulet blessed by her priest that she gave to me when I was sick. The cook—who baked decadent chocolate cake for Sonny and coffee cake for me when we visited as newlyweds and cookies for my children when they were little people—comforted and saved me long after I had grown up. She loved my father so much that when he died, she refused to attend his funeral. Afterward she worked for her parish priests, who remarked that they never before had eaten so well.

I try not to let my collections languish—how quickly treasure becomes junk—but instead put them to good use. (There are some things I don't house, like Frieda's wedding ring, which I wear every day. She wouldn't like that, because she herself wore it only on her weekend days off. Her white aprons, however, are still in the dresser drawer where she left them.) Sometimes that proves quite a challenge. I have a drawer full of monogrammed handkerchiefs—truly a thing of the past—that were made for my mother, my father, and me. I can't throw any away, even the ones that have holes. Instead I fill them with lavender or rose petals, tie them into balls, and use them as sachets to line my drawers.

When Carol Luiken, now retired from costume design and living on Cape Cod, bemoaned the fact that she couldn't find handkerchiefs anywhere, because she always carries real hankies, never tissues, I had an idea. Well, I had maybe fifty embroidered handkerchiefs with my mother's name, Carol, and they weren't getting any younger lying in my drawer. So I sent them off north, bound, of course, in ribbon and accompanied by a sachet, for a surprise Christmas gift.

Carol was thrilled with the beautiful hankies and even more with the thought. It is a pleasure to attach one person to another through an item. I have often given what was new when purchased—a Chester Weinberg dress, a Comme des Garçons coat, a needlepoint handbag from Venice—to a young friend who looks so good in vintage clothes. I still wear the navy-and-white Geoffrey Beene dress that once belonged to my client Estelle. It gets better every season!

Not long ago, Dena Kaye—the daughter of the wonderful comedian, actor, singer, dancer, writer, and cook Danny Kaye—came to see me to find something to wear for an evening at Carnegie Hall in honor of her father. The upcoming public appreciation for her father's many talents, which she felt was long overdue, made it a difficult time for Dena, who as one of the event's speakers wanted something graphic for the occasion. We plumbed the store's contents and came up with nada; she had her own very strong thoughts. Having known Dena for more than twenty years, I could sense she also wanted her clothes to pay tribute to her remarkable family. Why not wear something that had belonged to her mother, Sylvia Fine, a brilliant composer and lyricist who wrote many of her husband's songs, I suggested. Of course, everything was in storage. So we agreed Dena would pick out what was salvageable, which turned out to be three huge garment bags that filled a fitting room. The garments were for the most part custom-made by the California designer Don Loper. Trying on all the very extravagant clothes was like internalizing a part of her mother. Finally we came upon a green-and-black striped full-skirted dress with a bolero to match. Finding the beautiful dress, fitting into it (the workroom performed a miracle), and looking sophisticated was a boost to her being.

Clothing is no different from traditions or memories; it's a blessing when newer generations take them on happily. I love when children of clients pilfer their mother's closet—same as I did to my mother's wardrobe as a young person. That's a true compliment to taste.

I now have three generations of clients. There are the originals, or what's left of them anyway (fitting their walkers and wheelchairs into the dressing room is the hardest part!); their daughters, whom I knew as children and are now into middle age; and now their granddaughters.

I consider it the best commendation when I win over the thirteen-year-olds, because they're my toughest customers. As soon as they enter my dressing room, I know they're thinking, "No way this old lady is going to dress *me*." My failproof method is to first send away the mothers, who nowadays hover and fret more than in the days when children got polio. I send these "helicopter parents" (a completely foreign notion, taught to me by my grandson) flying right out of my dressing room. These young people get to try their wings—and taste—with me. I will let them choose the outrageous, and I'll pull what *I* believe is appropriate, and we end up sometimes in their corner, sometimes in mine. But the end result is always sheer happiness for both of us.

The young girls of today all dress way too maturely, but you can't take one and make her stand out from the others in an ador-able little chiffon dress. That would make for some kind of misera-ble evening! They dress for their peers—don't all women?—not for what I or their mothers want. I forget my own daughter and her smocked dresses, another life, when a thirteen-year-old chooses a silver bandage dress. I simply do it in good taste and show alterna-tives. I try to steer them away from the herd and make them under-stand the beauty of individuality.

When we did a sequin dress for one of my long-standing clients' granddaughters . . . well, her face lit up. And it kept getting lighter and lighter as we continued to make the dress shorter and tighter. She kept looking up at me in the mirror, and I kept saying, "That's okay." It's dress-up. I don't have a problem with it. I love that age group and what they have to teach me. They were the first who layered two T-shirts on top of each other, which I adore and utilize from time to time with clients of all ages.

I can still learn, even though Lord knows I've observed a lot over the years. Once, when a woman in the elevator found me familiar and asked, "Did you used to work here?" a buyer exclaimed, "Work here? She was *born* here!" (The reason so many people feel they know me is from my presence up and down all day in the elevator; I have considered wearing a red carnation and greeting people at the elevator banks, for all the times I get stopped.)

Indeed, it seems to many that I'm older and more steadfast than the limestone that makes up the store's edifice. It's been sev-enteen years since Jeff Kurland packed up his costume shop and moved to California, but whenever he's in town, he always stops by the office, because I'm like "a monument," he says. People from all over the country—Texas ladies who lunch, political types from Chicago, the wives of Oklahoma ranchers—do the same, because they know, even if we don't find clothes, they're going to have a great time—and I will give you lunch served on sheets of the store's white tissue paper in lieu of a place mat (with not a linen napkin in sight!).

My longevity in a business where most things are in one minute and out the next is astounding, even to me. So many people have come and gone through my life. My goodness, the presidents I have reported to alone! I'm still very strict and disciplined in my work, but at this point I hearken to no man. (They're scared to death of me here; that's the fun part.) I have been at Bergdorf so long that it has become my store.

People often ask me the same question: "How do you do it?" I don't feel so great every day. But just like Jeanne the fitter, I rise, dress, and am off to work, rain or shine. Aging can be scary if you let it obsess you. As soon as I turn the key in the office door, I'm alive and ready for the fight of the day.

Idle hands and brain make for unhappiness. I have known a lot of that. One exorcises the bad in pulling the heavy wagon. Everything must not be set and easy, otherwise life becomes sedentary. "Challenge" is the word. Some people do Pilates; I get under the bed and look for old Kleenex. Going to the gym to work out with a trainer is not stimulating to me. Walking through seven floors each day, arms loaded with clothes, is. (No wonder my doctor remarks on my strong upper arms. To this day he doesn't fully understand what I do for a living.)

The last years have brought not only the aches and pains of old joints. They have also brought out the humor I've become known for. I no longer censor myself in any way. Some call my one-liners bluntness—maybe—but I find that in my dotage I like to leave people laughing, or at least bewildered.

A tech entrepreneur from Silicon Valley, and a new client, said, "Talk to me about color."

"I like it."

For heaven's sake, I wasn't going to give this woman a lesson in color theory. Instead I smoked out her true predicament, even though *she* didn't know what it was. A woman in her fifties, surrounded at work by people who, in jeans and tight tops, were young enough to be her children, she followed their lead. In her mind it meant she had joined forces with the "youthful set." But to me that was insecure and misguided.

I understood my client's dilemma perfectly. I'm probably the oldest woman in the store. I could walk around thinking everyone around me is so hip. But I don't. I like to be different—even if "different" means older and especially if it means better. (Of course, this is coming from a woman who thinks all the people at the store look like they're going to the beach.) I have very high standards and want my clients to as well. There is nothing wrong with aspiring to an elevated style, the kind that has nothing to do with money or labels.

With my Silicon Valley entrepreneur, I let her have her jeans and tight tops (she had a figure kept youthful by much running). But I insisted, "You always have to wear a jacket."

"You bring something to the table that your younger counterparts don't," I explained. "You have intelligence, beauty, experience. You should also bring something to the table in the way you dress."

That's when I slipped a sumptuous yet streamlined leather jacket over her. The entrepreneur understood immediately. She had come in for an evening dress and left with a leather jacket.

After saying good-bye to André the carpenter, I walk back into the office where Emily, my assistant, an unflappable girl from the Midwest, hands me one of those telephone message slips that I have come to loathe; they often read "Urgent problem!"

"Jimmy Fallon's wife's stylist is coming. She needs a black dress," Emily says.

"Who?"

"Jimmy Fallon."

"I don't know who that is."

"He's on TV."

"Oh, you know I don't watch those reality programs."

How much I have seen from my office—even the planting of what were once saplings and are now sprawling trees. Funnily enough, my dream of standing at the window with a gun is gone—dissolved—although I often think about it in my waking hours. I described it to Joan Rivers not long ago. Having run into her as she shopped for nightgowns for her sister, who was desperately sick with cancer, I brought her down to my quiet sanctuary. Somehow the subject turned to my rifle dream, which I made a joke out of; I'm not exactly a sheriff type. I simply wanted to provide a moment of distraction. Joan, naturally, had the last laugh. The next day a package arrived by messenger: a chocolate pistol and a card from her that read "Don't shoot. Eat."

Emily relays to me yet another message from My First Bride. (She has already called twice today. The first was about a dress with elephants on it that she saw in the store. A die-hard Republican, she said, "I think I should really have it.")

"She wants to know what movie she and Jock should go see."

"Oh, dear God. Information, please."

Suddenly a voice, not unlike the sound of a car coming up a gravel driveway, rasps loudly from down the hall to my office: "Did you hear when the producer said, 'Make the clothes believable?' It always scares me when they talk like that."

In walks Pat Field, long fire-engine-red hair ablaze. A very low-cut, sleeveless shirt, a lace push-up bra, and skinny green army pants reveal a figure that would be the envy of most twenty-somethings, let alone seventy-somethings. She has come in with Paolo Nieddu for a movie. We catch up on the latest. She's just re-turned from setting up a *Sex and the City* exhibit in a Melbourne, Australia, mall that she wants to take on the road like Barnum & Bailey. But only where there are a lot of big malls, no museums, so no Europe. "If I am going to work, it has to be for money," she says from behind the green sunglasses she wears even indoors. "I didn't invent the rules, I just play by them."

Pat is bereft because her beloved veterinarian died recently, and when I ask about him, he turns out to be the very same vet I went to for my schnauzer Max, who has been dead for twenty years! What are the chances? Dr. John Higgins was good to me in my time of troubles; when Sonny left, I ended up with the dog and used the vet as a psychiatrist. (Eventually he had me hold Max when he administered the lethal shot so that the dog died in my arms. I walked home crying with Max's empty leash, which is still in the hall drawer where it was kept while he was alive.)

I am so sorry to hear about Dr. Higgins's death, but there is work to do. Paolo and Pat are shopping for a romantic comedy in which Cameron Diaz, Kate Upton, and Leslie Mann join forces after realizing that they're all in a relationship with the same man. Each actress is an archetype—wife, sexy power broker, ingenue—and their clothes have to tell the story. "I want original, not trendy," Pat growled. "I don't want them to look like they came right out of the spring collection."

Oh, and shooting begins in two weeks.

"We're in the prepping stages," says Pat, who is beyond unflappable.

"Rather."

The three of us hit the floor. The store has shrunk to me. I know most every corner (even though it's like the musical-chairs game—every day there's a move). Almost right outside my door, I show them a long black silk crepe oversheath with a large circular gold closure at the breastbone. You won't see yourself coming and going in this. I have whetted Paolo's and Pat's appetites, but almost immediately I put on the brakes.

"What size is Cameron?" I ask about the actress, who plays a high-powered attorney.

"She says she's a twenty-five or twenty-six, but never a twenty-seven," Paolo says.

I can't imagine she's that tiny.

"These clothes run *really* small."

"She seems to know what she's talking about. She was a model before she became an actress."

"So she knows how to squeeze into clothes."

While Paolo and I confer, Pat is diverted by a coat with a cutaway front in a patchwork design of calf leather, lambskin, and bonded snakeskin panels.

"Don't go near it," I say.

I have eyes in the back of my head.

She veers away from the coat but heads for something just as dangerous—a yolk-yellow fringe-front T-shirt. "That's left over from your last TV show," I say. This could take days. We need to get the hook and rein her in.

I pull a red dress. Bright in color, masterful in structure; it is deceptively simple-looking.

"Gorgeous," Pat says. "But what shoes? They're all so obnoxious."

"Aren't they awful? They're like hooker shoes."

"Hookers are classic. They wear a nice leopard or patent pump. Upstairs, one pair of shoes is more ludicrous than the next. They scream, 'Look at my feet!' Please, someone give me a nice five-inch Manolo."

A cell phone hanging around her neck on a string rings, and Pat answers. Pat is *always* on the phone. She absentmindedly starts poking at a square scarf with an abstract print in purples, pinks, yellows, and oranges so bright it would make a sunset ashamed, then sits down at the desk in the boutique she's entered.

"No. This is a fine time. I can talk for a minute," she says into the phone. "We've been taught that men can be bold but women should be demure."

Now she's giving an interview!

"We need to get her out of here," Paolo says.

". . . having gay male writers' words coming out of the mouths of women was liberating and revolutionary."

"We should pull her plug," I say.

Pat discusses the seminal nature of *Sex and the City* with the journalist on the phone as Paolo and I scour the racks and keep her from getting lost in the sweater section. We take oversize cashmere sweaters, upscale chinos, flirty dresses, and clingy silks. While contemplating whether a pair of pants is bell-bottomed or boot-cut, I see it. The missing piece to a now beautifully complete puzzle. A dark red ribbed sweater set. Where on earth has that been hiding? It's *the* perfect thing to go with my client's palazzo pants! I can tell without a doubt that its scoop neck will flatter her décolletage and the length of her hips. I pluck it from the rack and place it atop the heap of clothing I carry over my left arm. I will organize it all when I return to the office.

Suddenly Pat, a chain smoker, takes a cigarette out of her pack—in front of Prada!

"Oh, dear God! She's going to light up right here and get me fired," I say. Just then the doors open to one of the elevators filled with tony shoppers, and in goes Pat with a slight push from yours truly.

Back in the office, I neatly sort the clothes for the movie, hanging the items for each character in separate fitting rooms as if the characters themselves will be by any minute to try them on. Then I hang the sweater set on the clothing rack next to my desk and label it for my client, not with satisfaction—I'm not and never will be satisfied—but instead with gratification.

Clothes aren't the be-all and end-all. They can be fun; they can be beautiful; you can put them on your head or wear them backward if you want to; they're feel-good. I expedite all that for others. I'm a saleslady. It's everything my mother said don't be. There is, however, much gratification to what I do. Like when people come back and tell me, which they do a lot, "You know that dress you sold me five years ago? I still wear it all the time." Or, "I love that jacket from two seasons ago. You can't kill it." Or, "Do you know how many compliments I get about that blouse I bought last time I came here?" I hope to make an experience called shopping a bit more than just trying on clothes. When I've helped a person like what she sees in the mirror, I'm fulfilled.

"Sheila Wolfe, Tom Wolfe's wife, called," Emily says as I sit down at my desk.

The phone rings, and I pick up; it's Mindy, my ex-assistant.

"Hi, dear, I just saw your mother," I say. "She wants a suit. . . . Why? Because she wants a suit."

Mindy is going to London with her husband and two children next week and wants to know if she needs to make reservations for restaurants before she leaves.

"I would," I say. "The shoes you crave are in." (Mindy is a 5½, and we will get maybe two pairs, so I know I have to watch the shoe department for her tiny feet!)

The irony of my travel advice on London restaurant reservations isn't lost on me; the last time I was there, Jim and I dined in cozy pubs and in our charming flat, not at five-star eateries.

But in the last several years, I have become, despite my better instincts, something of a woman about town. I never contemplated beginning another life after my dear Jim died. How many restarts does one woman get? It simply appeared.

There are so many people who have picked me up when I saw no hope whatsoever. Charlotte, my first friend in New York, died from breast cancer long ago, but her son Jimmy (the one who was evacuated as a baby from the Atlantic Beach vacation house after I contracted polio), and his wife, Nancy, call me all the time for dates, always to a great, new, and trendy restaurant. God knows the maître d's and waitstaff must think they are dragging around their grandmother, but they've become dear friends as have their wonderful children, Charlotte and John.

Thirty years later I'm still enjoying Susie's impeccable taste and force of imagination that astonished me when she worked at the store. Now it is at the most glorious house that she and her husband Stuart bought in the Berkshires, where they invite me for weekends with their amazing daughter, Emmelyn. There all her talents are trained on a garden the like of which only occurs when a person loves and tends to it herself, the kitchen with food that is as delicious as it is lovely and plentiful, and decorating that is never finished— nor should it be.

I still have my oldest friend in Chicago, who was captain of my team at our all-girls summer camp. Dorie, who drinks a martini with an olive, is *still* captain. My second-oldest friend, Claire, whom

I met sixty years ago, is another force of nature. She's been known to drive herself to Greenbrier in West Virginia for her medical examination. The last time she did this, the amazed doctors wrote on her chart, "88-year-old woman drives from N.Y. for physical and she made it in eight hours!" In addition to her driving abilities, Claire makes extraordinary sculptures in alabaster—that's when she's not running to the Union Square farmers' market or down to some late-night comedy club in the Bowery. She is always up for an adventure, no matter what part of town it's in. One evening after coming out of a movie when it was still too early to go home, we landed at the Le Cirque bar. All of a sudden, while talking bar nonsense to the patrons around us, the woman next to me turned and asked, "Are you two a couple?" We almost fell off our barstools, but we didn't respond yes or no. The two of us have certainly grown into our own. Whenever I'm out with Claire, the doorman always gives me that peculiar nod when I arrive home after midnight.

I often wonder what Jim would make of this new me, so different from the one cloistered in his quiet country apartment. I'm out so much these days that I've become like a streetwalker. I don't know where the courage came from, but another person emerged yet again after he died.

I was a child for the longest time, but I have finally grown into a proper person. Learning how to be alone, truly alone, was the last step. My being an only child, this should have been easy for me, but it wasn't. My mother and father fussed over me too much and then left me alone too much. When I first came to New York, I was so frightened of being alone that I didn't want to leave the little apartment I loathed. It's funny, but on the street in a city of millions, at a cocktail party full of friends, or surrounded by family in a country house, one can still feel lonely.

Sophistication has nothing to do with the ability to go to the movies, eat in a restaurant, pass the weekend without drowning it in busywork, or face going home alone. The terrible fear of loneliness kept me from knowing myself, but now I am happy, because I do know myself. I know I have an unpredictable stomach. I like vodka. I'm overly neat. I know I dress well and with ease. I can finally talk to me, although, like my clients, sometimes I listen and sometimes I don't.

I'm not a religious person, but as I grow older, I'm more appreciative of the very fact that I'm able to rise from my bed, dress—appropriately—and appear at work five days a week. I dislike, however, when I'm called a legend. That overused word, which means absolutely nothing to me, should be retired or at least reserved for people who have built skyscrapers—not an eighty-six-year-old broad who is still standing. I'm a working grandmother, which I will admit is unusual. (My grandmother lay in bed putting on violet perfume when she was my age!) But I need to work: I would absolutely collapse if I didn't. When people stop me in the store having read about me in the paper or seen me on TV, I laugh at the recognition. I'm still the same nutcase. They all should see the real me, on my hands and knees doing a floor or standing over my sink scouring a pot; my hands tell the whole story. Where do you go when you're up? Down and out. What is fame? A fleeting moment. Who remembers Bella Abzug?

Sometimes, however, being recognized is a chance for a true human encounter, and those I relish. Last weekend I went to Coney

Island because an old friend had a huge desire to taste a hot dog from Nathan's. It reminded her of her wonderful husband, Charlie, who three weeks before he passed away had also wanted to visit Nathan's.

"But you're not dying," I said.

Nonetheless, off we went on a very hot summer Sunday afternoon to the beach. We were on the boardwalk amid throngs of people when I heard someone from the crowd say, "Are you Betty?" I thought I must have misheard. My hearing is not what it once was. Who could I possibly know in the very nether regions of Brooklyn? But there was a young girl, scantily clad, covered in tattoos, and accompanied by a boyfriend wearing dark purple nail polish, who told me, "You are my idol." How she knew me, I have no clue.

In the last few years, I seem to have become the Most Wanted Woman. I get many requests from the media for interviews, which I do easily and happily—because after they're done, I still go home and wash out my stockings in the bathroom sink. (I also never read or watch my own press.) A lot of people come to the store just to look at me, and I welcome them, same as I do the piles of e-mails and letters I receive from correspondents as wide-ranging as monks from an abbey in upstate New York who wrote to say keep up the good work, to owners of a deli in Denver who sent me a delicious coffee cake, to a young girl from Phoenix whose mother told her she isn't worth anything. I answer them all.

Yet I was completely taken aback by the fact that these two very young people on the boardwalk knew who I was. I've always liked accolades from people in the street. Is there any greater honor than being acknowledged—in Coney Island, of all places? The young woman went on to say that she hoped she could come to the store one day to be dressed by me. I quickly told her she did not have to wait. There was a door open to her anytime; I would be so flattered if she visited.

And that is absolutely true, because for me dressing someone well is as divine as helping someone to walk, to see, to smile, or to bake a tall, light angel food cake.

I'll drink to that.